Unrepentant

Peter Edwards

Unrep

entant

The Strange and (sometimes) Terrible Life of
Lorne Campbell, Satan's Choice and Hells Angels Biker

Vintage Canada

VINTAGE CANADA EDITION, 2014

Copyright © 2013 Peter Edwards

Published in Canada by Vintage Canada, a division of Random House of Canada
Limited, Toronto, in 2014. Originally published in hardcover in Canada by Random House
Canada, a division of Random House of Canada Limited, in 2013. Distributed by
Random House of Canada Limited.

Vintage Canada with colophon is a registered trademark.

www.randomhouse.ca

Library and Archives Canada Cataloguing in Publication

Edwards, Peter, 1956–
Unrepentant : the strange and (sometimes) terrible life of Lorne Campbell,
Satan's Choice and Hells Angel biker / Peter Edwards.

ISBN 978-0-307-36257-5

1. Campbell, Lorne, 1948–. 2. Hell's Angels. 3. Satan's Choice Motorcycle Club.
4. Gang members—Ontario—Biography. 5. Motorcycle gangs—Ontario—History. I. Title.

HV6248.C335E98 2014   364.1092   C2012-904498-9

Text design by Andrew Roberts

Image credits: Richard Nixon / Arcangel-images.com

Printed and bound in the United States of America

8 9 7

Contents

It was actually pretty simple. They like to make it complicated. People have embellished it a lot. We went to the bar. I sat with one other person. We ordered a drink. . . . Mike Everett, he said, "He's sitting with a gun pointed at Rick and Gary." . . . I got up right away and went to the table and I said, "How are you doing, Bill?"

As soon as I said "How are you doing?" he went for it. . . .

I totally wish he hadn't gone for it. I've had to live with it. It hasn't been easy. But he went for it and I happened to be faster. . . . It happened so fast that I just reacted. When you see somebody going for a gun and you've got one, with the upbringing I've had, you'll be fast. I'm glad I had the gun. . . . I never questioned my decision. Not once. Not for a second.

You're kind of helpless to change anything, but I just wish it hadn't happened. Just a waste of life.

LORNE CAMPBELL, outlaw biker for forty-six years

To Barbara, Sarah and James

For making me feel blessed.

P.E.

AUTHOR'S NOTE

I t might sound more authentic, given the subject matter inside these covers, if I said this book was written between snorts of cocaine off a tattooed biker chick's belly. In reality, the pages that follow are mostly the product of lengthy interviews that were conducted over several months across the kitchen table of a friend of Lorne Campbell's, between feedings of comfort food such as spaghetti with meat balls or freshly baked lemon meringue pie.

I heard about Campbell years before we ever spoke. I knew of him primarily from author Mick Lowe's *Conspiracy of Brothers*, as the outlaw biker who tried to take the rap for the fatal shooting of Golden Hawk Motorcycle Club member Bill Matiyek back in 1978. I also knew that, to some bikers, lawyers and even police, he embodies the old outlaw biker code of sticking up for your brothers, shunning the justice system and ignoring the press.

Naturally, I was curious when Mary Liscoumb, a retired educator who's a mutual friend, suggested a meeting with Campbell in the summer of 2011. In my profession, curiosity often trumps brains, and so off I went. I had written a lot of unflattering things over the years about the outlaw biker world, including the two clubs Campbell had belonged to, the Satan's Choice and Hells Angels. As I drove to the meeting, I couldn't stop wondering if I was in some sort of trouble.

It was immediately obvious when we started talking that Campbell was the real deal. He was sixty-three years old and had spent his entire adult life as an outlaw biker. He joined the Satan's Choice at age seventeen, the youngest-ever full member of that club, and he had seen and done plenty of things inside and outside the law between that time and his retirement in good standing from the Hells Angels in June 2011. (Yes, you can retire from a biker club and ride away intact.) Campbell had plenty of stories from those four decades on the streets and behind bars. He smiled in a way I couldn't decipher and said he was thinking about telling them in a book.

I said to Campbell that I was interested in his story, but I would only want to write a full and honest account. That meant I would double-check the truth of those stories. I would dig up material on my own and I would have the final say on what was published. I also told him that I had co-written a book, *The Encyclopedia of Canadian Organized Crime*, with one of my journalism heroes, Michel Auger, who survived being shot six times in September 2000. Auger was almost killed for the "crime" of doing his job as a crime reporter honestly, and the gunman was working for Maurice (Mom) Boucher of the Hells Angels in Quebec. I am proud to share this line of work with Auger and I wanted Campbell to know that I blamed some Hells Angels for the near murder of a friend. He needed to be clear that I could never condone or forget that.

I wouldn't have been surprised if things had ended here. That's what I expected and that would have been fine. My curiosity was already at least partially satisfied. Instead, Campbell pleasantly surprised me. I learned quite quickly that he enjoys surprising people, although not always pleasantly. He said he had no problems with me telling a full and honest story about himself, adding, with a smile, "I've got plenty of bad stuff."

Campbell knows more about what makes a good story than many people who have spent as much time in classrooms as he has spent in prisons and jails. In another life, he could have made a fine editor. I was a little taken aback when he spoke about the importance of character development and the need to present people as rounded human beings—not something I expected from a former drug debt collector who has broken more bones than he can remember.

As we continued to meet, I found I actually liked him, even though I still shudder at the thought of many things he has done. I often wondered how, with a different start, his life could have turned out far differently. The qualities that made him stand out as an outlaw biker, such as toughness and loyalty and intelligence, would have won him awards in sports or the military or business. I also liked how Campbell didn't whine about the life he did have. We only have this life and have to play the hand we're dealt. Still, at many points during our meetings he made me think about the important role fathers play in shaping their children's lives. Many of the saddest stories he told me were about people he knew with missing or abusive fathers. Too often in his own story, Campbell is one of them.

In time, I came to respect his brand of honesty. Through months of lengthy interviews, I double-checked his stories and never caught Campbell in a lie. He was never late for an interview and always gave his full attention to questions. He also never ended an interview, even though our average weekly talk lasted more than six hours and the questions were often intensely personal. There have been times when I felt he was leaving out a name or two when describing a crime so that he wouldn't be ratting anyone out, but he is largely comfortable with decisions he has made in his own life and didn't feel the need to embellish or cover up. He was often tough on himself and volunteered things about himself that I had never even heard as rumours. That included details of the Bill Matiyek shooting and how he came close to executing three other men who ran afoul of the Satan's Choice. He doesn't dispute what he has done; he just wants to explain why he did it.

Throughout our months of lengthy interviews, I found that Campbell has an extremely accurate memory that is aided by novel reference points. Sometimes, when I asked him a question, he would look at one of his many tattoos to try to figure out a date based on when he had had that particular image inked onto his body. He would also think back to how the timing of events related to his entry or release dates from jail or prison. I learned fairly early on in this project that prisoners who are fuzzy on other details invariably have sharp memories when it comes to when they were locked up or set free.

Most conversations in this book are re-created from his memory, while others are from police wiretaps.

Now that this project is completed, I find that I genuinely like Campbell and wish the best for him. It's still hard to reconcile the friendly, intense guy across the kitchen table with the man who appeared in police files and in newspaper stories, some of which were written by me. Both versions of Campbell are true to a point. The more I talked with him, the more I thought of the Catholic idea that we can love a sinner while hating the sin. I never expected my chats with Campbell about his crimes and capers to remind me of lessons from a priest. For all the delight he takes in surprising others, Campbell helped me to surprise myself.

CHAPTER 1

Growing Up Hard

All the time I was being beaten, I thought, "I'm not going to be fourteen forever. I'm going to grow up."

LORNE CAMPBELL

Lorne Campbell has shot and stabbed and punched out and hammered and clubbed more of his fellow human beings than he can remember. It would be easy to conclude that he fell into a hard life. That would be wrong. As Campbell tells it, he didn't fall into violence; violence is where his life began.

Campbell recalls a time when he was about six, and his dad was beating his mother yet again. This time, Campbell's father held a knife, threatening her. "I was screaming at my dad to kill her. It wasn't because I wanted my mother to die—I just wanted it to stop. I loved her. I just wanted it all to end. All of the violence and the beatings."

If the violence that typified his decades as an outlaw biker was bred into his bones, so was the sense of turf. For as long as he could remember, there was something righteous about hating the town of Whitby, a ten-minute drive towards Toronto from his native blue-collar Oshawa, a city that billed itself as "the Automotive Capital of Canada." He had barely left his mother's breast when he was hearing stories of how, during the Great Depression of the 1930s, Campbells huddled in tents near Whitby harbour, where the poorest of the poor gathered. The family felt abandoned by the town as they shivered by the shore of Lake Ontario. In future years, when someone from the family—like Campbell's cousin, superstar jockey Sandy Hawley—did well, others in the family would stress the connection to nearby Oshawa and try to omit any reference to Whitby. "It was like the municipality was being two-faced. Like, 'There's only two things I don't like about you, and that's your face.' We always fought people from Whitby, Scarborough, Dunbarton. It wouldn't matter if the person was a nice person. What's the matter with Dunbarton? I don't know. They ain't from Oshawa."

Campbell's father, Lorne Sr., was the youngest boy in a family of thirteen children, who were close in their own way. "They were all living in a tent, my aunts and uncles and father and grandparents." Campbell's paternal grandfather, Matthew, was a stonemason who immigrated to Canada from Scotland, where he was a Highlander. His hands were so huge he could pick up Campbell's father by his head when he misbehaved as a youngster. "My aunts and uncles would often praise him for being a hard worker. The whole family would sit around and play penny-ante poker. He'd spit chewing tobacco in a pail. We didn't think it was gross then."

Campbell's father was just nineteen when he enlisted on November 11, 1941, and his military records say he was motivated by "sense of duty." At that point he had already worked for almost five years, having left school after grade eight at age fourteen. He first worked for his father in construction for $18 a week plus room and board, and then for a Pickering construction firm for $43 weekly. Lorne Sr. was a tough man, and his military records show that while training for eight months at Camp Borden before being shipped overseas, he wasn't a model of discipline. He was punished four times for taking off from camp. In his records, one of these escapes is called "breaking out of camp while under open arrest." As Campbell puts it, "My father liked his freedom." He was allowed out another time to marry a nineteen-year-old woman named Rose Patricia Prest.

Campbell likes to joke that he was born at Oshawa General Hospital in 1948 "right beside my mother." The point of that joke is that they didn't really seem connected like a mother and child right from the start. If his mother hugged him and said she loved him on the day of his birth, it was perhaps the last time she did so. "My mother never in her life said 'I love you' to me. In that, she was distant."

Campbell grew up with two sisters: Lyne, two years older, and Loretta, who was born in 1954. There was also a younger sister named Roberta, who died of pneumonia when she was an infant and he was five years old. His mother took a photo of six-month-old Roberta in her tiny open casket and never mentioned her name again. The picture of Roberta was put away somewhere, safe from eyes and fingers and conversation. "Never was it talked about."

In later years, after Campbell jumped with both boots into the brotherhood of outlaw bikers, he was sometimes asked if he wished he had biological brothers as well. "You deal with what you're dealt in life. People who grow up like I grew up, you don't realize there is any option. If my parents stayed together, things would have been different. If I had five brothers, things would have been different. If, if, if. It would have been nice to have a more loving family. I envy people—not to the point that I'm depressed—that are brought up with a loving family."

One of his first childhood memories is of being decked out in sixteen-ounce boxing gloves when he wasn't yet old enough to go to school. Those gloves were heavier than the ones adult pros wore for fights, and it was tough for little "Lornie" even to hold them up, let alone punch. Lorne Sr. was only five foot seven and a half on a lean frame, but he seemed massive as he would feint and then hit, feint and then hit, while his son's skinny arms were weighed down at his sides. "He would punch me in the head and I'd go sliding across the floor."

The violence in his home was different from the heroic onscreen kind Campbell loved to watch John Wayne act out in Saturday afternoon cowboy movies at the Biltmore, Marks, Regent and Plaza theatres in downtown Oshawa. The violence in his home was so all-pervasive that Campbell grew up thinking it was normal. He can't remember a time when he cried in front of his parents. Instead, he vividly recalls the time he and Lyne laughed hysterically while their father rained down blows on them with a belt as they lay under their covers. "We couldn't stop laughing. It was hurting, but we were looking at each other and laughing." Laughter didn't make the blows any less painful, but it did give Campbell a sense of control in the situation. "When I was getting beatings by my dad, I would never cry. They were often. I got used to it."

Until the age of five, he went regularly to Calvary Baptist Sunday school on Centre Street in Oshawa. It wasn't his parents who took him but rather the next-door neighbours, who were eager to reach out and try to save his little soul. Inside his home, religion wasn't promoted, but it wasn't treated with a lack of respect either. "We weren't taught to fear anything like the devil." Campbell kids were expected to defer to grown-ups. "Be polite, respect your elders. It was just bred into every Campbell. It was 'Mr.' and 'Mrs.' You never called older people by their first name. Never disrespected elders."

There was a method, however misguided, to the violence that permeated his childhood home. It was clear from as early as Campbell can remember that he needed to grow up tough. Lorne Sr. had been an amateur boxer, both in and out of the army. In later years his fingers were stained nicotine yellow from smoking three packs of Export Plains a day, but Lorne Sr. could still make a fist and use it with speed and power. "Every time I turned around, I got hit by my dad. He said, 'When you grow up, you're going to learn to be a fighter.'"

In the Campbell household, there was no greater insult than to be called a schemer or a conniver. That he should run headlong towards something frightening rather than flee from it was bred into Campbell's bones. This could mean a spectacular flame-out, but at least he would go out like a man. "If there's a problem, confront the man," his father would say. This approach became central to Campbell's fighting style. A good shot to the solar plexus or a hook to the jaw was enough to take the knees out of most fancy dancers, in or out of the ring. "I wasn't ever deked by anybody. I couldn't ever be faked by anybody."

Campbell was handy with his fists on the schoolyard, but he never considered himself a bully. "Bullies are cowards and weak. I was never a bully. Not me. I would hate if I was ever thought of in that context. . . . I hate cowards. I despise cowards. You don't have to be a tough guy and go out and kill somebody to not be a coward." During one schoolyard scuffle he was caught totally by surprise when another boy booted him quick and hard and deep between the legs. When he told his father about it, Lorne Sr. sloughed it off. "He said, 'If you can't fight with your dukes, you're not a man.'" Still, the sudden nausea was real and the kick was undeniably effective. Campbell began practising kicks on his own, when his father wasn't watching. By the time he was a young man, he was able to leap up and boot the top of a door frame, although he wouldn't brag about it to his dad. "Everybody loves their father when they are growing up. So did I. I was his only son. He wanted me to grow up being a fighter. His heart was in the right place. I think that I'm a lot like him."

Campbell got his first bicycle when he was about six from his uncle Bob Chaten, who worked at the General Motors plant in Oshawa. The bike was so big he had to ride with one leg under the crossbar, but it brought a sense of freedom he would never forget. "My dad never had a car. Most of my uncles never had a car." Campbell would put empty cigarette packages in the spokes to make motorcycle sounds. For longer excursions he would take a second empty cigarette pack for when the first one wore out. Sometimes he rode with other kids and often he rode alone. "I rode everywhere on it."

As he grew older, Campbell developed a pronounced sentimentality about birthdays and anniversaries, but as a boy such markers of time didn't seem to matter much to those around him. It wasn't until he was about ten that anyone actually celebrated his birthday, when his aunts and uncles pulled something together. "There were no other kids there, but I did get a present or two. I can't remember what they were— I think it was a sweater or some piece of clothing. But I got ginger ale. The main thing that sticks in my mind is a glass of ginger ale with a trick ice cube with a fly in the cube. I drank the whole glass without even noticing it. They told me when I was done. That was fine with me. I didn't get ginger ale very often."

Campbell's mother told him little about her side of the family. She was born Eileen Chaten, a dour combination of Pennsylvania Dutch and English, and looked quite a bit like the young Queen Elizabeth, although any comparison between herself and royalty stops there.

Perhaps the proudest, most vibrant time of her life was during the Second World War, when she was single and worked at General Motors. The Oshawa factory had been temporarily converted into an aircraft plant, and towards the end of the war, workers like Lorne Campbell's mother proudly built a fighter aircraft there every day.

Years later, when American war veterans from California started up a biker club, they named it the Hells Angels after World War II fighter pilots. Years after that, police called the Hells Angels urban terrorists and Campbell couldn't understand how the term could be applied to him, even if he broke his fair share of laws. He considered himself and his family patriots, in their own fashion, and never saw any disconnect between his parents' service for their country and his years as an outlaw biker.

Lorne Sr. could be a charmer and fill a room with laughter and the air with a promise of better times ahead. "He wasn't big, but his presence was. Everywhere he went, he was liked." He certainly charmed women out of their inhibitions overseas, and later bragged that he had fathered children in France, Germany and England while serving in the Lorne Scots Infantry, a proud old Canadian regiment whose motto *Air-Son-Ar-Duthchais* translates to "For Our Heritage." Campbell's mother learned of these wartime escapades from her brothers- and sisters-in-law, which made it all the more embarrassing and painful for her. What Lorne's mother also didn't know when she met his father was that he'd been married to a woman named Rose when he went off to war. While still married to Rose, Lorne Sr. fathered a daughter, who was born in England in 1944, by a woman named Doris. He promised to bring Doris home when the war ended, telling her they would marry in Canada.

When the war was over, Lorne's father didn't bother to tell an army counsellor the extent of his romantic complications. The counsellor was duly impressed by what he *was* told, writing: "A neat responsive young man clean cut in appearance and sturdy in build, Campbell is wisely returning to his father's construction co. Experienced in most phases of the business, he intends to learn blue-print reading and then will be able to take over from his father whose health is poor. Thus it would appear that this man is well on the way to a satisfactory re-establishment in civilian life."

Lorne Sr. returned to Canada alone and promptly divorced Rose. It was around this time that he met Eileen and married her. All the while, he was still writing Doris and receiving love letters from her, which he hid in a secret cache.

Lorne Jr. grew up in a string of small rental homes in downtown Oshawa, on streets around Centre, Bloor, Albert, Celina, Simcoe, and a number of others whose names he can no longer recall. He does recall sticking up on the schoolyard for his first cousin Sanford [Sandy Hawley], who was six months younger and considerably smaller. "Nobody ever picked on Sandy." Sandy was so small that when he tried out for the football team, some of the larger kids suggested using him as the ball. Even back then, Sandy was tough and focused and dreamed of life as a jockey, while Lorne always wanted to be a cowboy.

The allure of cowboy life certainly had little to do with riding horses. Once, when he was about five, he was taken to a farm and plunked down on the back of a towering animal. "I remember my uncle slapping it and me falling off. It was a big horse." The draw of cowboy life was the notion of living at a time when the law was made according to what men felt was right in their guts and when agreements were sealed by handshakes, not indecipherable contracts. Perhaps that age never really existed, but going to the movies every Saturday encouraged him to think that it did. "Do I ever wish I had been a cowboy? I've often said that. There was more free-dom back then. There weren't as many luxuries, but you wouldn't have known that if you were alive back then—that would just be the way things were. I'm a romantic." In adult life he took to wearing cowboy boots, even though their soles scrape down quickly on asphalt when you're riding a motorcycle. He learned to wear them for a month or so and then attach an extra sole so they could handle the wear and tear of riding a bike. But it's not a cowboy thing, Campbell insists. "They're just comfortable."

Campbell's parents split up when he was eight. Certainly the beatings at the hands of his father were a factor in Eileen's decision to finally leave. Her eventual discovery of the secret stash of love letters from Doris in England likely didn't help either.

A single man again, Lorne Sr. phoned overseas to Doris. She had since married a Scotsman and was now leading what appeared to be a secure, if bloodless, life in England. Doris and her husband slept in separate beds and she dressed formally, even for breakfast.

Her sister answered the phone when he called.

"You know who this is?" he asked.

"Yeah, it's Lorne," the sister replied.

Within days, Doris flew to Canada, abandoning her life in England. Not long after that, she and Lorne Sr. were married. Maybe he had once been as much of a romantic as his son, but it didn't last. Romance was soon replaced by anger and abuse, just as it had been for Lorne's mother. "Doris took a lot of abuse from my dad. The same abuse as my mom. But [she] loved him to death."

After the breakup of his parents' marriage, Campbell wanted to live with his father, but a court ordered him to stay at his mother's home. It would be years before he was reunited with his father. Whatever respect for the law Campbell may have felt up to this point now disappeared. The law kept him under a different roof from his dad, and he loved his dad, beatings and all. His father hit him, but at least he didn't ignore him. Years later he would try to explain why he wanted so badly to live with his father, despite the violence: "In a child's mind, you think that's the way it is. That every family is like that. My dad wasn't a good dad, but I thought he was. He'd take me to the boxing club and box with me. I would always hear, 'You're going to be a fighter when you grow up.' My mother never had much to do with me in that way. . . . I was just devastated when my parents split up and it was decided I had to go with my mother. Just devastated."

Campbell was a smart if often angry student at South Simcoe Elementary School. "I fought every day at that school." Getting the strap was just another part of school life, like recess and homework, and on one particularly hard day when he was eleven years old, he and the principal set what must have been a school record. Fellow students counted to thirty-two as the strap slammed down on Campbell's hands. The principal had taken off his jacket and tie and leapt into the air to give his blows extra force. "He was trying to make me cry. He didn't. 'My dad can hurt me more than this,' I was thinking. The kids were counting. He felt so bad, he told me to wash my hands in cold water when he was finally done. And I got a beating from my mother when I got home."

During those years, Campbell lost contact with his father, even though they lived in the same city. He often thought of how his life would be better if the courts would only allow them to live together. He didn't reflect on his father's failure to pay child support even though he had well-paying factory jobs. "He had a beautiful personality. He was really funny." Campbell was intelligent enough to realize in later years that he had romanticized his dad in a way that didn't quite line up with reality. "In truth, my dad wouldn't have wanted me anyways and the beatings would have continued. . . . Everybody overlooked the idea he was beating my mother and he'd fuck anything that moved."

Campbell couldn't get comfortable at his mother's home, especially after a new stepfather moved in. The stepfather wasn't a bad man, but his arrival made a small house even more crowded and Campbell preferred to wander by himself at night. "I wasn't into anything, I would just stay out and walk the streets."

Two weeks before Campbell's fourteenth birthday, Eileen told authorities she couldn't handle him anymore. He hadn't been charged with any crime, but was classified as "unmanageable" by a judge. He spent that night in a steel-meshed cell. "I felt like a caged animal. A woman came down and sat with me. She talked to me for the longest time. I don't remember what she said, but she was a nice lady." He was stunned that he was about to be sent to a training school on the site of a Second World War prisoner-of-war camp in nearby Bowmanville, about twenty-five kilometres east of Oshawa.

"It was scary. It was two cops that drove me to Bowmanville. One of the cops said, 'You think you're tough? There's guys down there who can take you apart and put you back together again.' I didn't believe it. I said, 'Oh yeah?'"

Two weeks later, officials realized they had made a mistake, since Campbell was only thirteen and Bowmanville was for boys fourteen to eighteen. He was transferred to nearby Cobourg, where the youngest detainee was just five years old. The little boy was nicknamed "Cookie" and all the others rallied around and protected him because of his age. Campbell himself had no problems in Cobourg because he was one of the older, tougher kids. Some of the cabins there were named after British military leaders such as Cornwallis and Nelson, and Cobourg boys were expected to march everywhere, their arms swinging like little soldiers heading into battle. Shortly after his arrival, an older boy named Mailans told him he could expect a beating soon. There were no gangs in the training school, but there was a pronounced tribalism. Campbell was housed in Ramsay House and was quickly known as "the Rock of Ramsay," the toughest kid there. As such, he was expected to defend the house against taunts and attacks from boys in the other houses.

Campbell declared his personal war on bullies. "You've got to stop it before it starts. I'd stare at them knowing they'd eventually have to go, 'What the fuck are you staring at?' I'd go, 'You.' I'd know they were bullies just by watching them."

One afternoon, Campbell was holding some cleaning supplies when Mailans bumped into him on purpose. "I turned around and smacked him in the head." A supervisor named Montgomery jumped in the middle and then encouraged Campbell and Mailans to continue the fight in a washroom. What stood out about the supervisor was that he wore large, cheap rings on almost all of his fingers. He routinely organized fights between the young inmates. No weapons were allowed and combatants were forbidden from kicking an opponent who was down. Other than that, it was pretty much anything goes.

Surrounded by a circle of spectators, Campbell pummelled Mailans while the supervisor watched. "I beat the shit out of him." When Mailans could take no more blows and the fight was no longer entertaining, the supervisor ordered the other boys to leave the washroom and pulled Campbell aside.

His first shot caught Campbell totally by surprise. His rings raked across Campbell's face as he smashed him with an open hand. The supervisor backhanded him again and again. Decades later, Campbell could vividly recall the sensation of the rings tearing his face and the feeling of abject powerlessness in his gut. But the supervisor couldn't drive Campbell to despair. "All the time I was being beaten, I thought, 'I'm not going to be fourteen forever. I'm going to grow up.'"

What did get to him were arbitrary, impersonal, smothering rules, like when he was ordered to sit with his knees together and his hands crossed for hours on end. Sometimes this would stretch on for weeks, with breaks only for food and sleep. "That's when I started crying."

Another supervisor told Campbell that he was going to be placed in a foster home. Campbell advised him to give up on that idea. "I told him, 'If you send me to a foster home, I'll run away in an hour. Best just leave me here. I'm going home.'"

Academically, he scored an 84 percent average, the highest of all the boys, and it felt satisfying even though there was no parent around to congratulate him and no award to put on his wall. His father did come once for a visit. It took an hour for him to get the necessary clearance from Eileen since a court order barred him from meeting Lorne without her permission. That day, Campbell was playing football with the other boys and Supervisor Montgomery. It was just a touch game, but Montgomery wore cleats anyways, and in one violent collision he knocked Lorne out cold. They played on as Campbell lay by the side of the field. "I woke up and they were still playing football."

Not long after that, Campbell was enjoying his father's visit. He didn't bother mentioning the football game and how he had just been knocked unconscious. "I would never have complained to him because it wouldn't have done any good." Besides, it was a good day now and he didn't want to wreck what was left of it with whining. "It was the best thing that ever happened to me in there, because my mother never visited me. Never." The father and son talked that afternoon of how much they missed each other, but Campbell's father never visited him again.

After ten months in Cobourg, Campbell was returned to his mother. His father had given him his wartime France and Germany Star, Defence Medal, Canadian Volunteer Service Medal and clasp, War Medal 1939–45 and puttees, but when Campbell got home they were all gone. He kept asking his mother where she'd put them, but he never found out. "She would never answer me."

CHAPTER 2

Simcoe Street Parade

He told me to call him the Supreme Commander. I wouldn't do that.
I called him John.

Satan's Choice Motorcycle Club president BERNIE GUINDON
describing tensions with a rival biker

Campbell's mother was living in a second-storey walk-up apartment at 38½ Simcoe Street North, above Berg's Men's Wear in the city's core, when her son returned from training school at age fourteen. Across the street were the Colonel R.S. McLaughlin Armoury and the Queen's Hotel, where just by walking past the doors you could pollute your nostrils with the stale odour of spilt beer. Campbell's father was years behind in child support and his mother didn't have much money for food or anything else. Dinner at Eileen's apartment often consisted of near-meatless spaghetti and tomato soup and cream peas on toast, or other plain things at the low end of the comfort-food scale. The only time they had steak, it was round steak, the kind she had to pound repeatedly to get soft. She struggled to keep the place tidy, but that didn't take the slant out of the stairs or the wobble out of the furniture, and it certainly didn't make the apartment anywhere near good enough for Lorne to bring friends around. "I was embarrassed to bring a girl—or anyone else—to our apartment. I would never take anyone there, except close friends."

At nights, however, it offered a great view out onto Simcoe, as members of the old Phantom Riders Motorcycle Club took over the city's main street with a strange and seductive nighttime parade. "I'd sit at the window and watch the bikers go by. Bikers rode together back then. They don't so much anymore. That's the thing I've always enjoyed: riding in a pack."

The bikers outside his bedroom window oozed an aura of freedom and power, and of rich lives lived outside society's rules, which had done nothing to benefit the teenaged Campbell. Something about the bikers cruising past his window seemed all-powerful, as if they could tell death itself to fuck off, like old-time circus performers who could stick their heads into the mouths of lions and pull them out again, smiling, without a trace of fear.

Often he looked out at Bernie Guindon, a bootlegger's son who would soon help guide Campbell's life. Guindon was just six years older than Campbell, but he already seemed to have arrived somewhere special as he cruised past the *Conqueror*, a World War II tank stationed for posterity on the armoury front lawn. Guindon was easy to spot at the front of the pack, with his little black beanie helmet and gold chopper, the *Wild Thing*, its handlebars so high that it would tire a weak man to ride it a block. His odd headwear was far more than his own personal fashion statement. In a brawl, Guindon could slip his fist inside it and make his punches even harder. Once, during a particularly spirited brawl, he punched his way right through his own helmet. Campbell didn't know Guindon but yearned to ride with him and his club and feel for himself that kind of power. "I thought, 'Holy fuck! That's my life!'"

Guindon was often accompanied by Carmen Neal, a Native ironworker, and Reg Hawk, a legless accountant who rode a three-wheeler motorcycle converted from a milk delivery vehicle. The plastic ghost cartoon crests on the backs of their jackets gave off an otherworldly glow from the street lights and headlights. "They'd have scarves around their necks. . . . I just thought it was the coolest fucking thing I'd ever seen."

Sometimes Campbell would see Neal riding in the early hours of the morning, fearless and alone, on guard against a rival club, the Black

Diamond Riders. "Carmen Neal was a very proud guy. He rode through Oshawa like a sentry. He set up his Harley so that flames would come out of the pipes when he turned it on. He'd rev it up and flames would come out of the stacks on one side. At two in the morning I'd look out and see Carmen patrolling the downtown."

Guindon felt something special too as he rode down the street at the front of the line of Phantom Riders as if on some unspoken mission. He had grown up in the city's gut, helping his father peddle moonshine from their apartment in the back of a store at 502 Simcoe Street South, which was later levelled to make way for a shopping complex. Guindon's dad alternated hours of operation with another bootlegger so the city would never have to be without cheap booze. Often his father over-indulged himself, leaving Bernie and his brother Jack (Banana Nose) in charge. For this, the Guindon boys were paid twenty-five cents each, enough for a bottle of pop and a seat at the movies, where Guindon particularly enjoyed Roy Rogers, the Lone Ranger and Hopalong Cassidy. "I wanted to be a cowboy," he told me when we met.

Sometimes customers would urge Bernie and Jack to fight each other for their drunken entertainment. Jack was ten months older, but Bernie was clearly the better fighter. "That's how I learned to fight. They'd get me and my brother to fight and say they'd give a quarter to the guy who won."

Guindon wasn't too impressed with the booze-seeking customers who frequented his home, which helps explain why he was close to being a teetotaller in later years. "Every day you'd see guys coming into the house. Guys would be fighting with [my father]."

He also wasn't too impressed by the local cops who showed up expecting discount—or gratis—liquor. He and his father were stopped once by a police officer while picking through the remains of a burned electrical store, looking for something worth lifting. The cop seemed ready to arrest them until he recognized Guindon's father. "I found out later the old man used to pull b and e's [break and enters] with the guy. The guy was a cop now and drove us home."

What did impress Guindon when he was a boy were motorcycles, and that feeling would never leave him. When Guindon was just fifteen, a member of the Golden Hawks named Bill let him ride his 1955

Harley-Davidson, with Bill on the back, thirty-eight kilometres, from Peterborough to Pontypool. Guindon's own first bike was a British AJS single-cylinder model, and he soon became good enough to leap cars and trailers as a member of Canada's Hell Riders, a trick-riding troupe nicknamed "the original crash test dummies."

So it had been a big deal for Guindon when he was allowed to become a hangaround for the Golden Hawks in 1959 and then a full member at just seventeen years of age. "It wasn't like today. It was totally different. You didn't have to kiss ass. You didn't have to strike [become a probationary member]. They had to get to know you. Know how you rode a bike."

It was a time when clubs formed and folded quickly, and Guindon was still in his teens when he helped found the Phantom Riders Motorcycle Club. By day, he worked on the assembly line at General Motors, but at night, as head of the pack of Phantom Riders, Guindon was free of bosses and schedules, making his own laws and daring anyone to say otherwise. "We always felt powerful. You'd go by the old Cadillac Hotel and all the rubbies and nobody ever knocked us. If they did, we'd be knocking them. You always felt like you had a club behind you, a bunch of guys that were friends."

One of those friends was Wayne Willerton, a fellow General Motors assembly line worker who had been making Chevelles and Novas ever since he dropped out of school at age sixteen. Willerton felt transformed at night as he tied a dirty rag over his head and pulled out his dental plate, leaving a tough-guy gap where he'd lost four teeth. Atop his 750 Norton Commando in Guindon's Simcoe Street parade, Willerton felt like a somebody: "I felt like I was on top of the world. I felt like we ruled the world. I just felt the power."

Power wasn't something the Willerton men had been familiar with since Wayne's father had arrived in Canada at age fourteen to work on a farm near Port Perry, north of Oshawa. Willerton's father was a "Barnardo boy," a ward of an organization started in Victorian times to transport ragged orphans and neglected and disabled children from London's slums to Canadian farms. The original goal of founder Thomas Barnardo was noble, but by Willerton's father's time the organization's practices were often shoddy, or worse. Barnardo boys worked for near slave wages, and many later complained of physical and sexual abuse. For his part, Willerton's father arrived in Canada with no more than a black briefcase and a severe limp from the polio that had left one leg shorter than the other. The experience left him with bitter memories of making just five dollars a month and having nothing more than a bible to read under a bare light bulb. Willerton's father also harboured severe misgivings about people in authority, those who purported to be looking out for him. "He used to always say the Queen's shit stinks like the rest of us," Wayne Willerton recalls.

Impressive as his club was in their late night parades, Guindon dreamed of creating something far bigger than the Golden Hawks. He wanted to eclipse the semi-mythical head of the Black Diamond Riders, a Toronto biker known as "Johnny Sombrero," or "Sombrero" for short.

Sombrero was nothing if not a cocky adversary for Guindon and his followers. His real name was Harold Barnes, but he preferred to be addressed as "Supreme Commander" of the Black Diamond Riders, apparently not blushing as he lifted Dwight D. Eisenhower's Second World War title. "I never seen him with a sombrero," Guindon said in an interview years later. Whatever you thought of Supreme Commander Sombrero's name and title, you had to be impressed by his spunk. He once wrote to the Queen asking her blessing for himself and his minions to rid Canada of outlaw motorcycle clubs—except for the BDRs—much like seamen in centuries past would seek a monarch's blessing to rid the high seas of pirates. For reasons Her Majesty kept to herself, she declined to get involved.

Things got off on the wrong foot between Guindon and Sombrero, and deteriorated from there. "He told me to call him the Supreme Commander," Guindon says. "I wouldn't do that. I called him John." In 1961, even without the sought-after royal charter, Sombrero was in the midst of his campaign against lesser biker clubs. The struggle was for status and bragging rights, since there was nothing to actually take from the other clubs. In Sombrero's world you defined yourself by your rivals, and by your ability to send those rivals running in fear. Sombrero had shut down a biker club of teenagers called Satan's Choice, yanking their patches of a grinning Satan from members' backs. Then he set his sights on the Golden Hawks, Guindon's first club.

Young bikers who had never heard of the Battle of Hastings or the War of 1812 would later learn about the treachery that took place at a field day one afternoon in 1962 at Pebblestone Park outside Oshawa. It was supposed to be a fun event, with bikers partying, carousing and racing around on their motorcycles. Guindon thought it odd that members of the Black Diamond Riders were not joining in the play but instead carving down branches from trees in the park. Guindon alerted fellow Golden Hawks that something nasty was afoot that afternoon but, as he recalls, he was told, "'They would never do that at a field day.' It was unheard of."

Not long after his warning was dismissed, the Black Diamond Riders charged, doing passable Mickey Mantle impersonations with their freshly cut clubs. One Golden Hawk suffered a brain hemorrhage. At least one member barricaded himself in a car. Others sprinted for safety. At the end of the day, Sombrero had a fistful of Golden Hawk patches and the once proud Golden Hawks had been rechristened the Chicken Hawks.

Guindon answered by forming a new club he called the Phantom Riders. Many of the members, like Wayne Willerton, were recruited from the General Motors assembly line. Soon, Guindon heard that Sombrero had placed a bounty on them, offering a case of beer for every Phantom Rider patch that was delivered to him. "After what they did to the Golden Hawks in '62, when they did take some patches, I had a hard-on for them."

Hope for Guindon came in the unexpected form of a young moviemaker. It was in 1965 that Guindon got wind that director Donald Shebib planned to make a film about outlaw biker clubs. Shebib sniffed around the Vagabonds, Para-Dice Riders and Canadian Lancers, with no success. "They either weren't interested or their clubs weren't big enough," Willerton recalled years later in an interview. Guindon was different. He loved the idea of being in a film.

Guindon was able to convince the Canadian Lancers, the Plague and the Apostles from the Toronto/Oshawa area, the Throttle Twisters from

the Galt/Hespeler area and a few Red Devils from Hamilton to come together to form a super-club worthy of the camera's attention and perhaps
even Sombrero's fear. For almost half a year they struggled to come up
with a suitable name for the new club. Guindon liked the sound of "Satan's
Choice," as did the other club presidents. He had been friends with the
Satan's Choice's original founder, Don Norris, since they were teenagers,
and Norris was ecstatic when Guindon arrived at his door with the presidents of the Canadian Lancers, Plague, Apostles and Throttle Twisters
and a request. Says Guindon, "We wanted to amalgamate the four clubs
under one set of colours and he wanted the SCMC [Satan's Choice
Motorcycle Club] colours to be the banner they would all ride under. I told
him we would never, ever lose it to the Black Diamond Riders." As Norris
remembers, "I was ecstatic. It pulled me out of a funk. The folding of the
original SCMC had depressed me for some time. I knew if anyone could
pull off a resurrection of SCMC, it would be Bernie."

With that, Guindon's new mega-club stitched the image of a grinning
devil on the backs of their jackets, a blunt statement that his pack of
bikers weren't to be fucked with.

It was also an unmistakable fuck you to Sombrero.

That summer, when the Satan's Choice arose from the dead, Shebib
and his National Film Board camera crew turned their story into a docu-
mentary, although some members had hoped for a feature film like *The
Wild One* that would play in movie theatres. "They were everywhere we
went," Willerton recalls. "They seemed to be having as much fun as us."

If the Choice were somewhat of a media creation, that wasn't a first
for bikerdom. As Hunter S. Thompson wrote in *Hell's Angels*, massive
publicity about the biker world in the mid-1960s changed both the
nature of policing and the biker subculture as well. "The Hell's Angels
as they exist today were virtually created by *Time, Newsweek* and *The
New York Times*," Thompson wrote in 1966. (Back then, the Angels
spelled their first name "Hell's," but it changed along the way to "Hells"
after a protracted internal debate about how many hells might exist.)
There was something fitting about life imitating art in the rebirth of the
Choice. Like most kids of his generation, Campbell had seen *The Wild
One*, starring Marlon Brando and Lee Marvin. He especially loved the

opening, with a rumbling pack of motorcycles riding right at the screen, as if attacking it head-on. He wasn't so impressed with Brando's main character, who seemed more pouty than menacing, even though Brando became the public face of youthful rebellion when he was asked, "What are you rebelling against?" and he replied, "Whaddya got?"

For Campbell and many in the outlaw biker world of one-percenters (the estimated one percent of motorcyclists who don't feel particularly confined by the law), the real star was Marvin's character, Chino, who rode an American-made Harley-Davidson as opposed to Brando's British Triumph. More importantly, Marvin's character was based on a real-life biker, Willie (Wino) Forkner, a member of the old Boozefighters gang. "That's the guy in that movie," says Campbell. "Marlon Brando acted like a faggot, a sissy. 'What are you rebelling against?' 'Whattya got?' What's that?" While he loved the movies, Campbell wasn't big on superfluous drama. His screen heroes while he was growing up weren't moaners and criers and hand-wringers, and they didn't speak unless they had something to say, like Lee Marvin in *The Wild One* and *Cat Ballou* and John Wayne in just about anything. They were characters who played the hands they were dealt without bellyaching. And when Campbell's onscreen heroes gave a warning, they didn't repeat it.

So it was with considerable pride that Guindon rode up to Sombrero's clubhouse near Steeles and Yonge in Toronto's north end as the head of the new, bigger-than-ever Satan's Choice. Backed up by some of his tougher members, Guindon marched up to the Supreme Commander and reintroduced himself. "We went into the clubhouse and we told him, 'You'll never take our patches again.'"

Sombrero seemed strangely uninterested, looking behind Guindon.

"There's a rabbit on the front lawn," he said.

Guindon suspected this was a ploy by Sombrero to get him to turn around so Sombrero could jump him. "I'm not turning around for that sucker thing."

He kept his eyes on Sombrero, but his head shifted ever so slightly. In his peripheral vision, he saw a bunny go hopping by.

Campbell was at a dance at Gord's A Go Go, on the eastern outskirts of Oshawa. He was seventeen and living on his own, hanging with a close group of friends. One of his buddies had been beaten up that night by three guys from Hamilton, and Campbell was now circling the building, looking to exact revenge on the trio.

When he returned to the front of the building, he saw two of his childhood heroes: Bernie Guindon and Carmen Neal. There were also the three guys from Hamilton he was looking for, and they were clearly talking about something serious to the Satan's Choice leaders.

CHAPTER 3

Growing Pains

I thought he was dead. . . . He just lay there. You could see the whites of his eyes."

LORNE CAMPBELL

ampbell could hear one of the Hamiltonians, named Scotty, asking: "Do you know any martial arts guys? Any karate guys?" Campbell had heard that Guindon ran a fight club, long before that term became a part of popular culture. The fights were held in the makeshift boxing ring in the basement of Guindon's red brick bungalow at 480 Browning Avenue, in an enclave of non-rental brick homes that was definitely a cut above anywhere Campbell had ever resided. Guindon's house was alternately known as the Satan's Choice clubhouse and the Oshawa Boxing Club.

"I said to Bernie, 'Them three guys just beat up John. Can I come with you? I'd like to fight one of those guys.'" It was the first time they had ever spoken, and Guindon said yes. Within a few minutes Campbell was in the back of Neal's car, heading to Guindon's home.

Neal took a quick liking to Campbell, and said with a wink, "Even if you lose, you don't lose."

Willerton remembered the Hamilton visitors looking queasy when they walked down into Guindon's basement, where they saw a "splasher"—a girl eager to provide sex to club members—a boxing ring, a heavy punching bag, a few dumbbells and a motorcycle repair area. Getting out of the basement intact would be far more challenging than they'd thought.

The first match of the night was boxing, with three-minute rounds, and it featured Guindon and the Hamiltonian named Scotty. Halfway through the second round, Guindon dropped his gloves and let Scotty hit him as hard and as often as he wanted. Guindon just grinned back, as if he was immensely enjoying his up-close view of the oncoming fists.

In the third round, Guindon got down to business and starched Scotty with a sharp, short hook. "He was just smiling at him and then he knocked him out. I was impressed. He was exactly the way I was brought up. He confronted everything. He was a far better fighter than I ever was."

Reg Hawk was also keen to fight, despite the fact that he had two artificial legs, donated by the local Kiwanis club. Hawk had powerful forearms, the result of walking on double canes his entire life. The grocery store bookkeeper was keenly sensitive about the fact that he had never had legs, lest people write him off as a born loser. "He kind of let people think it was a motorcycle accident," Willerton said. "That kind of made him look tougher. I guess people would think, 'What a huge man he would have been before the accident.' But he was born a little guy with no legs." Hawk had devised his own form of self-defence based on cane swinging, Willerton recalled, and his unique fighting skills would do a ninja warrior proud. "He was brutal. He knew how to use those canes."

Perhaps word had already travelled to Hamilton about Hawk's prowess with his canes, as one of the visitors immediately rushed him. There was no room to swing them and Hawk's artificial legs splayed as the two men hit the floor. Unfortunately for the Hamiltonian, Hawk's backup plan was just as formidable as his caning powers. "He grabbed the guy and it was all over," Willerton remembers. "He had big arms. He just grabbed him and started squeezing."

Campbell was up next with a bout against a Hamiltonian called Billy. It was a modified street fight. Kicking was allowed, but not when the opponent was down on the floor. Campbell's father wouldn't have

approved as he opened with a hard boot to Billy's groin. He had practised the move often, and it worked as planned that evening, tenderizing
Billy considerably for Campbell's next shot. "He threw a right. I ducked
once and came across with a left. He went down."

Scotty, the biker Guindon had dispatched in the first bout, was conscious and feisty again. "Scotty thought I was going to kick him [Billy],
but I wasn't. He grabbed me from behind."

That was just the permission Guindon needed to get back into the
fray. He grabbed Billy, spun him around and landed another crisp, hard
hook. It was the defining shot of a night of semi-organized violence. "I
thought he was dead. His head hit the concrete when he went down and
he was out before he hit the floor. He just lay there. You could see the
whites of his eyes." Billy wisely declined a rematch with Campbell. "He
was finished."

The next day, once the bloodied Hamiltonians were gone from the
clubhouse, Guindon nominated Campbell to become a "striker," or probationary member, of the Satan's Choice Motorcycle Club. Later that
year, Campbell became their youngest-ever full member. "I didn't nomi-
nate many guys. He had parts." Guindon made this comment during an
interview in a room full of women. Asked what "parts" meant, Guindon
whispered, "It's not polite to use 'balls' in front of ladies. The slang word
would be 'parts'."

"Right away you thought this guy would be a good candidate for the
club," Willerton agreed. Eighteen years after that, Campbell would run
across the man he had beaten in the fight. Billy was then an inmate barber
at Collins Bay Penitentiary and cut Campbell's hair and shaved him with
a straight razor. He either didn't recall Campbell or didn't bear any hard
feelings as he applied the sharp blade to Campbell's cheeks. Whatever the
case, Campbell started shaving himself in prison after that.

Back in 1966, in his new status as a full-fledged Satan's Choice member,
Campbell rode a Triumph Bonneville he bought from another member.
For their initiations, some new members had outhouse buckets emptied
on them at a club property near Coboconk, in cottage country, while
others held them down. "Guys would fight back. They'd run and fight
and everything," Willerton says. Campbell says that members often

joined in the dirtying of their colours. "Everybody was trying to get their crests nice and dirty. Have everybody at a party pour beer on it, step on it, urinate on it. One guy, Pigpen, puked on it."

Campbell's initiation was relatively tame compared with what was inflicted upon other members. It wasn't that fellow bikers were in a polite mood the day Campbell joined their ranks; they just didn't want him to punch them out. The day he became a full member, Campbell bought beer for a party while others dirtied his club crest. "I got food and mustard thrown on my colours. Mine was dirty five minutes after I became a member."

Campbell took to wearing his Choice patch on the back of a brown buckskin jacket he bought at Berg's Men's Wear, beneath his old family apartment. It cost eighty-four dollars and had eighteen-inch fringes. Girls riding on the back of his bike would pull off handfuls of fringes as souvenirs. Within four months there were just a few of them left hanging from the jacket, so he cut off the sleeves to make it into a vest.

It seemed like no time before the Choice had swelled to thirteen chapters and some five hundred members, easily making it Canada's biggest, baddest outlaw motorcycle club. They chose Canada's colours—red and white—as their own and Guindon nourished the dream of expanding from coast to coast. Membership was fluid, with a high turnover in the ranks. "In a year or two you'd lose at least a hundred members," Guindon recalls. "They'd come and go so fast." A rumour circulated that prospective members had to murder someone to get into the club. Long-time member Bill (Mr. Bill) Lavoie joked that the body count would fill a cemetery the size of the city of Cobourg if this were true.

Campbell and Guindon were particularly proud that they were from the "Mother"—or founding—chapter of the club, and that they rode together, in formation, two abreast. "The Oshawa chapter always stood proud," Guindon says. "We'd fight anybody and ride to the fight." Adds Campbell: "There wasn't machine guns or knives back then, but there were pretty serious fights."

Guindon wanted plenty of fresh blood in his club, but he didn't want druggies, who reminded him of the annoying rubbies from his father's old bootlegging operation. "I didn't allow drugs in the club, believe it or not." Pain-killing Percocets and green speed pills were particularly common back then, and both drugs produced addicts. "I didn't want guys like that." He threatened anyone caught with drugs with a baseball bat beating, but that wasn't really necessary. "I had these," Guindon says, holding up his fists. "The bat was merely a backup system."

Despite the warning, Campbell and Willerton once tried smoking a nickel bag of particularly low-grade marijuana while riding in Willerton's white 1957 Chevy convertible, which had *Barbarian* painted on its side. For all the hype about marijuana, they were decidedly underwhelmed as they puffed on a joint.

"Do you notice anything different?" Campbell asked.

"The posts seem to be coming slower," Willerton said, motioning towards the oncoming street lights.

"Yeah, I see that," Campbell replied.

"Maybe I'm just driving slower," Willerton observed.

They mulled over that possibility and soon decided that non-premium pot wasn't worth the effort.

Campbell and Willerton were among the hundred or so Choice at a field day in Heidelberg, near Kitchener, in the summer of 1966. There were plenty of laughs when a salesman in a suit, who had been peddling condoms, bolted after bikers absconded with his products, blew them up like balloons and launched them into the air. There were more laughs at the expense of Alex Trebek, future host of the television game show *Jeopardy*. Trebek, then a television reporter covering the event, went red-faced when a splasher approached him and simulated oral sex on his CBC microphone.

"Weren't you the splasher we were with last night?" Willerton asked her when she was done with Trebek's microphone.

"Yeah, I didn't mind, but one of them stole my panties," she replied matter-of-factly.

As the weekend wound down, a young biker who wasn't with any club tried to impress other riders by doing an extended wheel stand. He wiped out, dying on the pavement.

On their way home, Willerton stole chocolate bars and chips from a gas station, more for the fun than the food. Not to be outdone, Campbell lifted a car tire with a Display sign on it. They knew there wasn't much point in stealing only one car tire, just as there wasn't much hope for a successful getaway when they were double-riding on a motorcycle, with Campbell holding the tire and sign.

Later that day, Campbell and Willerton occupied neighbouring jail cells and Willerton was able to slip Campbell some chocolate bars and chips. The charges were eventually settled with a fifty-dollar fine for possession of stolen goods.

Back at the GM plant after weekend escapades like these, Willerton was treated like a rock star, as he showed up for the assembly line with steel-tipped cowboy boots and plenty of stories. "Guys would always come around. [They'd say,] 'What did you do? Where did you go?'"

"That guy must be in a band," said one worker who didn't know about Willerton's Choice membership.

"Oh, he's in a band all right," another worker replied.

Willerton could barely contain himself one evening when he was home and the television news came on with a story of a fresh biker bust.

"Mom, we're going to be on TV."

She saw film footage of her son being escorted out of a paddy wagon.

"She was not impressed," Willerton recalls.

Campbell had *Elinor* tattooed onto his upper right arm for his girl-friend when he was seventeen, along with Japanese characters on his left leg that meant "the gentle art of karate." His father wouldn't have approved, but he was now practising karate daily. Getting this ink work was a far more pleasant experience than some of his earlier ventures to tattoo parlours. At fifteen, he'd had *Lorne* inked onto his arm at Don Spicer Tattoos at the corner of Simcoe and Bond streets in Oshawa. "I thought I was going to pass out." His queasiness about the needle was offset to a point by the sight of the panty-less artist inking his skin. "She had a miniskirt pulled up. I was thinking, 'Should I go for it?' I didn't. I wish I would have went for it."

At sixteen, he added a cross for his sister Roberta, who had died at six months, and Pegasus, the winged mythological horse. The tattoos at age seventeen—including *Elinor*—were done in the basement of a building next to the Warwick Hotel in downtown Toronto, on Jarvis Street near Maple Leaf Gardens, legendary home of the Toronto Maple Leafs hockey team. Literary types knew the Warwick as the one-time home of novelist Hugh Garner, while sleaze aficionados were familiar with it as the base of operations for a "No cover. No minimum" strip club and an assortment of weary prostitutes.

The tattoo artist who worked next to the Warwick was known as "the Chinaman," and he was one of a small and select group of local skin art professionals that also included Sailor Joe ("the most tattooed man in the world") and the Beachcomber. The Chinaman was a fine artist, but he was no stickler for sanitation. "He had a fish tank. It was so dirty you couldn't see the fish. [I thought,] 'And you're getting tattoos there?'"

When Elinor became pregnant, Campbell moved in with her and her father. The latter was a factory maintenance man, and it was a solid Oshawa house with two upstairs bedrooms. He was also a Second World War veteran and a divorcee who smoked heavily and was prone to bouts of binge drinking. More than anything else, he was a protective father. "I don't think he liked the idea that Elinor was pregnant, but he loved our daughter, Janice, to death after her birth."

Riding season officially began each year with the Victoria Day weekend in May. That's when all club members were expected to have their bikes on the road for a major party, generally held at Wasaga Beach on Georgian Bay, north of Toronto. Elinor was expecting the baby to arrive that weekend in 1967. Campbell was eighteen years old, a year older than Elinor. Campbell drove her to the hospital when she went into labour. Then he collected his mother and drove her to the hospital too. Immediately after Janice's birth, he rejoined his biker buddies for two days of hard partying, something he would later regret. "That's a real prick thing to do."

The Choice rode into Wasaga Beach that weekend a hundred bikers strong, like modern-day Cossack warriors. Cabins had already been rented by a girlfriend of a club member, since no one in their right mind would rent rooms to a patch-wearing outlaw biker for the May Two-Four weekend (the Victoria Day holiday, which occurs as near as possible to May 24, nicknamed May Two-Four like the twenty-four case of beer).

On the ride into Wasaga Beach, two Red Devils somehow offended Guindon. When they pulled over to the side of the road, he levelled one of them with a short, hard shot. Then he turned to his buddy and laid him out too. "With Bernie, there was no waiting," Willerton recalls.

At the back of the pack was a jumbo-sized Choice member with a squeaky voice named Crash, who was a legend of sorts in the outlaw biker world. He was surrounded by bike-riding experts who could maintain a tight formation at a hundred kilometres an hour with no stress, like an asphalt version of the Royal Canadian Air Force precision flying team, the Snowbirds. Crash, by contrast, was a remarkably bad rider even by regular standards, and remained uniquely unable to master the most essential part of motorcycle riding: coming to a full stop without smashing hard into something or somebody.

Guindon wasn't a patient instructor, but he was a knowledgeable and enthusiastic one. He genuinely liked Crash, whom he met at GM. He tried to tell Crash that it was important to use the brakes and to gear down if he wanted to pull over safely. He might as well have been explaining advanced physics to a goat. More than once, when riding at the back of the pack, Crash simply zoned out and lost control. "Crash came from the back of the pack and ran into the side of this guy," Willerton says. "The guy flew off his bike. Crash flew off his bike. That was Crash."

On a tour of Manhattan with other Choice members, Crash once managed to lurch with his growling chopper onto a crowded sidewalk, sending horror-struck New Yorkers scrambling for their lives. Yet another time, Crash barrelled through a tent set up by the Para-Dice Riders at a field day and came to a stop with a hard collision that put their bikes out of operation.

Years later, at a Christmas get-together at Campbell's home in December 2011, Guindon, Willerton and Campbell were reminiscing about the old days when the topic turned to Crash.

"It's a wonder he didn't get a shit-kicking," Guindon said.

"Everybody knew he was your friend," Campbell replied.

Guindon made Crash ride far to the back of the pack, but that just delayed the inevitable, as he kept running hard into the backs of other members' bikes.

"Crash! What are you doing? Hit the brakes!" Guindon would shout at him.

"I don't know what happened, Bernie," Crash would reply, his voice as high as a schoolgirl's.

Crash's personal life was as jarring as his motorcycle riding. "Crash started going out with a splasher and he was going to marry her," Campbell recalls. "During that same time, she had been with a whole bunch of guys, splashed all of the time."

Crash went to Guindon with a personal question that had been gnawing at him.

"Remember when the guys were with her?" Crash asked. "There was only three or four guys, wasn't there?"

"Yeah," Guindon lied, not wanting to hurt his friend's feelings.

In 1967, Campbell broke his foot and split his ear when running an intersection while doing a wheel stand. That was also the year the club got news that Neal had died out West in what had started as a prank on a construction site. Workers were throwing water back and forth at each other when someone threw a bucket of a flammable liquid on Neal. It ignited, and club members heard how Neal had kept walking while on fire, and how his body was cooled with ice in hospital until the pain ended only when he stopped breathing. Fifteen clubs from Montreal to Windsor showed up for the funeral, with about two hundred members putting on a show of respect. In outlaw biker fashion, the bikers didn't wear helmets in the funeral procession in Durham Region and shovelled the dirt onto the grave themselves.

Club colours were as sacred as anything in their world, so Campbell was upset when two Red Devils from Hamilton showed up for a party in Scarborough with jackets over their patches. The Red Devils liked to bill themselves as Canada's oldest outlaw biker club, but this evening it was as though they were ashamed of their identities. "These guys are hiding their patches, so they ended up getting a beating. In all fairness to them, they got beaten, but they fought." They didn't fight well enough, and so after Campbell punched them out, he rolled them over and yanked off their club crests.

The captured patches were hung on the wall of the Choice clubhouse alongside patches from the Warlords, Outcasts, Satan's Martyrs ("They were cocky, but only for a few minutes"), Hell's Creation, 13th Sin, Wheels of Destruction, Wild Rebels, Lonesome Rogues, Trojans, Vikings, Prophets of Hell and plenty of other clubs.

It was survival of the fittest and a culling of the herd; a two-wheeled version of Charles Darwin's theory of natural selection. For his part, Campbell doesn't get bogged down in theoretical terms when explaining why they pulled the other clubs' patches: "We were the biggest guys on the block. We didn't want any other clubs in the area. We wanted to be the only boys on the block. It was just, 'We're Satan's Choice and don't fuck with us.'"

There were hippies who considered outlaw bikers to be the noble savages of the 1960s counterculture. Choice members may have liked psychedelic music and free love (or at least sex), but they weren't so big on the flower-power philosophy of the largely middle-class hippies. "I didn't like hippies," Campbell says. "They were professing peace and love and everything and I didn't advocate that at all."

Campbell's crowd was quasi-militaristic and attracted to the power of packs, drawing a strict line between themselves and "civilians" who weren't in clubs. They looked like a leathered army of sorts, travelling in a line of roaring Harleys, trailed by a green hearse filled with beer. "Back in those days it was all about freaking people out," Willerton says.

Part of freaking people out was wearing Nazi memorabilia, which was relatively common and cheap in the 1960s. There was a widely circulated story that the Canadian Nazi Party thought they had fascist political allies in the Satan's Choice, and that they offered them land for muscle. Guindon says he wasn't aware if it was true but that he would have told the Nazis to fuck off if he had ever been approached. For his part, Willerton bought a German soldier's helmet at a flea market, then had it chromed lest anyone not notice it. He relished the attention until an elderly veteran shouted at him, "Look at that trash." Willerton couldn't help but sympathize with the old soldier.

Campbell would later cringe while recalling the lengths to which outlaw bikers went to inflict shocks on civilians. "Guys have eaten their own shit. Drank their own vomit. That was part of what people did to freak people out." The most shocking of the one-percenters, without peer, was Howard from Peterborough, the original "Pigpen" in Canadian outlaw biker circles. He patrolled the outer frontiers of crazy all by himself. There would be a host of other bikers called Pigpen over the years, just as there would be a waddling parade of 300-plus-pound guys called Tiny. Each of these Pigpens was revolting in his own right, but no one embodied the essence of the name better than Howard. Once, while visiting the Hamilton clubhouse, Pigpen went out to a corner store to buy some cigarettes. "He put his hand down his pants. He had shit himself. When the girl turned around to hand him cigarettes, he handed shit to her. She ran out down the street." Shocking people was like oxygen for Pigpen. "He was eating Tampax. Not Tampax just out of the box. Even eating dog shit. He wouldn't try stuff like that with me. I told him, 'If you ever try that with me, I'll kill you.'"

Back when he was a striker for the Peterborough chapter, Pigpen had seemed relatively normal. He was a good-looking, well-groomed, tattoo-less man with a solid education and an obviously high IQ. Somehow, the rush of being an outlaw biker surrounded by other rebels was too much for him. "Within six weeks, he was a nutcase. . . . It never impressed me, people like that. . . . They called it 'pulling class.' It was freaking the public out. Now, clubs own their clubhouses and they are always tidy. They're cleaner than most houses. Back then, the clubhouses were always rented. The guys would get scabies in them.

"He'd flip out at meetings. They'd [Peterborough members] jump him. Knock him out cold. He'd either wake up and sit down or they'd have to do it again." Pigpen's craziness was directed towards himself as well as others. He pulled out his teeth with pliers lest dentists insert listening devices into his mouth. In one of his increasingly rare moments of relative normalcy, Pigpen appealed to a jailhouse doctor.

"You have to help me," Pigpen confided. "I'm starting to eat my own shit."

Campbell heard from Pigpen that the plea for psychiatric aid didn't go well: "The doctor just ended the interview. He said, 'I'm not ready for you yet.'"

Once, while awaiting a court appearance in a holding cell, Pigpen decided that he just wanted to be left alone. Normally, guards would force reluctant prisoners to go to court, but Pigpen had a plan. He stripped off his clothing and smeared his body with feces, from head to toe. Not surprisingly, the ploy worked, and guards kept him at a distance and out of the courtroom.

"When he told me about that, he was proud," Campbell recalls. "He said, 'Who won?'"

"You did, Howard," Campbell replied, not wanting to excite Pigpen further.

Greatness of any sort seldom goes unchallenged. At one get-together, Windsor Satan's Choice members rolled out their own Pigpen, billed as "the Classman from Windsor," whom they considered the most disgusting person on wheels. "He had eaten a mouse. Howard [Pigpen] would not be outdone. He said to the guys, 'Go out and find a mouse.'"

The bikers managed to catch a live fieldmouse, which the Classman grabbed. "He bites the head right off the mouse. The mouse was squirming. He put the body on the table. He's not spitting out the head. Howard won't be outdone. They both kept breaking it apart, taking the intestines, eating them like it was caviar [or] sirloin steak. I went outside, thinking I was solid. I couldn't get out fast enough, just turning to the left and letting her go."

Sometime in the early 1970s, Pigpen fled to the Carolinas, staying ahead of Canadian charges. While there, he joined up with the Outlaws Motorcycle Club, changing his biker name from Pigpen to the alias "Garbage." The Outlaws and the Satan's Choice were on friendly terms and had a brotherhood pact, which made it fairly easy to make the switch from club to club. "Whatever happened to him?" Campbell said when asked. "He's running a restaurant with his lovely wife." Campbell chortled at the absurdity of the notion.

It was common for bikers to ride into a town in a pack and leave shortly afterwards with an eager police escort. "They just wanted to get you out of their jurisdiction," Willerton says. "They didn't want to touch us with a ten-foot pole."

Not all the police were so accommodating. There was an Oshawa officer named Forchette whom Guindon insisted on calling For-Shit. It didn't help that Forchette was an aspiring boxer and that Guindon had seriously tuned him up in the ring. They fought on the lawn outside Guindon's home one day and Guindon paid for the tussle by spending the next few months in jail. When he returned to General Motors, Guindon was told he was out of a job unless he mended his ways. "If I would quit riding my bike to work, then they would give me my job," Guindon recalls. He told them to stick it and climbed back on his motorcycle. With that, his five-year career as an autoworker was over in 1968. Years later, Guindon said he could understand why they wanted him out of the plant. "I wore my colours to work and I started a lot of other guys wearing colours to work."

At the age of eighteen, Campbell found work on a tobacco farm northeast of Oshawa. The job occasionally involved riding a horse, something he hadn't tried since he was five years old. Now, on the cusp of adulthood, he was told to ride a Morgan draft horse. "The horse wouldn't obey me, so we headed back to the barn, where I fell off." He fell in slow motion, as if in a cartoon. He quit the job that day and thereafter confined his riding to motorcycles. "My dreams of being a cowboy were over."

Next, Campbell drove trucks for Canada Dry, Pepsi and North American Steel, and worked on the loading dock for the steel company. When he wanted a break, he deliberately sliced his hand, took four or five stitches, and enjoyed a week of recuperation.

"I want some time off, but I want more," said a co-worker Campbell didn't particularly like. "Can you help?"

"I can. How much time you want off?"

"Six months or so."

Campbell prepared to swing a sheet of 18-gauge steel across the man's arm. It would be more than enough to leave a bloody stump and take him off the job forever. At the last second, the man saw the steel about to cut into him and yanked his arm away. "He had no idea what my mind was about," Campbell says.

The Satan's Choice lost their leader in 1968, when Guindon and five other bikers were convicted of raping a fifteen-year-old girl in an Ottawa home. He was twenty-four at the time. There were so many sexual assaults committed by outlaw bikers back then that the Hells Angels felt the need to draft a rule specifically forbidding rape. There were also plenty of orgies, when willing women and girls serviced whole groups of club members.

As Guindon tells the story, the charge that sent him to prison was for an encounter of the second variety. His relatively light five-year sentence suggests the court believed at least some of his account. "She was at the clubhouse. She was a groupie. Everything's okay. Everybody had fun, but we all left and left a couple guys who were hangarounds. These guys had taken this girl to one of the guy's houses and the guy's wife was gone and she came home and caught the guys doing whatever they were doing. That girl told the wife that she got raped."

It didn't help his case that she showed up for court in little-girl pig-tails, Guindon says. Guindon found himself in Kingston Penitentiary, where one of the few other outlaw bikers was Lockey MacDonald. He was a member of the 13th Tribe Motorcycle Club from Halifax, convicted of a similar charge. As they were both in prison on "skin beefs"—sex-related crimes—they were fair game for other convicts to attack under the unwritten but undeniable code of conduct that governs prison life. "They would sic the older winos on them," Guindon says. "Say, 'Here's a knife. Use it or else.'"

One day, MacDonald staggered into his cell with a knife wound. He dragged with him the old convict who had stuck him. Guindon said it wasn't hard to get the old-timer to talk, and he told them: "I stabbed him and so-and-so told me I had to."

The prisoners behind the stabbing were two Italian criminals from Hamilton. Guindon didn't know whether or not they were mob, and that didn't particularly matter. "I went in the common room and punched them out. I hit them with a nice left hook." One of the punches was particularly crisp. "I put his nose on the other side of his face."

Guindon says it made sense to carry out a very public pre-emptive strike on the Hamiltonians: "I was on a skin beef. [I said,] 'Why don't you all come after me?' Nobody bothered me." Things got decidedly better after that, Guindon says. "They didn't bother me. I don't hold grudges. The only time I hold grudges is when somebody comes back for a second one."

When Guindon confronted the Hamiltonians, he showed that outlaw bikers weren't to be fucked with either behind bars or on the streets, Campbell says. That made things safer not just for Guindon and Lockey but also for generations of club members who would do hard time in the future. "That particular incident paved the way for other bikers."

Guindon trained hard in boxing while behind bars and managed to qualify for the 1971 Pan American Games in Cali, Colombia. He won a bronze medal at 157 pounds, despite fighting one weight division above his usual. When he was freed on parole in January 1972, he moved several hours northwest to Thunder Bay, and it wasn't long before he was on bad terms with local police. He told them, "If you keep harassing me, I'll start a chapter here." The war of words continued and Guindon made good on his threat. But establishing a Thunder Bay chapter of the Choice made it easy for his parole to be yanked for criminal associations, and he found himself back in prison by November 1972. He was now known inside the club as "Number One Frog" or simply "Frog," from the *French Connection* book and movie.

This time, Guindon ended up in Stony Mountain Penitentiary in Manitoba, a nineteenth-century stone-and-brick dungeon on a tiny hill outside Winnipeg. "The day I got there, a guy from Ontario got killed." Guindon kept training, despite not having real boxing facilities. For a punching bag, he had an obliging First Nations behemoth who let Guindon whale away on his midsection. To toughen his own core area, Guindon did a series of ab exercises he'd picked up while watching the Cubans train at the Pan Am Games.

During the time Guindon was away in prison, Campbell quit the club. There had been an ugly brawl between two Choice members over a woman, and the intensity of the anger was too much for Campbell. Somewhere, the promise of brotherhood seemed lost. "I didn't want to belong to a bunch of guys who are fighting like that."

Campbell had his grade twelve and completed a drafting course at Oshawa's Durham College in 1972. Then he started a two-year mechanical technician course, but never completed it. Despite quitting the club, he never stopped hanging around with his friends from the Choice. He also didn't stop riding bikes. In 1973 he bought a 1969 BSA Thunderbolt motorcycle for eight hundred dollars. The next year he bought his first Harley-Davidson for nine hundred: a 1948 panhead chopper like the Captain America cycle Peter Fonda rode in *Easy Rider*. It was a rigid, heavyweight ride with no shocks or swing arm, which left its rider feeling every bump on the road. It also screamed badass from blocks away.

The use of drugs was up in the early 1970s, but it didn't seem that anyone in their circle was making money selling them. Sellers would become users, and people using drugs just got stoned and violent a lot.

The times were changing. As Willerton entered his twenties, he found that membership in the club was taking money out of his pocket and focus away from his plans to someday become wealthy. His father made auto glass for the GM plant and Willerton wanted something far better than the merciless boredom of life on an assembly line. When he had signed on with GM after dropping out of high school, he told his friends he might stay two years before setting out for something better. When he reached his mid-twenties, though, he was still on the assembly line, and restless. "You can't leave GM. That money for no education. The habit becomes a ditch, and the ditch becomes a grave. We had that saying in GM."

Willerton bought himself a three-piece suit and a Cadillac and set out part-time to try to sell soap franchises in Montreal, hanging on to his GM job as insurance until his outside ventures took off. He decided it was time to stop wearing the Choice patch on his back and focus on making real money in the mainstream world. "I figured to get rich I had to get out of the club and get a suit. I wanted to get rich and I knew I had to be playing the game and leave the club."

And it wasn't just Willerton who was changing. There were also seismic shifts under way in the outlaw biker world, and Willerton wasn't comfortable with what he was seeing. When he had joined the Phantom Riders as a teenager, he had convinced himself that the biker world offered a balance to his life as an assembly-line drone. In its best light, it represented an oasis of honesty in a hypocritical world and a chance for juvenile fun and near rock-star glamour. That life officially ended for Willerton one day when he was expected to fly down to Montreal and pick up a gun to help settle an inter-club beef. To that point, the Choice had largely been about mindless hijinks and punch-ups and splashers, but now the club was heading in a more dangerous direction, from which there was no turning back. "The guns were starting to come out. That was the turning point for me."

Campbell's life was moving on an opposite track, as he answered what felt like an irresistible pull to re-enter the ranks of the club. Not long after he rejoined, Campbell was appointed sergeant-at-arms of the Choice's Oshawa chapter, and his new official duties included punching out guys who got out of hand at parties and enforcing club discipline in general. He had no doubts he could handle the job. "I know when a guy is out of hand and needs a shot in the head." Unlike many of the outlaw bikers, he didn't take on a nickname to go with his club persona. "I was known as 'the Hick from Oshawa.' They never called me that to my face. I was from a small town. Never did drugs. I was thought of as a hick. Then I started fighting and people saw how loyal I was."

It was around this time that Campbell happened to bump into a girl he had known in elementary school, who had somehow seemed even poorer than Campbell. She always wore ratty clothing and was the constant butt of jokes, ostracized to the point that other kids refused even to touch her while square dancing during physical education classes. Since those awkward, unhappy days, she had blossomed nicely, finding a loving husband and building a good life with him. That day when they met by chance, she approached Campbell and made a point of saying some kind words to him. "She just remembered that I was nice to her back at school. It was a nice feeling. It was nice, very nice, for her to say that."

The iconic gangster movie *The Godfather* came out in 1972, ushering in a public fascination with organized crime. There was a fair amount of crime in Campbell's biker family, but still not much organization. At Choice meetings, talk was about club runs, not drug deals, he says. Any cop trying to predict the club's movements by using organizational charts and economic analysis would have had just as much luck relying on a dart-throwing monkey. "They'd call it organized crime. We'd say, 'Fuck, if they only knew.'" Steve Earle, the American roots musician who spent many of his formative years in Texas biker circles, later wondered about the effect Marlon Brando's performance as Mafia boss Don Corleone in *The Godfather* had on biker culture in general and Hells Angels leader Ralph (Sonny) Barger in particular. "He saw Marlon Brando in *The Wild One* and he wanted to be scooter trash. He saw the same actor in *The Godfather* and decided he wanted to be a gangster."

Something about the Satan's Choice still appealed to Campbell's romantic nature, but the reality of the club often disappointed him. To an outsider, it may seem odd to call someone romantic when he talks wistfully of the days he punched out bikers on a regular basis and rode in a snarly pack that scared the bejesus out of civilians. It's tougher yet when those days also included bumping shoulders with the likes of Pigpen from Peterborough. But romance isn't an exclusive thing, limited only to well-behaved lovers of Keats and baby's-breath bouquets.

At this point in his life, Campbell wasn't looking for employment in the underworld; he already had steady work. He sought something more precious and elusive. He wanted a family, he wanted fun, and he wanted to be a part of something big that mattered. "When I was a kid and we would make a wish when we broke a turkey wishbone, I've always wished for happiness. I never wished for money."

CHAPTER 4

Anger Mismanagement

I bit a chunk out of his arm.

LORNE CAMPBELL talking about competition during biker field day

C ampbell's daughter Janice was eight when he split with Elinor in 1974 at age twenty-six. That made Janice the same age that Campbell had been when his parents broke up. For most of his time with Elinor he had been out of the club, but he never really left the lifestyle. By the time the relationship ended, Campbell was back wearing a grinning devil patch on his back and living at the Choice clubhouse on the sixth concession north of Oshawa, a modest Ontario-style cottage with tarpaper siding on a semi-rural acreage. Since the days in the basement of Guindon's home, the clubhouse had shifted from a cleaned-up barn in tiny Nestleton to a downtown Oshawa house and then to a century property outside Port Perry near Lake Scugog. The closest neighbour on the sixth concession was the landlord: former pro wrestler Bill Stack, a Maple Leaf Wrestling regular best known for unmasking the Red Demon.

One evening, Campbell called Elinor and there was no answer. He drove to see her with no particular purpose in mind; he just felt a need to be there. Elinor and Janice still weren't home when he arrived. He ordered a pizza and ate it alone. The next thing he knew, he was walking through the empty house they had once shared, cigarette lighter in hand, setting the curtains ablaze. It was as if he were watching another person. He crossed the street to his sister's house, where he sat in the kitchen by the front window as his former family home went up in flames. "I watched the TV explode, go right through the front window and land on the lawn," Campbell says. "I got a kick from it."

Squad cars fanned out over the city in pursuit of the arsonist as Campbell watched firefighters quell the blaze. Eventually, he crossed the street and walked up to the cop. "I just said, 'How are you doing? I'm Lorne.'"

When the cop realized whom he was talking to, he tried to draw his gun, but he was too nervous to get it out of the holster, fumbling with it like Don Knotts's Barney Fife character on the old *Andy Griffith Show*. Then he tried to call in other police officers, but they were too busy hunting down Campbell to listen. Campbell stood by quietly with the nervous cop until he and his fellow officers sorted things out. "Finally he screamed, 'He's here! He's here!' He was scared shitless."

Campbell told the cop that he hadn't originally set out to burn the house down and had only planned to get a pizza. The fumbling cop regained his nerves by that point. "He said it must have been a bad pizza."

Campbell could be glib about many things in his life, but he would profoundly regret his conduct during much of his time with Elinor. "I wasn't cruel to my daughter, but I was abusive to her mom. I was too nuts, too radical. She was just a beautiful mother and everything. I was too wild to settle down. I was abusive to her mentally and physically. It's not an excuse, but it's a learned behaviour from seeing how my dad treated my mother."

Long before he set the family home on fire, Campbell knew he had a serious problem. He wasn't worried about his habit of punching out other outlaw bikers; they all deserved it, in his opinion. What scared him was the thought of repeating the angry pattern of domestic abuse in his childhood home. From the age of eighteen, Campbell had sought out psychiatric and psychological counselling on his own, something he would continue for decades. "I've seen at one time every single psychiatrist in Durham Region."

One psychiatrist nervously blinked and twitched as he sat at his desk and read Campbell's growing history of assaults. After what seemed like several minutes of watching him read and twitch, Campbell said, "I'm outta here," and got up and left.

Another psychiatrist diagnosed him as having "phobic anxiety." Somehow, Campbell's violence was linked to his need to be protective and his deep anger was often misdirected against those he loved. He presented Campbell with what Campbell called his "crazy papers," which spelled out this diagnosis. Campbell was told to present them to police officers or others, should the need arise.

The psychiatric analysis may have provided fascinating reading, but it didn't really help Campbell cope with the violence. The first counsellor who really clicked with him said he wasn't going to waste time trying to catalogue the many possible causes of Campbell's deep anxiety. His specialty was relaxation therapy, which was considered cutting edge at the time. This approach appealed to Campbell because it sought definite results, not just interesting explanations and excuses. Campbell paraphrased the psychiatrist as saying: "It could be hundreds or thousands of reasons. Who gives a shit? Let's learn how to deal with it."

He found ways of getting Campbell to unwind, such as listening to a tape of running water. "He gave me the key. Try to find out what your body's feeling. Learn how to deal with it. I said, 'It's not the rest of the world, it's me.'" It was a breakthrough, although not a total solution. Campbell only went to one more session and then felt he could start applying the doctor's teachings on his own. "I was still violent after that, but more controlled. It took time. He gave me the key. I took about a year to learn how to relax with people."

Campbell made a conscious and determined effort to face down his boyhood fears on his own, just as he had been taught by his father to confront problems head-on. He suffered a phobia of heights, which he tackled by finding jobs as an ironworker, repairing smokestacks. He addressed his deathly fear of spiders by purchasing a Mexican redleg tarantula as large as his hand, and holding it each day. He had Mother McEwan of the Choice tattoo a tarantula onto his right calf along with 1% in 1974. "It was a spur-of-the-moment thing." The same year, he had Elinor's name covered with an eagle tattoo and inked a Choice devil's head onto his left shoulder, with space to record each year he was in the club. "I thought I'd be in for the rest of my life, for eternity."

The pet tarantula died when he went to Thunder Bay for a couple of weeks and forgot to leave it water. He would never learn to love spiders, or even be comfortable with them, but by that time he at least had his arachnophobia in a tight mental box. He bought replacements for the dead spider, lest his fear well up again.

Campbell remained fiercely competitive, always feeling the need to prove himself. This was never more obvious than during Satan's Choice field days near Kitchener, when members of different clubs came together to party and show off their bike-riding skills. Field day events included one in which bikers competed to see who could push a beer keg farthest with a motorcycle. There was also a hot-dog race, in which a woman riding on the back of a bike has to reach up and bite off a wiener dangling from a scaffold. The wiener was made more slippery with mustard. Another event was called Pick Up Sticks, and it involved a biker cruising slowly in a circle with a passenger on the back, riding sidesaddle. The passenger would scramble from the motorcycle to retrieve sticks thrown into the centre of the circle and then jump back on the Harley. Whoever rode off with the most sticks won. It sounds simple, even gentle, like a Sunday school Easter egg hunt, but it was little more than a human cockfight. Campbell won the event against two dozen other bikers by wearing spurs and kicking often and hard, like a rooster engaged in bloody combat.

If Campbell couldn't win field day games himself, he helped fellow Choice members defeat bikers from other clubs. In 1975, the Choice celebrated their tenth anniversary with a field day just north of Oshawa, by the clubhouse. Campbell lined up for a drag race between Guindon, fresh from prison, and Bobbo Gray of the Para-Dice Riders. Campbell was riding his 1948 panhead while Guindon was also atop a Harley-Davidson, a brand of motorcycle he loved so much that he named his own son Harley Davidson Guindon. Guindon was an excellent rider, but Gray's knobby-tired, self-built racer, *Brain Damage*, made him the prohibitive pre-race favourite. Campbell deliberately crashed his bike into *Brain Damage*, taking Gray out and ensuring Guindon's victory.

There was also the turkey race, which involved fighting to see who could pull off the biggest chunk of a freshly beheaded turkey and run to a finish line. "This sounds simple, but it takes hours to rip apart a turkey." It had evolved from the chicken race, a much-maligned contest in which live chickens were sacrificed. In the old chicken races, the competition began when a biker lowered his arm and contestants raced after the live birds. After a huge furor from the media and the Society for the Prevention of Cruelty to Animals, races now began the instant an axe swung down, beheading the turkey.

Bikers were almost sacrificed as well. In one turkey race, Campbell pressed down on the neck of a member of the Detroit Outlaws as they fought for the same poultry chunk. Eventually, teenaged Joe Ertel of the Satan's Choice pried Campbell off the motionless Outlaw and threw him backwards. The Outlaw was an odd shade of blue-grey and Ertel shouted, "Look, he's dead! The guy's blue! His tongue's out!" The Outlaw was loaded onto a St. John's ambulance that had been hired for the event and was eventually revived through an emergency tracheotomy.

The near killing of the Outlaw didn't quell Campbell's competitive juices at the field days. "I knocked out four teeth from a particularly tough club member. If you're a biker, lose some teeth—you look too good." Years later, when he was forty-four, Campbell competed in a field day against a boxer who was almost half his age. "I bit a chunk out of his arm. I thought, 'This 25-year-old, he's not going to win. I've been fighting all my life.' He had no hard feelings. He lived to fight again."

The only race that couldn't be mastered by trickery or extreme violence was the slow race, in which bikers deliberately rode their motorcycles as slowly as possible. "I never won the slow race. My mind would never slow down enough."

They camped out in tents for the anniversary field day, and one morning Campbell had a rude awakening. Bill (Mr. Bill) Lavoie, Jungle and others had tied a rope to his legs while he was sleeping and fastened it to Mr. Bill's Harley. Campbell's wake-up call that morning was the unfamiliar sensation of bouncing across a field. "I was being pulled at thirty miles an hour over grass. It was in retaliation because I was bugging people for days. I couldn't sit up. They stopped before the gravel road. I thought, I'll fucking shoot him if they drag me on the road."

As the new version of the Satan's Choice Motorcycle Club wheeled into its second decade, it developed a certain amount of structure, almost despite itself. Members drafted a national constitution, which filled just one page. It had nine rules, mostly about crests, tattoos and bikes:

1. Every member must have a bike over 650 c.c. in running condition (no Jap scrap etc.).

2. Any club wishing to strike for S.C.M.C. must hand in one set of colours for each recognized chapter, and wear sponsoring chapters' side flashers. Striking clubs must strike for a minimum of three officer's meetings and pay $100.00 to their sponsoring chapter. Individuals wishing to strike must strike for a minimum of six weeks.

3. There must be a 75% vote for rules to be passed or changed at an officer's meeting. New rules must be proposed then taken back to individual chapters for members votes, then returned to an officers meeting. Any chapter not represented will lose its vote.

4. If a chapter misses two consecutive officers meetings or three in a year, its vote is automatically called. Excuses will be considered and left to the president's discretion as [to] whether it shall remain a chapter.

5. All new presidents must have twelve or more months in the club (excluding ex-members). All other officers positions are left up to chapter discretion.

6. Any Satan's Choice chapter folding must appear at an officers meeting, with a complete explanation, colours, all club property, and bills paid.

7. Any members leaving the club must have tattoos dated or disfigured.

8. After five years a member of S.C.M.C. in good standing may become an honorary member with the approval of his chapter and then the approval of the officers at an officers meeting (75%). [Honorary members couldn't vote but could attend club parties and other events.]

9. Any member found to be using a needle for the purpose of shooting anything will be automatically expelled from the club.

Life at the farmhouse on the sixth concession was bucolic, in a bikerish way. Campbell had a new girlfriend who was a frequent visitor and nature lover, after a fashion. "We used to screw under the willow tree."

At one club meeting, Oshawa chapter president Peter (Rabbit) Pillman was visibly upset as he spoke of a complaint from their landlord, Bill Stack. Pillman got his nickname more for his enthusiastic appreciation of women than for any resemblance to the Beatrix Potter character.

"Somebody's fornicating on the front lawn and Bill don't want that," Peter Rabbit announced.

"You know, Peter doesn't know what 'fornicating' means," a member piped up. "It's too big a word. Peter, do you know what 'fornicating' means?"

Peter Rabbit didn't miss a beat. "No I don't, but I want it stopped."

Apparently, Campbell and his girlfriend had been ratted out by members of a family who boarded their horses in a nearby stable and who went for weekend rides together.

Campbell saved Peter Rabbit from further aggravation by speaking up. "Peter, it's me," Campbell said. "'Fornicating' is fucking, and I'll stop."

CHAPTER 5

Friend for Life

They're not innocent people. They were aware of the consequences.
I was totally without remorse. They chose to be in this world.

LORNE CAMPBELL on collecting drug debts

At club parties, Campbell and Guindon always seemed to be the first to get up and grab partners and dance. That's how it was at a party held by Doug (Chicklet) MacDonald, president of the Toronto chapter. Campbell soon found himself guiding Kay Foote around the floor. It was a slow dance, but nothing grinding or disrespectful. Kay was the old lady of someone in the club, not some anonymous splasher, and Campbell treated her accordingly.

When the tune was over, club striker John Foote walked over and punched his wife Kay in the face, ignoring Campbell altogether. Campbell was shocked and primed to defend her when MacDonald stepped in and pulled him back.

"Lorne, this is normal for them," Chicklet MacDonald said.

Kay wasn't screaming or crying and didn't seem particularly upset. It was almost as if she expected to be hit. Campbell looked towards Foote and saw no anger in his face. When Foote turned to Campbell, his tone was matter-of-fact. "He said, 'No hard feelings. That's just the way we are.'"

Campbell later concluded that Foote must be a sadist and his wife a masochist. It was a match made nowhere close to heaven, but they both seemed fine with it.

The incident didn't even appear to be that big a deal for Foote, who clearly had other things on his mind that evening. He had already heard of Campbell's ability with his fists, and he said: "Lorne, with my strength and your fighting ability, we can make a lot of money."

He was referring to the profits to be made in the ever-expanding trade of underworld debt collection. The commission was 50 percent of any unpaid debt they managed to recover. Not long after that, Foote gave Campbell visual proof of what he meant. "Within two or three weeks, he brought down forty thousand dollars to the Oshawa clubhouse."

Foote wasn't just good at collecting money owed by street drug dealers to their suppliers; he was also heavily into drug rip-offs, which were planned robberies of drug dealers. On the upside, these were crimes for which the victims could be counted on not to call the police. On the downside, they were also crimes in which the targets were hard-core criminals who could be expected to fight back.

Foote lived in an apartment at 399 Markham Road in Scarborough, on the eleventh floor of a high-rise, just down the hall from the temporary clubhouse of the Choice's Toronto chapter. The old Toronto clubhouse had burned down and these were the club's temporary digs. Foote's apartment wasn't in his name, but it was clearly his place and he had customized it in the same way bikers personalize their Harleys. The front door of Foote's apartment was heavily reinforced and backed with sliding steel bars on a hinge. The walls of the front hallway were painted black so that anyone peering in the peephole could see nothing. Razor wire ringed the balcony, in case anyone felt like climbing up or dropping down from a higher apartment. The Choice clubhouse down the hallway was easy pickings by comparison, with just a regular lock and nothing protecting the balcony.

One of Foote's two bedrooms was set up as a motorcycle chop shop, for dismantling the motorcycles that he stole. He limited his thefts to Harleys, as if they were the only bikes worth stealing. He would get them up to his apartment through the main elevator and then wheel them into his place, as if this was part of a normal workday.

Campbell wasn't a motorcycle thief himself, except when he thought a bike needed liberating from a particularly bad owner. Once, a biker couldn't control his chopper and asked Campbell to ride it back to Toronto for him from northern Ontario. Campbell obliged—but then kept on riding once he reached the big city. He also would accept Harleys to settle debts, but in his books that didn't count as theft either. "I've never stolen one. Never would. I've done a lot of things. It might not make sense, but I wouldn't steal one."

For tax purposes, Foote ran a business that involved painting murals on the walls of muffler shops, but by the time Campbell met him he had settled into the role of full-time gangster. Foote was the undisputed master of the don't-fuck-with-me expression, squinting hard and talking out of the corner of his mouth like a character from a James Cagney movie. He'd pinch the front of his mouth tightly shut and squeeze out words from the sides so that no one could read his lips. Sometimes the tough effect was heightened by the presence of a cigarette stuck in his mouth. Maybe this was a trick he'd learned while serving time in Texas and Michigan prisons after he'd got in a shootout with police. Or maybe he picked it up from the movies. Or perhaps that was just the way he always talked. Whatever the case, no one knew and no one was asking.

There were plenty of things you didn't ask John Foote. You certainly didn't push him about the rumour, never proven in court, that he shot a prowler dead and drove around for a time with the corpse in the trunk of his car, looking for an appropriate final resting place. It was better just to leave that story alone, since it certainly wasn't beyond the realm of possibility and there was always room in his trunk for another body. "He was a very tough, serious individual. Feared by many."

Foote didn't take up a lot of space, but he radiated power, as if he was a much bigger man jammed into a five-foot-nine frame. He set weight-lifting records in U.S. prison and could do repetitions on the bench press at 350 pounds. Strength is impressive, but it is often explosiveness that separates the good from the great in physical pursuits. Despite club rules against needle use, Foote liked to inject liquid speed into his veins for an added boost.

Foote also had ingenuity. On the job, he packed a sawed-off 16-gauge shotgun that fit neatly into a quick-draw holster he designed himself. He also built guns, including palm-sized, double-barrelled shotgun pistols that sprayed out wide so they could disable but not kill several people at a time. Some of his personal arsenal was hidden inside walls of his apartment, stored away for whenever he might need them.

While working, Foote eschewed the flashy, attention-grabbing jewellery of many in his milieu, preferring a businesslike appearance in a suit and trench coat. Sometimes, when he was trying to keep a particularly low profile, he would dye his hair and comb it differently. "He was indefatigable."

No matter how he looked, Foote displayed a sphinx-like countenance, betraying little emotion. As Campbell got to know him, he could detect a slight shift in his new friend's appearance when he was on the verge of violence. "If Foote smiled at you, be scared."

Others in the club certainly learned to take him seriously even before he got full member status. Full members sometimes kidded probationary members that they were going to strip them of their patches and demote them back to civilian status. Established members made the mistake of trying that joke with Foote before he got his full membership patch. "John had four or five members against the wall with a handgun pointed at them. . . . When the vice-president came down, he said, 'Tell these guys they ain't taking my striker patch.'" They didn't.

When Foote stalked drug dealers, he'd find those in the low end of the drug trade often flashing their wealth and bragging about their business. They were as sloppy as Foote was relentless. "In the drug world, people talk." Campbell heard that Foote had once gone to a residence in Toronto to rip off some drug dealers only to find that half a dozen police officers had arrived just before him. He caught the cops by surprise, handcuffing them together at gunpoint. He then proceeded to rip off the drug traffickers as planned, and left with the loot as well as the cops' guns.

Not long after that, he placed a call to the officers' detachment. "I'm John Foote and you're looking for me," he announced. "I've got six handguns of your police. You're looking for them."

The stunned officer on the phone professed ignorance.

"Okay, then I'm keeping them," Foote said.

He was never charged for ripping off the dealers of their money or relieving the police of their guns. Shortly afterwards, however, he was pulled over by police and beaten. "When they were beating him, he was laughing. He was a pretty neat guy."

Foote was five years older than Campbell and treated him as an understudy of sorts. Campbell quickly came to regard him as a solid friend, whose loyalty was beyond question. Like Foote, Campbell didn't feel bad about putting fear into people when collecting drug debts. "I collected money for people. I just look at it like they were playing the game. They're not innocent people. They were aware of the consequences. I was totally without remorse. They chose to be in this world."

Foote sometimes spoke to Campbell about fear, and how it was their worst enemy. He wasn't talking about their own fear; he was talking about the fear that often consumed their targets when they showed up to collect money. Such fear could drive men to do dangerous things. That connected with another key lesson from Foote: if things went sour, there was no point in beating someone up just a little bit. "'If I give a guy a shot, he may come back with a gun. If I beat him senseless and break a couple bones, he ain't coming back. It's just human nature.'"

When attempting to collect drug money, Foote and Campbell often had to determine if they were dealing with someone who was just acting crazy or someone who was truly nuts. "I always thought, if someone's going to be crazy, I'm going to be crazier. That's not the same as insane. I treat them differently. If they're crazy, I'm two times as crazy. I hurt them so that they'll never come back to me. I've always got along with crazy people. But insane people, you handle them altogether differently. You have to do one thing or the other: kill them or walk away from them. I'm nervous about insane people."

Foote and Campbell both felt at home with violence. Breaking the fingers of someone who was tardy in his debt repayment wasn't a problem, nor was more serious violence. "My heart's never pumped any faster when I fought or was involved in gunplay. But I have fear for people around me. I worry about the people who are close to me being hurt—my loved ones and my friends." They also both felt a certain professional pride in their chosen trade as drug debt collectors. "They already had been threatened by the time I got to them. I would hurt people and they always paid. I would hurt them first. It was people who were always making excuses, running away. I used to say, 'There ain't nobody I can't find.' When people used to try to intimidate me, I'd say, 'That's *my* game.'" To find missing debtors, Campbell would go to bars and houses where he expected to find friends of his prey. "I'd beat up their friends. They're drug dealers. Drug addicts. After a while I'd just walk in and they'd tell me right away."

Campbell and Foote also both accepted that spending time in jail went along with their line of work. Time with Foote in the Whitby jail on an assault beef was a fresh experience for Campbell, although he was already accustomed to jail. It was as though they were the ones with the power, even though they were on the wrong side of the bars. That came across once when a guard tried to bully Foote, blaming him for the loss of a pillow.

"What do you think I did?" Foote asked. "Shoved it up my ass?"

The guard declined to speculate or give Foote another pillow. Other prisoners, including Campbell, managed to secure one for Foote anyway. They also got a light bulb. They crushed half of it down to a powder and poured it into a pot of tea the guard routinely drank from. "He drank it and didn't come to work for two weeks. When he came back, he wouldn't say fuck all. He just stared at us. We smiled at him."

Campbell was driving on November 4, 1976, to the Kitchener Choice clubhouse on Weber Street, where he had been partying regularly. The news came on his car radio that his friend John Foote had been shot to death at 4:40 that morning in the Markham Road clubhouse apartment. It was as though Campbell was shot too. "I was supposed to be with him that night. I heard it on the radio: 'John Foote was just shot and killed.' My head hit the steering wheel and I turned around and went right back to Toronto. I really believe that if I had been there, it wouldn't have happened. It was just a fear thing. Fear can be your worst enemy. If someone's scared of you in that world, you could be shot because of their fear."

There were three bullets in Foote's body and Campbell had no doubts about who put them there. Foote had argued earlier that night with a

23-year-old clubmate named John Harvey, a surgeon's son. Harvey had the unsettling habit of scaring people with his pistol in the evening and forgetting all about it by morning, by which time the Valium he often took had worn off. In one incident, he levelled his pistol, which had a notorious hair trigger, at member Jeff (Boom Boom) McLeod's head for what felt like an eternity before he was finally convinced to put it back in his shoulder holster. "All he had to do was twitch and Jeff would have had half his head blown off. It was scary. Was he joking? Who knows?"

On the final evening of Foote's life, things escalated to the point that he whacked Harvey with a pool cue. Harvey left the clubhouse and Campbell was certain he'd returned with his pistol. Ironically, there was a good chance that it was Foote himself who had modified the handgun to make it even more sensitive.

It was just like Foote's warning: it was the fear of other people you had to worry about. "Who else would have gotten close enough to Footie? Who would he open the door for?"

Campbell was out on probation for the arson of his home at the time of Foote's funeral. His probation officer chewed him out for attending the service, which meant he'd violated the conditions that stated he couldn't associate with clubmates.

"It was my best friend and I went to his funeral," Campbell told him. "Go fuck yourself."

"You don't care about anything, do you?" the officer asked.

"No," Campbell replied.

Oddly, Harvey didn't appear to realize what he had done. A heavy Valium user, he seemed oblivious to the fact that he'd fired the fatal shots, even though he was eventually convicted of manslaughter. The funeral was a blur and Campbell didn't say much to anyone. He just kept his eyes on Harvey. "I watched him all through the funeral. I was a pall-bearer and I was so upset I couldn't grab onto the casket."

Foote's death made Campbell think a lot, but he didn't consider leaving the club. Instead, he sewed a patch on his vest over his heart that read, "In Memory of John Foote." Campbell now understood why Foote tried to teach him about preparedness. "From his death, I really learned that saying: 'Fear is your worst enemy.' In anyone else's lifestyle it wouldn't make any sense. But it did make sense in mine. It was a guy who feared him who shot Foote. In other words: be prepared."

In the end, Harvey was killed by a drug overdose, dead from his own demons.

The passing of John Foote meant Campbell was now collecting drug debts alone. Campbell was just as serious as his mentor. "If I died at that point: don't feel bad for me, because I was playing the game." Naturally, he took it seriously when the club's president, Peter (Rabbit) Pillman, told him in the mid-seventies that he had been ripped off by a young biker named Shaun Robinson. Campbell stuffed a sawed-off shotgun into Robinson's mouth, making it clear he expected the money to be paid promptly. The gun was rammed in so hard Robinson's cheeks popped out like a chipmunk's.

The next day, Robinson rode up to Campbell's place to renew the discussion. Robinson clearly looked whipped, but he felt compelled to talk nonetheless. Campbell had the sawed-off shotgun to guarantee himself the last word in the conversation.

"What do you want?" Campbell asked.

"I came up here to tell you that you were wrong yesterday." Robinson protested that he had paid the money to a third party, who was supposed to deliver it to Peter Rabbit.

"Who was it?" Campbell demanded.

"I can't tell you, but you'll find out," Robinson replied.

Campbell was impressed that Robinson had the balls to approach him. He was further impressed that Robinson refused to rat anyone out when he removed the shotgun from his mouth. That was a solid, if dangerous, thing to do. "It took balls. I was nobody to be fucked with."

Campbell asked around and determined that Robinson was telling the truth. Robinson had paid Peter Rabbit's money to a third party, who took off to Florida with it, making Robinson look like the crook. When the third party returned to Durham Region, minus the money but sporting a suntan, Campbell hauled him into the Cadillac Hotel by the CPR tracks, just north of Highway 401 on Simcoe Street South. When it was built in the early 1950s, it was considered the place to be by movers and shakers, but by Campbell's time it was known by a new generation of patrons as a bucket of blood. Campbell worked there as a bouncer, and the Cadillac doubled as an office of sorts for him. "I beat him so badly I put him in the hospital."

Two weeks after the beating, Campbell heard that the man had committed suicide. "I didn't have any bad feeling over it. I didn't feel any remorse. Good for him. He killed himself. He was a cheat. A scam artist. Always dressed in a suit. Just a guy out for himself."

As for Robinson, Campbell grew to consider him a valued friend. "He was one of my favourite guys in the club. He's true blue. He's been time tested."

As he rose up through the ranks of the Satan's Choice, Campbell harboured a particular fantasy. He dreamed of the day he would meet up again with the supervisor from the training school in Cobourg, the one with the rings, who used to beat him. When that day came, Campbell was twenty-eight years old, weighed a solid 185 pounds on a compact five-foot-ten frame, and had earned a fearsome reputation for his ability to settle scores and collect debts with baseballs bats, pistols and the hard, precise punches he had learned at the hands of his father.

Campbell was leaving the British Hotel in Cobourg around last call with fellow Satan's Choice member Brian (Babs) Babcock, and didn't recognize the supervisor at first. The British was the type of place that gave rundown dumps a bad reputation, and Campbell was a weekend regular, best known for pounding out its patrons. He beat up so many of them that Bill (Mr. Bill) Lavoie asked him to ease up a little. "Then quit sending stupid people to my table," Campbell replied.

That night, the former training school supervisor looked like a shrivelled old man, even though he must only have been in his late thirties. He and a buddy were obviously drunk, and it was clear from his puffy grey face and bloated body that getting pissed drunk was part of his daily routine. His eyes were glassy, he had just wet his pants, and he leaned on his friend to keep from falling over.

"You know who that is walking in front of us?" Babcock asked.

"Who?"

"That's Montgomery from the training school."

Babcock had known Montgomery from around town and recognized the face. As Campbell watched the man stagger across the hotel parking lot, he remembered the feel of the drunk's ring-covered fingers on his face.

Montgomery didn't recognize Campbell. He was having a hard enough time just making it across the parking lot.

"It was a pathetic sight," Campbell says. "He was a drunk and he died of cirrhosis of the liver shortly afterwards. If he was in better shape, I would have beaten him up right there. But I just smiled at him."

CHAPTER 6

Turf

In my heart, I knew I was dying.

LORNE CAMPBELL after he is shot

C ampbell added a tattoo to his left forearm with the letters *FTW*, which could alternately be translated as "Fuck the World," "Fight the World" and "Fight to Win." All interpretations were correct in Campbell's world. The biker violence of the sixties and seventies was almost always about turf rather than profits, and largely reflexive, reactive, ultra-harsh and utterly pointless to anyone but another biker.

One day, Campbell heard that the Choice had been permanently cut off from being served at the Plaza Hotel tavern. It was the nicer of two drinking holes in Cobourg, the other being the British, and Campbell wasn't about to have the club's drinking options limited. He also wasn't keen on being told where he was and was not welcome.

He turned to a biker called Fat Frog (not to be confused with Bernie Guindon, the Number One Frog, or Guindon's cousin from Quebec, the Bull Frog). "Go over to the Plaza and open the door," Campbell said.

Fat Frog did as he was asked, and Campbell rode through the door on his growling 1948 panhead chopper. He weaved around the tables before gliding to a halt in front of the bar.

"Give me a rye," Campbell ordered.

The bartender gave him a rye.

"Are we cut off here?"

"No."

"I know you cut our guys off. Are we cut off now?"

"No."

Campbell downed his rye.

The other Plaza patrons kept chugging their draft, as if this were somehow normal. "Who knows if they were afraid?"

"Fattie, open the door again," Campbell said.

Fat Frog opened the door again as Campbell revved up his chopper.

"See you later," Campbell called, and cruised out of the Plaza into the pouring rain in a scene worthy of Lee Marvin himself.

Much of the biker fighting wasn't of the one-on-one, fair contest variety. When Campbell was faced with a threatening group, he reasoned that it generally made sense for him to attack the biggest enemy first. A quick, brutal knockout tended to calm down smaller would-be tough guys. That was the guiding principle late one night on Thickson Road, on the Oshawa–Whitby town line, when Campbell and another Choice member overheard what they took to be disparaging comments about them from inside a car while stopped at a gas station. Campbell and his friend were wearing their club colours, so group honour was at stake and playing deaf wasn't an option.

"What'd you say?" Campbell shouted. "Get the fuck out of the car!"

There were six men in the car and they all got out. They clearly weren't intimidated by the two bikers.

Campbell pasted one of the bigger men with a boot to the groin that would have done a Canadian Football League kicker proud. The pointed toe of his cowboy boot focused the kick and made it all the more nauseating at the receiving end. The man appeared out on his feet when the cops arrived and ordered Campbell and his buddy to get lost.

Campbell met the recipient of his right foot a couple of months later at a party. It was far more pleasant than their first encounter, until the man proffered a baffling comment.

"If it had been just me, I'd have punched you out."

"Bill, don't say anything more," Campbell said.

"If it had been just me, I'd have punched you out."

It was a decidedly odd comment and Campbell wasn't about to waste time and brainpower deciphering it. Instead, he replied with a left hook that sent Bill down hard, between the fridge and the counter. On the counter sat a huge man, who packed considerable muscle and girth onto what Campbell guessed was about a six-foot-four frame. This Goliath couldn't help but gawk at the violence a few feet away.

"You got a problem with this?" Campbell shouted.

The Goliath didn't reply fast enough, and Campbell let loose his best shot. The big man wasn't able to block it and Campbell's knuckles collided squarely with his head. But he didn't go down. He didn't even appear to flinch. "He grabbed me and like a rag doll he threw me down," Campbell says.

Then he cocked a mammoth fist directly over Campbell's head. There was just enough time for Campbell to think of the damage that fist would cause to his cranium, like a sledgehammer on a coconut. Once the Goliath was sure he had made his point, he calmly lowered his fist and returned to the party. Throughout the altercation, the big man had looked bewildered, not angry. "You talk about grateful," Campbell says.

Big violence frequently bubbled up from little things in the outlaw biker world. Infringements on their turf, and real and perceived slights against the honour or security of them and their clubmates, often served as detonators. Bikers sometimes didn't have much beyond their Harleys and an exaggerated sense of honour, so they guarded those things with their lives. That's the way it was when Campbell heard that Jimmy Brockman, a former Golden Hawk who was no longer in a club, had threatened a Choice member named Pete. Campbell couldn't just leave that threat against a clubmate hanging in the air. He needed to take Brockman aside and tell him that such talk simply wasn't acceptable.

Campbell had just downed a mouthful of beer at the Royal Hotel in Whitby when Jimmy Brockman walked by. A comic named Kangaroo was due to perform that night and Campbell had been looking forward to the start of his show. Now he'd have to miss at least some of the comedy.

"Jimmy, I want to talk to you outside."

Brockman stepped outside, where Campbell asked: "Just what were you doing at Pete's?"

Campbell hadn't taken a hard look into Brockman's eyes and didn't yet realize that he was revved up on speed. Campbell also didn't know that Brockman was sitting that night on a stash of pills that would be worth a considerable amount on the street. Campbell did understand that he was dealing with a dangerous man.

Brockman was too slow to answer. Campbell recalls: "He never got more than two words out and I hit him. He went down."

Brockman barely touched the pavement before he bounced up with a gun in his hands. Now Campbell was the one caught off guard. "You never know what you'll do when a gun's pointed at you," Campbell says. Brockman pulled the trigger from point-blank range. "The first one went through my arm. The next two went by. I knew he had a six-shooter and that he had three left."

It was the perfect time to sweat and panic and beg for the chance to go on living. A very different feeling overtook Campbell as he faced the gun with its three remaining bullets. The sensation surprised him. "There was such a calmness, I couldn't believe. I said, 'Finish it now, because I'm going to come after you.' In my heart, I knew I was dying. I was sure he was going to shoot again." In that moment of kill-or-be-killed, Campbell didn't feel any hatred towards the man firing at him, just an odd, hard-to-define sense of regret: "Too bad that happened, because I liked him."

Jimmy Brockman didn't want to be a killer that night. Perhaps he too had gone into the Royal relaxed and eager for an evening of comedy. Brockman had never hated Campbell and now he was a finger squeeze away from ending Campbell's life. In that instant, when he literally held the power of life and death in his hands, Brockman did something totally unexpected: he threw down the gun and ran away.

Campbell's bullet wound was treated by the mother of a club member, who also happened to be a nurse, which saved him from going to hospital, where the injury would have been reported to police. Still, it's hard to keep a shooting in a downtown parking lot quiet, and so it wasn't long before a cop appeared at Campbell's door. It was the same cop who had had so much trouble with his nerves while arresting Campbell after he burned down the family home. The police officer appeared to have gained a little confidence since their last meeting.

He asked Campbell about his wounded arm.

"I fell on a nail against a wall."

"Expect me back to arrest you."

"Don't bother, because I fell against a nail. That's all you'll get."

Not long after that, Campbell was pulled over by RCMP officers. They too asked who'd shot him, and Campbell also told them that he hadn't been shot. Then, according to Campbell, a Mountie said something chilling.

"You know what? If you keep this up, we can shoot you."

"Well, you had better be faster than me."

The cop continued, noting that other bikers would be suspected if Campbell's life ended with a fresh bullet in him. But again, they didn't arrest him.

With the police out of the way at least for the time being, Campbell set out on the hunt for Jimmy Brockman, to settle their unfinished business. He was confident that he was now the hunter and not the hunted. "At the risk of sounding like a braggart, I figure if I'm packing and there's a threat, let's get it on. I had no fear."

Campbell was taking a break from the hunt early one morning with his Choice friend Rick Smith, better known in biker circles as Smutley (pronounced Schmut-lee), in an Oshawa booze can owned by a man called Jewels. Booze cans are the watering holes of the biker world, the cool shores to which everyone—hunters and hunted alike—is drawn to refresh themselves. It was at Jewels's booze can, between sips of beer, that Campbell finally laid eyes on Brockman sitting on a couch. It was just luck, and perhaps no small measure of stupidity on Brockman's part, that brought them back together. Brockman had been living out of his car, with a machine gun on his lap, fearing the day when Campbell would finally call out his name again.

That night in the booze can, Campbell went after Brockman with his fists, not his pistol. "I pounded on him. I heard, 'Click, click.' Jewels had got a shotgun." Campbell didn't nourish false hope that Jewels was on his side since the shotgun was clearly pointed in his direction.

Smutley wasn't packing a gun and the best he could muster was a large ketchup bottle, but he brandished it mightily, like a club. At least it was glass and not plastic, but few lunatics would consider it a deterrent against a loaded shotgun. "I started to laugh," Campbell remembers. "I said, 'Just what are you doing? It's a 12-gauge shotgun. You're going to run up with a ketchup bottle?'"

Brockman saw the humour too, and also started to laugh. The mood for murder and revenge was irreparably broken. The shotgun and ketchup bottle were lowered and they all returned to their drinks.

Decades later, Campbell still cherishes the story of how Smutley tried to come to his rescue with a ketchup bottle. He doesn't expect many from outside his world to find it amusing, but it's hilarious to him. "I realize, to other people who didn't live that life, that's not funny."

Campbell didn't hold a grudge against Jimmy Brockman for shooting him. At the time he put the bullet in Campbell, Jimmy was stoned and figured Campbell was trying to rip off his stash of speed. In their world, that was a reasonable fear. "In his mind, I'm ripping him off. I liked Jimmy. I would have done the same thing. Only I would have pulled the trigger again. I wouldn't have thrown away the gun."

Life was too short to take such murder attempts or beatings personally. It wasn't as if Brockman harboured some particular ill will against Campbell. "He had shot people before me, and he shot people after me." Things remained that way, on a friendly, live-and-let-live basis, until years later, when someone killed Jimmy Brockman with an axe.

One night, all Campbell wanted to do was work himself through a hangover in a downstairs bedroom of the Oshawa clubhouse. This wasn't so easily accomplished, as a childhood friend named John had pounded on his bedroom door several times earlier that night, rudely interrupting his sleep. When there was yet another knock at his door, Campbell's bleary eyes settled on the .22 semi-automatic rifle he kept by his bed.

"Get the fuck out!"

Knock, knock, knock.

"How many times do I have to tell you to leave me alone?"

Knock, knock, knock.

Campbell emptied a clip into the door and the pounding stopped. He had no clue it was Peter (Rabbit) Pillman at the door, along with one of Campbell's long-time friends. He didn't really object too much when the club fined him five hundred dollars for pumping eleven bullets in the direction of his president, but he wasn't happy either. "I didn't think it was fair, because I didn't shoot anybody—but I did shoot the door right between them. You've got to accept what you've got to accept."

Campbell was alone in the Oshawa clubhouse another night when his old friend Larry (Beaver) Hurren and another member named Randy came home late one night with two women they had met in a bar. Members all had keys to the clubhouse, but they had both forgotten theirs. There was also a way for members to sneak in, and that was their means of entry that night. By the time they were on the stairs, Campbell heard them.

Campbell didn't ask the intruders on the stairs to identify themselves before he fired a shotgun in their direction. "All four of them ran upstairs," Campbell recalls.

"Who's up there?" Campbell demanded.

"It's Larry."

Once satisfied that they weren't thieves or invaders, Campbell invited them down for a drink to show there were no hard feelings on his side. They wouldn't budge or socialize with him. This time Campbell wasn't fined, because chapter members ruled that Hurren and Randy should have brought a key. "They should have woken me up first. I was pretty security conscious."

Tough as he was in a fight, Campbell didn't have a particularly strong stomach. His friend Larry Vallentyne from the Toronto Choice was even more queasy. That said, they were both holding up well at an all-Canadian run in the late 1970s in Thunder Bay, which brought together members of the Choice, the Vagabonds of downtown Toronto, Los Bravos of Winnipeg and the Grim Reapers of Alberta. They mixed together and sampled a concoction of yellow jackets, black beauties, bennies, LSD, whisky, rum and vodka. It was called, simply, Concoction and was set out in a punch bowl and jugs with the warning, "Don't drink this unless you're ready for it."

There was a live rock band playing in a field, and Campbell and Vallentyne were the function's shuttle service, driving attendees out to the bandstand in a souped-up Oldsmobile. They attacked their duties with ferocity, hitting speeds that felt like a hundred miles per hour and crafting dramatic stops worthy of a Hollywood stunt driver. Somewhere along the line they managed to tear off two of the Oldsmobile's doors and back over a new Harley, which had been driven only once. The Harley's owner was a good sport, letting his insurance company handle the damages, while riders in the shuttle service seemed overjoyed just to step out of the vehicle alive. "Larry is a very good driver. People were freaking out."

Part of the biker shtick for freaking people out was to kiss each other on the lips in plain view of others, so it wasn't a shock when Vallentyne turned to Campbell and said, "Give me a little kiss." It was a shock, however, when Campbell felt something live crawl into his mouth at the culmination of their smooch. "He had a live field mouse in his mouth and spit it into my mouth. I started throwing up. It ruined my whole day. My whole evening. I couldn't stop barfing."

Potent as the Concoction was, there was likely no drink anywhere that would have been strong enough to wash the taste of rodent from Campbell's mouth. A girl at the party kept asking him, "Why are you sick?" Answering her question only threatened to make him relive the experience and become sick again, but she wouldn't back off. Finally, Campbell recalls, he replied: "'He shoved a mouse in my mouth and it's still stuck in my fucking mouth.' Now *she's* getting sick."

Campbell had noticed that Vallentyne was queasy whenever he was around a regular called No-Face in a bar they frequented. No-Face got his name from the day he tried to commit suicide with a .306. Through good fortune or bad shooting, he missed his brain but blew off much of his face, including his nose. No-Face got his life back on track, and now Campbell saw him arrive at the get-together in party mode. "He's all dressed up. He's sporting a fedora but no jaw. Two holes for a nose."

Campbell was chatting with some Vagabonds when he saw Vallentyne crawling out of a tent with a titanic hangover. "I'm talking about Larry being upset by seeing No-Face. I know Larry's approaching. I said, 'Then Larry turned around and gave him [No-Face] a French kiss right on the lips.' Larry just started puking.

"What a good party that was."

CHAPTER 7

Biker Chick Magnets

I heard a guy blindfolded his girl—a dancer—every night when he took her home. I asked him why he does it. He says, "Yeah, I don't want her to know where I live." Like it was normal.

LORNE CAMPBELL

B oy Scouts get merit patches for knot tying, semaphore and other crafts. At one field day, the Satan's Choice awarded Campbell a patch on his club vest for performing cunnilingus on a menstruating woman (a red wing patch) and another for having sex with a woman with a sexually transmitted disease (green wings). Campbell scored a biker's daily double of sorts that day, getting both his patches from contact with the same woman at the same party. To make it official, the event had to be witnessed by a club member, much like the Guinness Book of Records needs an official spotter before recording an achievement in its books. With that accomplished, Campbell declined to go further in his patch earning and didn't seek purple wings, for sex with a dead person—not that there was a corpse available anyway. "The other ones are just too weird for me. I never saw anybody wear a purple patch. Nobody in Canada ever did. There was a white patch for sex with a virgin. I never saw that either."

When it came to their treatment of women, Campbell was actually disgusted at the conduct of some clubmates back in the 1960s and 1970s. He remains troubled by the memory of how young girls would show up at biker clubhouses as if expecting some sort of protection. If a girl looked too young, Campbell says he would give her a stern fatherly lecture. "I've sent many underage girls home in cabs."

Plenty of women willingly arrived at biker clubhouses, eager to party with the bad boys. One of the wilder biker parties of the 1970s was in the apartment of an Oshawa woman who had a framed eight-by-ten photo of her father on top of the television in the living room. What made the photo stand out was that her father was wearing a police uniform. It wasn't until later, when evidence was revealed at a biker trial, that Campbell learned that the orgy had been electronically recorded by police, and that the officers who listened in on the bacchanal included the woman's father. It might break another man to listen to his daughter in mid-orgy with a biker gang while flanked by his peers. However, the father in the picture that watched down from his daughter's television was nothing if not zealous, and he rose high in policing after the incident. "They [police] call us sick. What would the other cops think? And we're the bad guys? Holy cow! Think moral. To bug your daughter, that's mind-boggling. Did his wife know? There's a thousand questions there." As Campbell sees it, much of the tension between police and bikers came from jealousy. "We've been with the nicest broads, we've partied heartier, and these cops sit there for days [in surveillance] just watching."

Campbell had an extremely low sperm count because of a case of mumps he contracted as a child, which made him doubt several claims that he made women pregnant in these late-night romps. "I've had four or five girls blame me for being the father. I just smiled at them." There were other stories about women that he didn't doubt, although they made his head spin nonetheless. "I heard a guy blindfolded his girl—a dancer—every night when he took her home. I asked him why he does it. He says, 'Yeah, I don't want her to know where I live.' Like it was normal."

One good spot for bikers to meet women was the bar of the Genosha Hotel on King Street East in Oshawa's downtown core. In Marvel comics, "Genosha" was a make-believe land populated by mutants that devolved into a full-fledged disaster zone. In Campbell's day, the real-life Genosha wasn't much different. It hadn't always been this way. The Genosha was conceived as an impressive place to house visiting auto executives and salespeople, and its name was a combination of "General Motors" and "Oshawa." Opened in 1929, it never rebounded after the stock market collapse later that year. Rescued from bankruptcy in the Great Depression by local notables, it was still grand enough that Queen Elizabeth, the consort of George VI, stayed there for a night in 1939.

Over time, however, furnishings were stripped and the once stately Chicago Style, art deco–influenced hotel was converted into a rooming house while the basement became a low-end strip club. The Genosha had been a rock-bottom dive for quite some time when Campbell and his friend Smutley arrived for a drink one afternoon in the late 1970s and overheard two men at a neighbouring table boasting that they were members of the Satan's Choice. It was clearly a ruse designed to impress a pair of nearby women. Worse yet, it appeared to be working, as if the imposters were writing a cheque on funds that weren't even theirs.

"The broads are going to go with them," Campbell recalls. "They're getting lucky. Smutley wanted to hit them right off the bat. We didn't have colours on, so they didn't know we were with the club.

"I said, 'You're Choice?' The guy answered, 'Yeah.' I hit him in the face and Smutley hit the other guy. I had had enough."

The fight was over before it began, as were the men's hopes of afternoon romance.

Of all the women in the bikers' party sphere, one particularly stood out. She was of elfish stature, standing barely over five feet and weighing a little over a hundred pounds. She was Smutley's girlfriend, and she was fiercely possessive of him, even though she was anything but exclusive. Her name was Daryle Noreen Newstead, and she loved having the same first name (albeit with a different spelling) as hockey star and Toronto Maple Leafs captain Darryl Sittler.

Daryle would sometimes find other women for group sex with Campbell and Smutley. Despite the adventuresome sex, Smutley eventually grew tired of Daryle and dumped her. On the rebound, she travelled to northern Ontario and hooked up with a man named Darryl Gerald Dollan, who at twenty-eight was three years older than her. It was never clear to Campbell if Dollan's first name was part of the attraction. Whatever the case, Daryle and Darryl soon headed south to avenge what she considered Smutley's insult to her honour.

Around four in the morning of November 18, 1978, Ontario Provincial Police constable Phillip Duffield noticed only one headlight shining from a maroon Datsun station wagon on Highway 17 near the hamlet of Thessalon, between the northern Ontario cities of Sudbury and Sault Ste. Marie. He called the car's licence number into his police radio and was informed that the Datsun was stolen. Duffield, who had been a cop for only fourteen months, pulled it over on a dark, lonely stretch of road. Then he did that most frightening thing for a police officer working alone at night: he walked up to the driver's side, shone his flashlight inside and asked the stranger inside to get out.

"Yeah," the male driver replied, and opened the door slightly, just wide enough for the barrel of a shotgun. The first blast caught Duffield in the left arm, while the second somehow missed him altogether.

Duffield was able to squeeze off a shot from his service revolver before he radioed in to his dispatcher that he had been hit.

The Datsun's driver fled north off Highway 17 onto side roads, eventually pulling up at a well-lit, one-storey home. It belonged to the Kehoes, a retired couple brimming with small-town goodwill, who never hesitated to open their door to anyone in need.

Newstead certainly wouldn't have looked threatening as she told 58-year-old Phyllis Kehoe: "There's an accident a bit down the road. There's a policeman been shot."

Phyllis Kehoe later recalled that she felt she wasn't dressed properly when she answered the door. Her mood shifted from hospitable and concerned to terrified when she saw the shotgun. She fled to their bedroom. Shotgun pellets ripped through the bedroom door, wounding her and knocking her 63-year-old husband, Robert, to the floor.

Dollan and Newstead tied Phyllis and Robert Kehoe together. When they saw that the couple's grandchildren—a thirteen-year-old boy and fourteen-year-old girl—were also in the home, they bound them together with their grandparents. Then they cut the phone cable and escaped in the Kehoes' truck.

The grandson freed himself and ran more than a mile to their closest neighbours. It was around this time that Dollan and Newstead were pulled over at a nearby OPP roadblock and arrested. By that time, Robert Kehoe was dead.

Newspapers quickly dubbed Newstead and Dollan "Canada's Bonnie and Clyde." They dug up information on them, which was far more sad than glamorous. Dollan had lived in fifty-two foster homes in Alberta before his tenth birthday, and had been diagnosed as suffering from a personality disorder with antisocial, depressive and schizoid features.

Eight years after their trial, Newstead was back in the news. This time it was for something positive: she received a degree in religion from Queen's University while an inmate at Kingston's Prison for Women, serving a second-degree-murder term for her role in killing Robert Kehoe. That made her the first woman in Canada and the first inmate in an Ontario prison to earn an entire degree behind bars. Her area of study was Buddhism, which encourages followers to lead moral lives and to be aware of their thoughts and actions.

In the biker world, club members are expected to ask permission to date other members' former girlfriends. That's what Campbell did before he began his relationship with a black-haired seventeen-year-old named Charmaine. Charmaine's family had moved to Oshawa from the Maritimes, and she was pretty and fun and hard-working and didn't seem to have an enemy in the world. Charmaine had dropped out of school, but always managed to find a job.

"I met Charmaine in 1975. She had gone out with [club member] Larry Hurren and I asked him if I could have her number. I saw that she was fun to be around. After we had gone out a few times, I told her she was a breath of fresh air compared to the girls I had been with up until then."

Campbell recalls with pride an evening with Charmaine and a friend and his date. The other woman clearly looked down her nose at

Campbell and Charmaine. The conversation was already more than a little strained when the topic shifted to fantasies.

"What's yours, Lorne?" the prissy woman asked.

"My fantasy is to be in a room with thirty or forty naked beautiful women," he replied. "I don't want to be fucking them. I want to be rolling over them. I just want someone to take pictures of me so no one can say I'm a liar." Campbell betrayed no trace of a smile as he pretended to confide his deep yearning. It took the prissy woman some effort to regain her composure, and then she asked Charmaine, "What's your fantasy?"

"I just want to be one of those women," she deadpanned.

The prissy woman had no clue how to react.

CHAPTER 8

The Biker with the Dragon Tattoo

I'm his sister and you slit his throat.

A WOMAN upon meeting Lorne Campbell in an Oshawa bar

n the late 1970s, Campbell was running Top Choice Tattoos on downtown Bond Street in Oshawa with his friend Joe Napolitano. Joe and
his brother John moved in mob circles, and Campbell was amused by
a story about Toronto area Mafiosi once kidnapping Joe over a debt John
owed to them, in the $30,000 to $40,000 range. The mobsters figured
that John would pay his debt for the return of Joe.

"You guys know him," Joe told his captors. "You know what he's like."

The mobsters did indeed know what John was like—and they freed Joe.

It was hard to be mad at John for any length of time. He had a certain
charm and flare, and after his brother's release he used a large portion
of the booty to buy drinks for the men he was cheating. "He would take
them to the bar and it was their money."

One of the employees at Top Choice Tattoos was Poncho, a skilled,
if light-fingered, skin ink artist. Poncho went on the run after stealing
money from the shop. One day, while Campbell was getting a dragon
tattooed on his back, he heard a commotion at the front door. The noise

kept getting closer to the chair where he sat. Then Poncho appeared, with a biker tight on either side of him. "I said, 'How the fuck did you get him?' They didn't say anything. They just went downstairs."

Campbell followed them down to help discipline Poncho. There, he saw his old friend Larry Vallentyne. "I went to punch him [Poncho] in the head and Larry kicked me in the hand. It wasn't meant for me—it was meant to hit the guy's head."

The fumbling continued. His co-workers leaned down to cut off one of Poncho's fingers, missed, and amputated a pair instead. No one but Poncho felt the worse for it. Campbell returned upstairs, nursing his sore hand, to finish getting his dragon tattoo.

Not surprisingly, the ten-fingered tattoo artist who'd been working on Campbell was too shaken to resume work immediately. "The guy who was tattooing me was nervous. I had to tell him to settle down."

One evening in the winter of 1976, at the Vagabond Motorcycle Club's clubhouse on Kintyre Avenue in Toronto's Riverdale neighbourhood, the music was so loud that Campbell was having trouble carrying on a conversation. He was trying to talk with a Vagabond nicknamed Beach because he looked as if he had just strutted off Muscle Beach. Beach didn't just look tough; he was a former mercenary soldier and had a well-deserved reputation to match his appearance.

Beach looked concerned about something that evening, but Campbell couldn't make out what he was saying.

"I can't hear you, Beach," he said, and they both walked outside.

As soon as they got outside, Beach caught him solidly with a punch to his face. "He's a powerful guy. It didn't hurt, but I went on my back and slid about ten feet. It was the-punch-that-didn't-hurt, but it sent me flying."

Campbell ran back at Beach, but Vagabond president Bambi jumped into the middle. "Bambi, he was a tough guy despite his name. I don't know how he got the name."

Bambi told Campbell, "He'll get a beating from us for doing that."

"Okay," Campbell replied.

In fact, it wasn't even close to okay for Campbell. He drove to Oshawa, picked up a pistol and returned to the party. "I'm not showing it, but they all know I have a gun."

Beach had already left the party, and things simmered until a run to Sault Ste. Marie the next year. Beach was there and immediately apologized, not out of fear but because he realized his punch to Campbell's head had been out of line. Campbell later learned that Beach was angry because he had heard that a member of the Choice who was in the United States, partying with some Outlaws, had called the Vagabonds "a bunch of faggots." When Beach corked Campbell, he thought that *all* of the Choice were saying that about *all* of the Vagabonds. Clearly, things were about to pop unless something was done fast.

At another party around this time, a man named Tom became enraged. The cause of his anger was the apparent theft of his girlfriend's purse or coat. Venting his anger, Tom said that the thief would suffer dearly if he ever caught him. In front of several people in Campbell's circle, Tom announced: "I don't even care if it's Lorne Campbell. I'll shoot him and cut his old lady's tits off." Tom felt bold enough to say this because Campbell wasn't at the party. Even so, it was a breathtakingly stupid thing to do. When word got back to Campbell, he had no doubts about his required course of action. "I went where he lived."

Tom wasn't there, so Campbell spent the night in the man's bed, awaiting his arrival. When Tom still hadn't appeared the next morning, Campbell joined up with his friend Smutley. There was a .45 pistol in a bag in their glove compartment when a Durham Region cop pulled them over. The cop recognized them both. He had no clue that what he said over the next five minutes or so would determine whether Tom lived or died.

"Hi, Lorne."

"How are you doing?"

"You're on parole?" the cop said to Smutley.

It was a hot afternoon, but Campbell didn't sweat at all. He felt certain they were going to be arrested, so why get stressed out about it?

Smutley confirmed that he was on parole.

"What are you on parole for?"

"Armed robbery."

With that, the conversation ended. To Campbell's amazement, the cop let them drive on, and the hunt resumed in earnest. "I was hunting him every day."

The pursuit of Tom consumed Campbell's life. He went to parties he figured Tom might attend. He went to bars that Tom frequented. In the end, Campbell couldn't stand the prospect of hearing Tom's friends say one more time that they didn't have a clue where he was. "I started hitting people. Finally someone told me."

Tom was reportedly in the Cadillac, the same Oshawa hotel where Campbell worked as a bouncer. It was too good to be true. Once again, the hunters and the hunted had returned to the same watering hole.

Before Campbell could get to him, Larry Vallentyne stepped in. He told Campbell that Tom had recently dropped Campbell's name, as if they were good friends, and then talked about someone Campbell wanted beaten up. Vallentyne, thinking he was doing a favour for his friend Campbell, went to the home of the stranger Tom had mentioned and brained him with a large glass coke bottle.

"Larry, you just got suckered in, buddy," Campbell said.

Now they both had a serious grievance against Tom, who didn't have a clue how much worse his fortunes had become. They approached him together, and before Campbell could do anything, Vallentyne smashed a glass across the front of Tom's neck.

"Phone the fucking ambulance," Campbell ordered a bouncer. None of the patrons seemed to notice the man bleeding all over the bar. "After it was over, we just sat down and drank another beer." Tom survived, although Campbell heard later that it was only because the ambulance arrived on the scene so quickly and the attendant was exceptionally skilled.

A couple of weeks later, a woman Campbell had never seen before appeared alone at the Cadillac. She had the type of good looks that Campbell would have remembered. Not long after she walked in, she was smiling at him.

"You Lorne Campbell?" she asked.

A few minutes after that, they were dancing together close.

Somehow, as their bodies pressed together on the dance floor, the conversation shifted to the man whose throat had been sliced open at the Cadillac.

"You know Tom?" Campbell asked.

"Yeah, I'm his sister and you slit his throat."

"I didn't slit his throat. I just held him."

Campbell then told her his side of the story, about how Tom had said things that simply couldn't go unpunished. The woman might be good-looking, but Campbell was too angry now to mince words. "Your brother is a conniving piece of shit," he said, and added, "I found out he was using my name."

The woman was a good listener. Later in the evening she admitted that she had brought a knife to the Cadillac, hoping to catch Campbell off guard so she could stick him with it. "That's the only night I ever seen her. I spent the night with her."

As for Tom, Campbell later heard that he died of a drug overdose.

Hamilton Choice member James (Wench) Kellet was a particularly loud partier. Part of the reason was his enthusiasm for drugs. Another factor was his out-there personality, which didn't bother Campbell. "I just thought it was funny."

Things got funnier in 1976, when Wench decided he should run for mayor of Hamilton, under the slogan "Choice in the Right Direction." Wench knew he had no chance of actually wearing the mayor's chain of office, but he sounded positively civic minded as he explained that getting involved in politics was better than just sitting around complaining. Not surprisingly, Wench proposed to curb police powers if he ever made it onto the police commission. "They have too much power and they're always bothering people," he told a *Hamilton Spectator* reporter.

All joking aside, Wench saw himself as an inspirational figure for the little guy. "I hope somebody will see that I'm a nobody running for mayor and I hope that moves somebody with something on the ball to run in the next election." Wench truly felt his city needed someone like him in the corridors of power. "Hamilton is in the dark ages with stuffed shirts at City Hall and some are just out of touch."

No one was shocked when Wench finished last at the polls, although some observers were impressed that he managed to get 1,000 of the 100,000 votes cast. A year later, Wench was back in the news. This time, nobody in the Choice was laughing. There had been a disturbance at Wench's apartment building, most likely a drug binge that got out of hand. When police arrived, shotgun fire from inside the apartment trapped them in a cruiser. Members of the Hamilton Choice offered to mediate, but police turned them away. The four-hour standoff ended with more gunfire. Wench was shot dead by the police.

CHAPTER 9

Family Breakup

Knives, guns or fisticuffs. Keep in mind that I am good at all of them.

LORNE CAMPBELL challenging a biker to a fight

C ampbell hated few things more than conniving. He liked to handle problems face to face, man to man. Conniving was especially rank to Campbell when it involved an attack on his extended family, the Satan's Choice, and there was plenty of that going on when the American-based Outlaws sought to woo away Choice members. The Outlaws were the oldest of the big outlaw motorcycle clubs. The group had been founded in 1935 in the Chicago suburb of McCook, Illinois, in Matilda's Bar on old Route 66. They were the second-largest outlaw biker club in the world, behind only the Hells Angels, with a particularly strong siren call for Canadian bikers living near the American border in Windsor, across from Detroit, and along the Niagara Peninsula.

The conniving really got going after May 1976, when Bernie Guindon was sent back to prison. This time, the Frog was sentenced in a Sault Ste. Marie court to seventeen years for conspiring to traffic what police said was between $33 million and $60 million in PCP, or horse tranquilizers. The conviction also deep-sixed Guindon's hopes of qualifying as a member of Canada's boxing team at the 1976 Montreal Olympics.

There wasn't any evidence directly connecting Guindon to the stash of drugs, but police put together a damning case nonetheless. Police had a letter he had written to clubmates while awaiting trial. It read: "What's really going to sink me is the undercover man from Buffalo, Kenneth Peterson, a special U.S. agent, if he shows up. If he sings the way I think he might, I'll be going away for at least a dozen. If you hear of anyone who might be of some help, let me know. I just found out his name, that's why the delay."

It was hard not to see the letter as an invitation—or even a plea—for others to rub out the prosecution's star witness. No one acted on it, but in the end the letter was enough to send Guindon away. "The only evidence they had on me was that letter," Guindon says, as if amazed at how a few sentences can alter the course of a life. Two others involved in actually trafficking the drugs got relatively light ten-year sentences.

Guindon suspected he was sold out by a man who had been introduced to him by Garnet (Mother) McEwan, a St. Catharines member of the Satan's Choice. Guindon won't say much about McEwan, as outlaw bikers are loath to criticize each other publicly. The Frog limits his comments to a terse six words: "Mother was a big fat sonofabitch." It stung Guindon that McEwan assumed his presidency of the Choice just as Guindon was heading off to Millhaven super-maximum-security penitentiary. Worse yet were his suspicions that McEwan was conniving to sell out his club to the American-based Outlaws.

The tensions within the club regarding the Outlaws were just simmering in 1976 when Campbell drove to a biker funeral in Montreal with Moose, a friend from the Para-Dice Riders. Campbell was bellied up to the bar in the Montreal Choice clubhouse when he heard a commotion in another room, where he knew Moose sat playing poker. Someone had stabbed Moose a half-dozen times in the forehead with a buck knife. The wounds weren't life-threatening, but it certainly didn't make Campbell or Moose feel welcome.

"What the fuck did he do?" Campbell asked someone in the room.

"He spilled a bottle."

Lorne made sure Moose was taken to hospital, then returned to the party, where things only got worse. Clearly, Satan's Choice members who were leaning towards joining the Outlaws were trying to stir up something with club loyalists and their friends. "They wanted trouble," Campbell says. "They wanted something to happen."

A Windsor Choice member said, not so far from Campbell: "You can say things in front of some of your brothers, but other brothers"—he gestured towards Campbell—"you can't."

Later that weekend, a Windsor Choice member named Dave Séguin seemed particularly bent on insulting Guindon's old Oshawa chapter. Oshawa was the birthplace of the Choice, and there was no chance that members there would be giving up on their club. It was to the turncoats' advantage to belittle them.

"If I broke down on the 401, I wouldn't phone anyone from Oshawa," Séguin said. "That's how much I hate Oshawa."

It was impossible for Campbell to remain silent after hearing that.

"You know what, Dave, you don't even know me," Campbell said.

Then Campbell introduced himself with five knuckles to Séguin's head, which dropped him onto the floor. A group of Windsor Choice supporters rushed in and began pounding on Campbell. "I've got six guys behind me, boot-fucking me, and I'm pounding on Dave. He's yelling, 'Let me go, let me go.' I said, 'Not till I'm finished with you, Dave. This ain't hurting me.'"

"Get the fuck out," McEwan shouted at Campbell, who recalls: "He hit me six times. I said, 'You have no idea what you're getting into.' I thought, 'You fucking coward.'"

Even without the nasty aftertaste of the Guindon trial, Garnet McEwan had never impressed diehard Choice members like Campbell. Mother seemed no more than a caretaker president, and a weak one at that. Where Oshawa had always been fiercely Canadian, McEwan appeared a traitor to the very club he was supposed to be protecting, eager to sell them out to the expansion-minded Americans. No Canadian club had ever folded into an American one before, but Campbell was certain there was going to be a split in his beloved Choice, with the Outlaws taking several of their chapters. There were grumblings that McEwan had been wined and dined by the Outlaws in the States and was sacrificing his old club for compliments, booze and women. "He was given young girls, things that he would never get as a big, fat, stinky guy selling pencils on the corner. When Bernie was sent to prison, it made it easier for Mother to sell out. It paved the way for the Outlaws to groom Mother."

When Guindon was around, the Oshawa chapter was not to be fucked with, in the same way that bikers had a particular respect for the Oakland Hells Angels, one of that club's original chapters and long-time home of Angels icon Ralph (Sonny) Barger. "Nobody fucks the Oakland guys wherever they go. You fuck with one Oakland member, you fuck with them all, and when they rode to somewhere, you know it's Oakland. You just don't fuck with Oakland."

Campbell had never been one for grey areas and he had often made it patently clear that he didn't respect McEwan, whom he considered a waddling insult to everything the Choice in particular and mankind in general should represent. Aside from teasing him about his very real pencil-selling past, he had occasionally ribbed McEwan about the fact that he wore a plastic leg, saying, "You never had a leg to stand on." There was no love lost between them that night in Montreal, as McEwan ejected him from the party after his dust-up with Séguin.

Shunned, Campbell walked twenty kilometres towards Dorval airport through the snow and sleet, wearing cowboy boots and just a T-shirt under his sweater. He hitchhiked some of the way, getting a ride with an elderly couple who wanted to take him to their farmhouse. He also walked on the median, and finally settled for the night in an abandoned, unheated house. "It was very, very cold."

A few weeks later, the Choice held an official meeting about the punch-up. Campbell travelled to the two-hundred-acre property owned by the club near a cottage town called Coboconk, northeast of Oshawa, along with most of the club's two hundred members. They were asked to decide whether Campbell should be allowed to remain with the Choice after his pummelling of fellow member Dave Séguin. Campbell didn't have any hopes of an impartial hearing. Presiding over the meeting was Mother McEwan, who had taken a half-dozen shots at Campbell before kicking him out of the Montreal clubhouse. Mother said no guns were allowed, but Campbell didn't recognize Mother's authority and packed a loaded .38 anyway. He wasn't expelled from the club that day, which was fortunate for all involved who weren't suicidal. "If I was kicked out, I was dying that day."

In true Canadian fashion, the matter was deferred until a later meeting back in Montreal. Again, it was open to the club's full membership. There, Campbell challenged Séguin to skip the formalities and settle the matter between them.

"Knives, guns or fisticuffs," Campbell said. "Keep in mind that I am good at all of them."

Seguin declined all three options. Campbell went up to the second floor of the clubhouse to await the result of the debate. In the end he was demoted to striker, a middle ground that wasn't a real expulsion. It was enough to keep Campbell from leaving the club—and the world— with guns blazing. "If I had been kicked out, I'm sure I wouldn't have come out of that clubhouse."

One day in the spring of 1977, Campbell was working on the carburetor of his Harley panhead outside the latest clubhouse, on Baseline Road in Oshawa. His driver's licence was suspended for unpaid fines and he wasn't supposed to operate any motor vehicle. That afternoon another club member rode on the back of the motorcycle during a test drive, to help push the bike if it stalled. Campbell was well-known in the area, and was wearing his Choice colours in case anyone had forgotten who he was.

When they were back at the clubhouse, two cruisers pulled up.

"You were riding your bike," an officer told Campbell.

"No I wasn't."

"Yeah, we saw you."

The biker who was with Campbell piped up: "I was driving it."

They told Campbell he was under arrest for driving under suspension.

"Can I go in and get my boots?" asked Campbell, who had been working barefoot.

The officers obliged, which wasn't surprising. "Even though I had problems with them, they knew I would never run."

At the police station, Campbell learned he was also charged with conspiracy to commit perjury. In effect, he was accused of counselling the other biker to lie about driving the motorcycle. At the time it seemed like little more than a nuisance. There was no way of knowing that such a seemingly trivial incident would soon affect his life and the lives of a half-dozen others in a massive way.

Campbell got a hint that things might be going south when he saw two ex-girlfriends of club members in the Whitby courthouse, ready to testify for the Crown. In the outlaw biker world, as in many cultures inside or outside the law, an angry ex-lover is not a force to be taken lightly.

One of the two women had gone out with a biker named Randy. They had no children, but during their breakup they had a particularly ugly dispute over custody of their fridge, which Randy had taken. The other woman at the courthouse was just plain angry about her own breakup with Larry Hurren. Campbell could sense it was going to be messy if they hit the witness stand, although he still didn't understand exactly what the Crown was intending by getting the two women involved. He had plenty of experience with the courts, but he had never even heard of a conspiracy to commit perjury charge. "That's like thinking about telling a lie," he says.

The women's hard feelings threatened to drag Campbell down if they took the witness stand and started spouting off about him and the club. His lawyer persuaded him it would be wise to plead guilty to the perjury-related charge, which carried a maximum fourteen-year term. He wasn't particularly concerned about it, so he followed his lawyer's advice. Friends organized a party for that night, anticipating his release from jail. Instead, in May 1977, he found himself starting a one-year term in the Whitby jail. It seemed like a joke, but it was a bad one and it was on him. "That fridge cost me a year of my life. He [Randy] took the fridge. I took the brunt." Within a few years, that perjury conviction would haunt the club big time.

At the Whitby jail, Campbell settled into a job in the kitchen. "It's a clean, good job and the food would be a perk." Jail staff planned the meals and inmates prepared the food. One day the menu read, "Fried liver or baloney."

"What do you think that means?" Campbell asked a co-worker.

"I don't know," the other man said. "It's kind of ambiguous."

"Let's just give them the baloney," Campbell decided. "I don't feel like cooking."

Not long after that, there was trouble in the cells. "The guards told me everybody was throwing their baloney through the bars."

Campbell got one of the guards to let him onto the range, at the epi-centre of the bologna tossing.

"Anybody got a problem with me, bring it on," Campbell said.

No one did. Despite the bologna incident, Campbell prided himself on his kitchen work and didn't let the near mutiny get to him. "It was all fucked-up food in jail anyway." He decided there was simply too much fat in pork roasts to prepare them for his fellow inmates. "I refused to cook it up. Refused to even touch it." He also refused to serve powdered milk, telling fellow inmates, "If you get powdered milk, it's not me, guys."

He took particular pride in his mashed potatoes. Preparing them in a large metal pot afforded him a chance for a vigorous workout. "There was no lumps in my mashed potatoes. I was really proud of that. I was sweating in them, putting in the milk and butter. There was sweat in them, but there were no lumps. People loved them."

While in Whitby jail, he was given a psychological survey that included questions about whether he had ever had sex with his mother, father or siblings. He checked yes to all of them, which amused at least one guard, who could see it was a joke. Campbell says he should also have added: "I fart in the bathtub too and I bite the bubbles."

Friday, July 1, 1977, was Black Friday in Campbell's world. That was the day half of the Satan's Choice Motorcycle Club patched over—or switched membership—to the Outlaws. The club's Montreal, Ottawa, Kingston, St. Catharines, Hamilton and Windsor chapters joined the American-based club. Remaining loyal to the Choice were the Toronto, Kitchener, Oshawa, Peterborough and Thunder Bay chapters. Like his mentor, Campbell was stuck in jail, powerless to do anything but fume and grieve. "The split never would have gone down if Bernie was still out. Bernie Guindon's influence was not to be challenged. When he talks about people having parts, he's got all kinds of parts."

On a happier note, Campbell was voted back into full membership in the club. Never before had a member had his full status returned while he was still behind bars, but Campbell wasn't a typical member—if there was such a thing—and these weren't typical times. "I took it that they had finally seen the light."

Campbell was into the final month of his perjury sentence when he got news that the Hells Angels had also expanded into Canada. Not to be outdone by their bitter rivals the Outlaws, the Hells Angels awarded death head patches to members of the Montreal-based Popeye gang on December 5, 1977. This move to turn the Popeye (there was no *s* in their name) into Canada's first Hells Angels charter (as the Angels call chapters of their club) made sense in the biker world of *realpolitik*. The Popeye were tough but isolated. Patching over to the Angels provided the former Popeye members no small measure of support and protection.

As the American-based clubs moved in, Guindon still faced several years before he could even hope for parole. The days when their biggest threat was the likes of Johnny Sombrero were long gone. At least Sombrero was local. Now, Campbell and Guindon could do little more than grind their teeth and curse the existence of Mother McEwan, who got the whole cross-border expansion mess started. "Bernie and I never wanted American clubs. We never wanted American influence. It wasn't a good feeling."

The Choice had a practice of holding general meetings, which were open to all members and not just ranking officers. Someone got a warehouse in the west end of Toronto for the Choice's general meeting in the summer of 1978, which focused on heroin.

Lookouts were posted at the windows at the top of the building as members debated whether they should be allowed to deal in heroin. Cocaine hadn't really made a major impression yet and heroin was the drug that attracted the most heat from police.

The two members most in favour of dealing heroin were Ken Goobie, a lanky, balding former Maritimer, and his friend and partner in crime Armand (In the Trunk) Sanguini, a fellow Choice member with tight

Toronto mob ties. "Their argument was that they snorted heroin and they didn't have a problem with it," Campbell says.

The debate was still under way when a lookout shouted from his perch at the windows, "Here comes the cops."

Cruisers filled the lot as the bikers attempted to bolt from the warehouse. Campbell didn't make it out of the lot before his car was pulled over. "Every one of these cops has got his gun out."

Campbell got out of the car with Larry Vallentyne. Nobody ever called Larry calm or discreet.

"You'd love to shoot me, wouldn't you?" Vallentyne shouted at the cops.

"No, we're here to look after things," an officer replied. "We don't want to shoot anybody."

"Fuck off," Vallentyne retorted, and slapped off the officer's cap.

Campbell walked up to the officer who seemed to be in charge and motioned towards Vallentyne. "Can I talk to him?"

"I wish you would."

Campbell approached Vallentyne and gestured towards another officer who was holding his cap in front of his body so that it covered his other hand. "The guy in the front of the cruiser has his throwaway right under his hat. I saw it."

A "throwaway" is an untraceable firearm that some officers carry. It's clearly illegal, but useful in a pinch. It can be dropped beside the victim of a shooting to make him look armed when he wasn't. It can also be used to shoot someone, since it's not easily traceable like a service revolver.

"Oh yeah?"

"Do me a favour and get back in the car."

It felt like a lifetime as Vallentyne considered his friend's advice. Most likely it wasn't more than a few heartbeats. "It's only about three seconds of my life," Campbell says. Then Vallentyne got back in the car.

It was clear that many police officers despised the bikers, just as many bikers hated the police. Just how far the officers would go to stick it to them was anybody's guess.

———

Campbell was shaving one morning when Charmaine took a phone call saying that his father had cancer of the pancreas. Treatment wasn't advanced at the time, and his father's chances of survival were slim. The call signalled a brief window to reconnect, and Campbell seized it.

Campbell was impressed by how his father refused to complain as his life painfully withered away. Once, Campbell offered him a joint in hopes that smoking it would improve his appetite.

"I don't do it myself, but I know it gives you an appetite," Campbell said.

It appeared to have the desired effect, as his father downed half a sandwich and a glass of milk. "It was a really happy mood."

As an adult, Campbell hadn't met with his father much, but the feeling was good as they finally sat together. "He was proud of me then. . . . He was proud of me that I didn't take any shit from anybody." He hadn't lost his feistiness. "He could always give me a slap in the head," Campbell says. "He was pretty fast. He would kind of smile and give me a slap."

Campbell's father grumbled that he was taking shit from plenty of people now, like when strangers cut in front of him in the betting lines at the racetrack when he went to watch his nephew Sandy Hawley ride.

"Nobody would cut in front of me if you were there," he told his son.

CHAPTER 10

Three Bullets

The provincial cops searched far and wide
And the outlaws ran but they could not hide
And they brought em in every single one
Save the man who actually fired the gun . . .

singer-songwriter STEVE EARLE, "Justice in Ontario"

The Golden Hawks didn't become extinct that afternoon in 1962 when they were tricked and chased and humiliated at Pebblestone Park by Johnny Sombrero and his Black Diamond Riders. It just looked that way, as they never regained the status they once held, back when no one dared call them Chicken Hawks. They were still one-percenters, and their parties were better than nothing, which explains why one evening in 1976 Campbell was drinking with some Golden Hawks in the Choice clubhouse in Oshawa. He was in the basement bar when Augie, the Golden Hawks' sergeant-at-arms, said right out of the blue: "You fucking asshole."

"What did you just call me?"

Augie was trying to joke, but Campbell wasn't in a joking mood and Augie wasn't a particularly smooth comic. Augie also wasn't the apologetic sort. Now that Campbell had got his dander up, Augie wasn't about to back down from the challenging tone.

"A fucking asshole," he repeated.

With that, Campbell dropped Augie with a shot to the face. The Golden Hawks' vice-president rushed in to help his fallen clubmate and Campbell dropped him too. "I fucking backhanded him. It was like something John Wayne would have done. He went right over the table. I thought, 'Lorne, good one.'"

Clearly, Augie hadn't been the perfect host and Campbell hadn't been the perfect guest, but what had happened up to this point wasn't that unusual. What followed was. Little did anyone at the Satan's Choice clubhouse that evening realize that the spat with Campbell set the stage for events that would dramatically alter the lives of at least nine men and contribute to the death of a tenth. The fallout would also make it into university law classes, under the subject heading Miscarriages of Justice.

A couple of weeks later, there was a party at the Golden Hawks' clubhouse on Baseline Road between Whitby and Ajax, the town immediately west of Whitby. This time, some members of the Saddle Tramps Motorcycle Club from Owen Sound showed up. Campbell was enjoying himself when he was abruptly told by a Golden Hawk named Bill: "You've gotta leave."

"Why?"

"You've gotta leave."

"Was it because of what happened?"

"You, you just gotta leave."

"I ain't gonna leave."

Bill wasn't about to back down, and they couldn't continue this back and forth all night. It's not much of a party when no one wants you to stay, even if the beer is cold, so eventually Campbell left. But he returned shortly before daybreak with John Foote, John Harvey (the man who later killed Foote), Wayne (Hobo) McCall and Peter (Rabbit) Pillman. The party was still under way, although considerably less sober than when Campbell was ejected. Campbell called out: "Everybody on the floor."

Some of the Golden Hawks were too drunk or stunned to appreciate that their visitors were armed.

"On the fucking floor!"

Campbell then asked, "Where's Bill?"

Bill's brother pointed at his sibling.

"I went over and beat him up. I hit him so hard and so many times his eye popped out."

The president of the Golden Hawks tried to calm things down, but Campbell said he wouldn't accept any excuse for kicking him out of the party. It was too massive a breach of etiquette to be smoothed over with a few "I'm sorrys." Golden Hawks didn't have the right to tell Satan's Choice what to do, even in the Golden Hawks' clubhouse.

"That should never have happened," Campbell said.

"What do you want?" the president asked.

"I want all of their colours."

Taking someone's colours is the ultimate humiliation in the outlaw biker world, equivalent to excommunication or shunning in religious orders, or dishonourable discharge from the military. The Golden Hawks' president wasn't willing to let this happen; there must be some compromise solution. Campbell replied that there was an alternative, but it would be even more severe.

He shut down the once proud Golden Hawks altogether.

Two years later, in October 1978, there were rumblings that the Golden Hawks were making a serious effort to take flight again. They were supported by the Outlaws in their efforts to re-establish a chapter around the small town of Port Hope, about half an hour east of Oshawa. One of their new members was 23-year-old Bill (Heavy) Matiyek, who had the habit of carrying a sawed-off double-barrelled shotgun up his sleeve or tucked inside a cowboy boot. Even without the firepower, Matiyek was imposing enough, standing over six feet tall and weighing in the neighbourhood of three hundred pounds. Perhaps he was hopped up on bennies one evening that autumn when he opened fire on Campbell's friend Smutley. He proved to be less of a marksman than a physical presence, and Smutley was able to duck behind a car door and save himself.

On the evening of October 18, 1978, Campbell was watching the Maple Leafs hockey game at the Satan's Choice Toronto clubhouse when a telephone call came through telling of trouble in the bar of the Queen's Hotel on Port Hope's main street. The Queen's was billed back in 1918 as "without a rival between Toronto and Belleville," but like the Genosha in Oshawa, the Queen's glory days seemed a million boozy Saturdays in the rear-view mirror by October 1978. At this point, the seedy three-storey dive was best known in Campbell's world as an Outlaws hangout.

Inside the Queen's that night, Matiyek was stoned on bennies, more than a little drunk, and had a .32 pistol tucked inside his coat. Perhaps emboldened by the pills and the beer and the gun, he was openly contemplating putting a hole in someone from the Satan's Choice.

Campbell and his clubmates rushed out the door of the Toronto clubhouse when they got the call about what was happening at the Queen's. "Back then, people moved when there was trouble." They stopped en route at a house near Port Hope. "Somebody else had a gun with them and was told to give it to me because it was a revolver and they were trying to figure it out. Somebody said, 'Give it to him, just in case.' We were told the Outlaws were in the bar and we went from there to the bar."

Campbell was a natural to carry the revolver, since he was considered calm enough not to panic and tough enough to kill if necessary. Semi-automatics eject cartridges, leaving evidence for police, so the revolver seemed the right gun to carry into the Queen's that night.

In the L-shaped, dingy bar were Sonny Bronson and Fred Jones, both former Satan's Choice clubmates who had patched over to the Outlaws. What happened next would become part of biker folklore. "It was actually pretty simple," Campbell says. "They like to make it complicated. People have embellished it a lot. We went to the bar. I sat with one other person. We ordered a drink. . . . Mike Everett, he said, 'Bill's sitting with a gun pointed at Rick and Gary.' . . . I got up right away and went to the table and I said, 'How are you doing, Bill?'

"As soon as I said, 'How are you doing?' he went for it. . . .

"I totally wish he hadn't gone for it. I've had to live with it. It hasn't been easy. But he went for it and I happened to be faster. . . . It happened so fast that I just reacted. When you see somebody going for a gun and you've got one, with the upbringing I've had, you'll be fast. I'm glad I had the gun. . . . I never questioned my decision. Not once. Not for a second.

"You're kind of helpless to change anything, but I just wish it hadn't happened. Just a waste of life."

Bill Matiyek's life ended at 10:55 p.m.

How it ended would be discussed for decades.

Campbell took the long way out of the Queen's, not noticing a side door near Matiyek's body. On his way towards the front door, Campbell saw his former Choice brothers Jones and Bronson. They had ridden with Campbell, partied with him and broken bread with him. Now they were on the other side of an unbridgeable divide, and Campbell couldn't help but think they were dupes and traitors. He had already fired three shots and there were three bullets left in his revolver. The thought flashed through his mind that maybe they would have to be shot as well, but Campbell kept his gun down and walked through the front door onto Walton Street, the same way he had entered. "What had just happened was totally self-defence. Shooting them would have been different. People who do that kind of thing are stone cold. They weren't a threat to me.

"I just walked past them on the way out."

Campbell drove back to Oshawa, dumping the pistol on the way, and spent the rest of the evening at the Cadillac Hotel. The next day, he was back at his day job as an ironworker on the Air Canada hangar at the Toronto airport.

He says it never entered his mind to flee the area. At the very worst, it would be a second-degree-murder beef, since it wasn't premeditated. "I would never run on anything that I've been wanted for or anything that I've done."

It took police a while to catch up to Campbell, and when they did, it was for an unrelated charge. He was dispatched to Toronto's Don Jail in 1979 for three months for an assault he described as "beating the snot out of a bar owner for pulling a gun." Larry Vallentyne also took part in the tenderizing. Since Campbell is left-handed and Vallentyne punches best with his right, they stood side by side, with Campbell on the left, and whaled away on the man. "We were still beating the guy when the cops got there. Every time he started sliding down the walls, we pulled him back up and hit him some more."

That meant Campbell was in jail for the Christmases of 1976, 1977, 1978 and 1979. He had stopped celebrating Christmas after he burned down his old house and lost contact with his only child. "After her mother and I split up, because of Janice I never celebrated Christmas all of the time I was with Charmaine. I didn't get sad, but I was happy to be by myself."

At night in Toronto's Don Jail, after the lights were turned out, he noticed a mouse sneak up to the bars of his cell, looking for crumbs. Campbell began gathering scraps for his visitor from the evening "jug up," slang for the prisoners' evening snack. He left crumbs by the bars and watched as the mouse—which he called Mouse—scurried close to eat them. He next placed the scraps inside his cell. Mouse ventured inside to eat them too. In time, he placed them inside his shoes, and watched as Mouse ran up to eat them. Campbell had to lie perfectly still so that he didn't scare Mouse away. To keep from spooking his new friend, the drug debt collector for Canada's toughest biker gang had to stay quiet as a mouse himself.

He was assigned to work as a garbage collector at the Don, under not-so-tight supervision. This allowed him to leave the secured jailhouse, a rare privilege. Other prisoners told him of a plan in which their friends would leave a pouch of Daily Mail tobacco filled with marijuana along his route outside on the jail grounds. He would pass through security heading out of the jail with a pouch of Daily Mail tobacco in his shirt pocket. When the guard wasn't looking, he was to pick up the pouch that was waiting for him, with marijuana hidden under the tobacco. He would put that pouch in his pocket and throw out the pouch containing only tobacco, so that he could bring the weed in for his fellow inmates.

The plan worked like a charm, and soon prison staff could detect the burnt-popcorn smell of marijuana wafting from the cells, and see that several of the prisoners now seemed to be floating on a druggy cloud. The only prisoner who was leaving the building was Campbell, and so he was pegged as the likely culprit, even though the guards hadn't figured out how the weed was being smuggled inside.

"You're not working anymore," a guard told him. Campbell was being moved.

"Okay, where are you taking me?"

Campbell was led to a range of eighteen cells. He did a double take when he saw male prisoners with nail polish, some of whom were doing other inmates' hair. Standing outside Campbell's cell was what appeared to be the lone non-transvestite on the range.

"How are you?" the man asked.

"Not too bad."

The man could see that Campbell was taken aback by the sight of the other male prisoners flamboyantly decked out as women.

"I don't mind the odd blow job," the man said.

Campbell stormed up to a guard. "Why are they putting me here? Why did they put me on this range?"

"There's no other room."

The guard seemed nonchalant until Campbell turned suddenly and walked away, saying, "Watch this. If you don't move me, I'm going to punch every one of them out."

"Campbell, come back here."

He was transferred back off the range before he ever set foot in his new cell.

CHAPTER 11

Busted

What breaks a chain, Rick, is a weak link. Don't be a weak link.

LORNE CAMPBELL

Baraang!

Baraang!

Campbell was on the second floor of the Toronto clubhouse on the evening of Wednesday, December 8, 1978, when he heard something crashing repeatedly against the front door. Outside was a police officer with a sledgehammer, slamming it hard into the steel-reinforced door and then struggling to regain control as the hammer rebounded sharply each time. There was no doorbell and he didn't feel inclined to knock.

Baraang!

Baraang!

"It's steel," Gary (Nutty) Comeau shouted out the window. "Come to the back door."

The cop either didn't hear or chose to ignore him, and kept bouncing the hammer off the door. Behind him were some seventy officers, in riot gear and looking ready to go to war.

"We'll open the door," Campbell shouted.

Before he could get there, a police truck with a mounted boom on the back reversed hard into the door, punching out a panel. "Then somebody opened the door and they all came in." Fortunately for the bikers, none of them was standing behind the door when the boom hit it. "It would have knocked somebody's head right off their shoulders."

Comeau, Jeff (Boom Boom) McLeod and Larry (Beaver) Hurren were among those led out in handcuffs. An hour west in Kitchener, David (Tee Hee) Hoffman of the Choice chapter in Waterloo Region was arrested at his home. All four arrests went off without incident, and police told reporters they put on the show of force because they expected to be met by some fifty Choice inside. It struck Campbell as odd that four members of the club were charged but he remained free. "I wouldn't say I was shocked, because not so many things shock me, but I was surprised. I had expected to be arrested."

The investigation into the death of Bill (Heavy) Matiyek had started badly and gone downhill from there. Police generally craft a case with a combination of forensic and eyewitness evidence. In the case of the Queen's Hotel killing, forensic evidence was sadly lacking. Beer glasses weren't fingerprinted, which would have shown that Campbell was in the lounge. Immediately after the December police raid, Nutty Comeau's black leather jacket disappeared after it was taken by police from his mother's home as evidence. Testing on the leather jacket would have shown that Comeau had been shot in the arm that night with a bullet that had passed through Matiyek.

Eyewitness evidence in the case was no better than the forensics. Perhaps it was fear or booze or the biker code against testifying against others. Or maybe it was that the shooting happened so suddenly, with the three bullets fired within seconds of each other in a corner of the room while many of the bar's patrons were distracted or drunk. Or maybe plenty of people were lying.

Whatever the case, about all the police knew beyond a reasonable doubt was that there were a lot of Satan's Choice members in the Queen's when Matiyek was shot and that they all hightailed it immediately after he slumped over dead.

At age twenty-six, Comeau was already an eight-year member of the Choice. In the early 1970s he'd been convicted for indecent assault, but as he explained it, he didn't touch a girl who was having sex with a group of bikers, he just didn't stop them. The Crown said the bikers could all plead guilty to indecent assault or all be tried for rape. Pleading guilty seemed like the prudent thing to do, but it meant he was still classed as a sex offender. Comeau wasn't someone Campbell hung around with a lot. He was loud and could joke about others, but was thin-skinned about taking a ribbing himself. That said, he was still a brother, and for Campbell nothing trumped brotherhood.

Fellow arrestee Jeff (Boom Boom) McLeod was a quick-witted 24-year-old *Toronto Star* delivery driver who tipped the scales somewhere around 315 pounds, give or take a couple of hamburgers. He and Comeau were men of big appetites, and the two pals could put down ten burgers each in a feeding. Boom Boom wouldn't back down from food fights in restaurants or real brawls in bars, but he was far more intelligent than his looks suggested.

At twenty-seven, Larry (Beaver) Hurren was three years younger than Campbell, who had sponsored Hurren into the club. They got to know each other when he lived in Campbell's home with Elinor, her father and Janice for a time while attending high school. He had been the best friend of Campbell's former brother-in-law and supported himself by working alternately as cab driver and factory worker. He was also the veteran of one amateur boxing fight. He might have won that bout at the Oshawa United Auto Workers hall if he hadn't been docked a point because his corner man, Campbell, shouted instructions too loudly and too often about how he should handle his more experienced opponent.

Not long after the raid on the clubhouse, police made another sweep of arrests, picking up four more Choice members. They included Rick Sauvé, who in the Crown's eyes was another of the ringleaders in the Matiyek killing. Those who knew Sauvé considered him an unlikely candidate for the role of underworld killer. Just twenty-five, he was a Port Hope boy who quit school in grade nine to take a local factory job, where he rose in the union until he was elected local president. He was married with a four-year-old daughter and coached minor hockey. He was also distantly related to Matiyek: his brother's wife and Matiyek's brother's wife were sisters.

Sauvé was a genuine motorcycle enthusiast, as opposed to a criminal with a motorcycle, and this passion led him to join the Peterborough chapter of Satan's Choice. Sauvé had been a member for only a couple of months when Bill Matiyek was shot to death, and the night he spent in jail after the clubhouse raid was the first time he had ever been in custody. While he was nothing close to a hardened jailbird, Sauvé was a solid member in Campbell's books. Years later, Sauvé would remember Campbell telling him: "What breaks a chain, Rick, is a weak link. Don't be a weak link."

The most noteworthy thing about co-accused Merv (Indian) Blaker of the Peterborough chapter was his quiet and respectful demeanour. Campbell wasn't sure if that was his natural way or an Ojibwa trait or a bit of both. Blaker's family moved to Port Hope from the Curve Lake reserve when he was young. At thirty-three, Blaker was the oldest of the accused and was considered a hard worker at an outboard marine outlet in Peterborough. He had been a Choice member since 1967, and was acknowledged by his fellow bikers as a top-level rider. At times, he truly seemed at one with his motorcycle, commanding it to do high-speed controlled wheelies, veering to the left and right, or to inch forward at what seemed like an impossibly slow speed. His skills reminded other experienced riders of the possibilities of true bike riding, and conjured up images of a Native warrior from an earlier age, doing tricks on a war pony.

Indian's biking was about function, not form. There was a competition in the Choice for the "Rat Bike" owner: who had the skuzziest motorcycle. It was an oddly respected award, because it was meant to be presented to a true biker, one who rode hard and kept his bike on the road and didn't care in the slightest about it looking pretty. Indian always seemed to win the Rat Bike award. Indian was slightly built and not considered a threatening man. Campbell still smiles at the memory of Bill (Mr. Bill) Lavoie trying to teach Indian how to use a handgun. That lesson ended suddenly when Mr. Bill accidentally shot himself in the finger.

Since Indian grew up close to the Queen's, it is hard to imagine he would have taken part in such a brazen crime in such a public place, where he would almost certainly be recognized.

Thirty-one-year-old Tee Hee Hoffman got his nickname for his distinctive high-pitched laugh. That laugh didn't seem in keeping with his stature as a champion super heavyweight powerlifter, but it was just as much a part of the man as his mammoth size. A bookkeeper at B.F. Goodrich in Kitchener, Tee Hee was known for his good nature, not for violence. His arrest was particularly baffling, since Tee Hee wasn't even in the bar—or Port Hope—that night.

Like Hoffman, Peterborough welder Gordon (Dog Map) Van Haarlem was facing charges despite a strong alibi: he was sharing drinks in the Grand Hotel in Peterborough with off-duty jail guards at the time when witnesses put him in the Port Hope bar. He would have been hard to miss, since he showed up at the Grand wearing his club colours. Van Haarlem had been nicknamed "Dog Face" by Comeau, a comment on how the Peterborough bikers weren't a particularly handsome bunch. Dog Face was actually on the good-looking side, however, and in time his nickname morphed into Dog Map, for the winding routes he sometimes took getting places.

Rounding out the "Port Hope Eight" was Armand (In the Trunk) Sanguigni, Campbell's 28-year-old clubmate from the Toronto suburb of Mississauga. His nickname came from his serious mob ties, which explained his dealing of bennies and his access to counterfeit currency and heroin. He wasn't physically imposing, but if you stared directly into his eyes he could look back in a way that made your knees buckle. He wasn't a drinker, but he liked his heroin, a drug he felt he could control. It wouldn't have been shocking to hear that he had taken part in an underworld hit, but the public nature of the Matiyek killing seemed much too sloppy for a mob guy.

As police probed the Queen's Hotel murder, Campbell was almost always in their sights and often in their custody on a string of other charges. One punch-up involved him trading blows with off-duty police officers after they directed Campbell's friend to quiet down in a Scarborough Chinese restaurant. Police might accuse Campbell of a lot of things after the Port Hope shooting, but no one could say he was hiding out.

After one of his many court appearances for assault during this time, Campbell and Larry Vallentyne were handcuffed together on their way to a prisoner wagon when the elderly guard leading them tripped and fell over into a snowbank.

"Come on! Let's go!" Vallentyne said.

"We're not going."

"We'll fuck off and go to the clubhouse," Vallentyne offered. "By the time they get there, we'll be drunk."

"They'll say we knocked him over."

At that point, the guard was crawling up out of the snow.

"Are you okay?" Campbell asked.

"The old guy just got up and said, 'Thank you.'"

With that, Campbell and Vallentyne were led into the prisoners' van and another night in jail.

CHAPTER 12

Stepping Up

And the guilty man stood free outside
When he took the stand to pay his debt...

STEVE EARLE, "Justice in Ontario"

uriosity propelled Campbell to attend the preliminary hearing in
Port Hope in February 1979 for the murder charges against his
eight clubmates. The site of the hearing—the town's quaint red
brick town hall—seemed a bit incongruous for what was being packaged
as a cold-blooded gangland hit. It was built back in the 1850s, when some
serious people thought Port Hope could one day be the capital of Canada.
By the time of the trial's preliminary, the town's glory days were long
gone. Rather than being a centre of power, Port Hope was fast establishing itself as a favourite destination for hard-core antique collectors and
visitors happy to eyeball its impressive architecture and soak in what one
newspaper described as its "pleasingly old-fashioned and somewhat
sleepy vision of civic orderliness, right down to the white picket fences,
lovingly-arranged flower gardens and cats napping on porches."

Campbell attended in the hope he could somehow insert himself into
the legal proceedings and get his clubmates off the charges. It baffled
him how eight Satan's Choice members could be charged for killing Bill
Matiyek while he—the real and only gunman—wasn't one of them,

even though it seemed every cop in the area knew who he was and that he was plenty violent. He had heard rumblings that so-called eyewitnesses were getting ready to testify, with reasons of their own for co-operating with the Crown. Perhaps after he took a look at things for himself, it might all make more sense.

Pillman came with him. Peter Rabbit was close to a dead ringer for Campbell, and sometimes Campbell himself had to squint when looking at a photo to see which of them was in it. Peter Rabbit was slightly taller and slightly younger-looking, but not much. He wasn't eager to make the trip, but he also knew it would be considerably less aggravating to go than to refuse Campbell's invitation.

Campbell was curious to see if any of the so-called witnesses would recognize him. He and Peter Rabbit attended on the day the coroner took the stand and other Crown witnesses sat in a room near the courtroom, awaiting their call to testify. No one seemed to pay them any attention as they walked back and forth past the open door of the witness room. "Three or four times I walked by with Rabbit. I didn't stare in, just walked by."

One might have expected a startled reaction from at least one of them. It wouldn't have been shocking if the police were called and told that the real killer—and his double—was parading past the witness room. What happened instead when they walked past the witness room was *nothing*. It was as if the people gathered inside had never seen either of them before. "None of them said, 'I believe it was him.' It just befuddles me. I thought, 'How the fuck could that happen?' They knew me. I hung around Port Hope."

The only real reaction from anybody that day came from Sanguigni, who clearly wasn't comfortable with Campbell's fact-finding stunt. He didn't explain why he was upset with Campbell in the courthouse and Campbell didn't ask. Whatever his objections, a complaint from Sanguigni wasn't to be lightly dismissed, so Campbell reined in his little experiment and went home, still wondering how the case could proceed without the real shooter in custody. It seemed the worst thing the accused had going for them was the fact that they were all members of Satan's Choice, and who—besides their families—would cry if eight bikers were packed off to prison on a flimsy case? Who would feel less safe? "We were the scourge of the country," reflects Campbell.

Campbell decided there was really only one thing left to do. So one day he announced to Charmaine that he was going to step up and confess to the shooting of Bill Matiyek. To that point he hadn't told her a thing about what had happened that evening in Port Hope. He believed in handling his business by himself, but this couldn't be kept quiet any longer. Charmaine now had a life-changing decision to make. It was likely that he would be heading for a serious stretch in prison, and it didn't seem fair to make her wait for his return. Charmaine was young and deserved a chance to start a new life. "I told her it was going to happen. [I said], 'We'll part. Get on with your life.'"

Charmaine refused the way out he offered her. "No," she said, "I'm with you."

The Crown appeared amenable to a deal. Their case was far from airtight, since they were trying to make first-degree murder stick without much evidence. They also didn't have a clear motive and were just guessing about the identity of the shooter. A month before the trial was to begin, the Crown offered a deal that meant everyone charged could walk free and Campbell would get a life term for first-degree murder, with no parole eligibility for twenty-five years. Campbell verbally agreed, but a few days later, without explanation, that deal was withdrawn and a new offer tabled: Campbell could plead guilty to second-degree murder—an acknowledgement that the shooting was reactive and not premeditated. That sounded accurate enough to Campbell. He would get a life term with parole eligibility after ten years. The rub was that everyone else, rather than walk free, would get four years as accessories to the crime.

The bikers were solid that they had to vote unanimously in favour of any deal or it would be rejected. The Crown also wanted a blanket deal: it had to be everyone or no one. Tee Hee Hoffman balked at the offer. He hadn't even been in Port Hope at the time, and a police wiretap at the Kitchener clubhouse would later back his alibi. The idea of serving prison time understandably didn't sit well with him, and the others respected that. The deal was rejected. Campbell waited for a new offer, but the Crown's mood had cooled. The optics of wheeling and dealing with the province's toughest outlaw biker club on a high-profile murder case weren't good. Far safer for the Crown to proceed to trial and take their chances with a jury.

Port Hope is a small town and the Queen's shooting was big news. All the local publicity could easily prejudice a jury, so the trial shifted down the highway three hours west to London. That meant the defence lawyers from eastern Ontario would be picked up in a chartered plane that hopped to London at the start of each week and flown back to eastern Ontario at the end of the week. It was highly unusual for the public to pay for lawyers' air travel, but it was considered acceptable under the circumstances.

The trial was now set for the newly built London courthouse, a mound of bricks and glass in the city's core that could pass for an insurance company's or bank's headquarters. Just a couple of blocks away, overlooking the Thames River, sits the old Middlesex County Courthouse, a local landmark with personality to spare. Resembling a gothic castle or medieval movie set, it had been the scene of a notorious miscarriage of justice a century earlier. The Donnellys were a nineteenth-century version of an outlaw biker club, known for fast horses, ready fists and rough, unflinching brotherhood. After a gang of supposedly respectable men clubbed and pitchforked them to death in 1880, truth took a holiday. Despite two trials at the Middlesex County Courthouse, a combination of lying witnesses, political meddling, police bumbling and widespread prejudice meant no one was convicted from the mob that murdered five members of the Donnelly clan. Campbell could only hope that the local delivery of justice had improved with the passage of time.

As the trial began, heavily armed members of the OPP's tactical unit could be seen on rooftops and on the streets and in the hallways of the courthouse. It was as though the paramilitary officers were standing guard against a modern-day horde of Cossack warriors on Harleys; in one headline, the *London Free Press* described the courthouse area as "like an armed camp." Inside, the Port Hope Eight were all neatly dressed in conservative suits or sports jackets. Their hair was groomed and beards trimmed or shaved off altogether. Despite their gussied-up appearance, none of them denied they belonged to the Satan's Choice.

Crown attorney C.J. Meinhardt showed the jury mug shots of their hairy, pretrial, bikerish selves, lest anyone be mistaken about how they looked the night Bill Matiyek died. Meinhardt told the jury he was about to prove that Matiyek was the victim of a premeditated, gangland-style execution; he was slain to make an example of him, and the guilt for his death was shared by at least eight members of the Satan's Choice. Bikers who guarded the doors to make sure Matiyek couldn't escape were just as guilty as the one who actually pulled the trigger—or so went the Crown's theory.

The jury also heard that Matiyek had a .32 calibre semi-automatic pistol in his left breast pocket, loaded with a clip of eight bullets. The breech of the gun was empty, meaning Matiyek hadn't cocked it for firing when he was hit with three close-range bullets. That was a mystery for the bikers, since Matiyek had talked about having "nine friends." The assumption had been that he was talking about nine bullets in his pistol. No one could name nine Golden Hawks. If there had been a bullet in the chamber, where was it now? Campbell wondered if it was ejected by a police officer to make Matiyek appear more like a victim.

The jury heard that one shot grazed Matiyek's upper left arm and shoulder, then hit his jaw and deflected down and out the right side of his neck. The second blast went in the back of his head and out his right ear. The third went in through his right ear and was stopped in his brain. That was the bullet that ended the life of Bill Matiyek.

All shots were fired from Matiyek's left side, and a pathologist said it was impossible to tell how many gunmen were involved. He also noted that Matiyek's blood alcohol level was double the legal limit to drive.

Under questioning from Comeau's lawyer, Howard Kerbel, 23-year-old labourer David Gillespie admitted that his statement to police the day after the shooting was made "with some haste and some fright . . . after I'd had a few drinks." Then he added a potentially damning statement. Gillespie told the court he'd overheard Comeau ask Sauvé and

Blaker: "Are we going to do it to this fat fucker now, or what?" If the jury accepted this, then the Choice members were on the hook for first-degree murder, since the comments suggested planning and deliberation before the killing. But despite claiming to have overheard Comeau say this to Sauvé and Blaker, Gillespie also said he couldn't be sure if he had seen Sauvé close to Matiyek's table on the night of the shooting. He also wasn't positive about whether Comeau was at the table either.

"Look at him!" Kerbel ordered. "Look at Mr. Comeau! Now, is he the man you saw at Mr. Matiyek's table before he was shot?"

"He looks like the man."

Upon further examination, the court heard that one of the witnesses had once said that another man, named Ray Snider, "could be the gunman," but he was never further identified or charged. The Crown's case appeared even shakier when a police identification officer admitted he didn't have any prior experience showing photographs to prospective witnesses. He also conceded that perhaps he should have shown individual witnesses the photos separately rather than as a group, although he added that he couldn't recall them talking while they viewed the pictures.

When Queen's Hotel waitress Gayle Thompson took the stand, she testified she was certain that Comeau was the killer.

"So there is no doubt in your mind that you were able to identify Mr. Comeau by his hair and by his beard?" Kerbel asked.

"Correct."

"No doubt—not even the slightest doubt?"

"No."

"And there is no doubt in your mind, not the slightest doubt, that Mr. Comeau is the man you saw get up from Mr. Blaker's table, walk toward Mr. Matiyek's table and shoot Mr. Matiyek."

"Correct."

Upon further questioning, she admitted that this was a change in her story from earlier in the proceedings, when she had told authorities that Comeau was only "possibly" the gunman.

Another Crown witness who pointed towards Comeau as the gunman was 23-year-old Port Hope Credit Union computer operator Susan

Foote. She also admitted her testimony had changed between early phases of the investigation and the trial.

Foote said that she was now positive she'd met McLeod at several Satan's Choice parties four years before the shooting.

Defence lawyer Bruce Affleck reminded her that she hadn't been so certain about some details when she testified during a preliminary hearing. As for meeting McLeod at a Choice gathering four years earlier, that was unlikely: "If I were to suggest to you that Mr. McLeod was not a member of the Satan's Choice four years prior to October 18, would that affect your story?" Affleck asked.

She still insisted she had seen McLeod that night in the hotel when Bill Matiyek's life ended.

Further questioning from Kerbel brought the admission that she had also heard talk that a man named "Smutley" might have been the killer. She was also sure that the killer was left-handed. The jury wouldn't know it, but Campbell was left-handed while Comeau and all of the other accused were right-handed.

Former Golden Hawks president Lawrence Leon told the court that Sauvé had threatened Matiyek and himself early in 1978, saying he would not live out the year if he didn't shut down the Golden Hawks in Port Hope. It was a potentially damning statement since, like the "fat fucker" quote from Gillespie's testimony, it suggested the premeditation necessary for a finding of first-degree murder.

Leon said he was no longer with the Golden Hawks and that Matiyek had been the club's sergeant-at-arms. There is a rule among outlaw bikers that they cannot testify against anyone, even an enemy. Perhaps Leon was thinking about this while he sat at the witness stand and told the court that he had thought a great deal about threats against Matiyek and himself. "If it had been me instead of Bill, he'd have come forward too," Leon told the court.

None of the accused were to take the stand. They were sticking to the outlaw biker code that forbids a club member from making any comments that might implicate someone else, whether a respected brother or a hated foe. The defence strategy was to open with Campbell as a surprise witness. His account of how he'd shot Matiyek should make more sense than anything the jury had heard up to this point. Even if his story wasn't accepted by the jury, Campbell could also bring out the fact that Comeau too had been shot that night. That was crucial for the defence lawyers. It had been established through X-rays that Comeau still carried a bullet in his body, but it wasn't proven that the bullet was fired from the same gun that killed Matiyek. Campbell's testimony could potentially compel the judge to order the bullet to be removed from Comeau for forensic testing, and this could be huge for the defence. How could the Crown claim Comeau was the shooter if he was shot with the same gun himself?

Campbell would be introduced to the jury by Bruce Affleck, Jeff McLeod's defence lawyer. It was a reunion of sorts for Campbell and Affleck. Back when he worked as a prosecutor, Affleck had nailed a sixteen-year-old Campbell with a ten-dollar fine for carrying a switchblade. More notably, Affleck had also parked Campbell in the Whitby jail for a year on that imaginative charge of conspiracy to commit perjury.

Despite their opposing roles, Campbell had found Affleck oddly likeable as a Crown attorney. Now, with them both on the same team, Affleck bubbled with goodwill at the sight of Campbell and gave him a vigorous thumbs-up biker handshake whenever they met. He explained to Campbell that he'd left work for the Crown because of a heart attack. Defence work would allow him more control of his hours, which should mean less stress. "His doctor told him that if he had another heart attack, he wouldn't make it."

Affleck was also an Oshawa guy. He paid his way through law school by working as a bouncer at the Brown Derby nightclub at the corner of Yonge and Dundas streets in downtown Toronto. Like Campbell, he had a sharp brain, and often bragged about his 149—"near genius"—IQ. In their new, jovial, relationship, Affleck loved to mention tough guys and then ask Campbell, "Can you take him?" Campbell would invariably reply, "I haven't fought him yet." And Campbell would always think to himself, "I could take that guy."

Unfortunately for the new friends, Affleck's old charge against Campbell was now working against them. He confided to Campbell that the Whitby conviction had been the result of a legal version of horse-trading, when a couple of accused men were set free in other cases in return for a lawyer convincing Campbell to plead guilty on the rare conspiracy-to-commit-perjury charge.

They spoke at a London motel the morning Campbell was to take the stand. "Are you nervous?" Affleck asked.

"No."

"Do you want some Valium?"

"No, I don't take Valium."

"I like to take them in court when I'm nervous."

Campbell relented and took a five-milligram Valium. He took it to quiet Affleck, not to calm his nerves. "He was bugging me so much to take them. He handed me four. I said, 'I'll take one.'"

Campbell felt clean, even righteous, as he prepared to take the witness stand. If things went as planned, then the eight Choice members would walk free and Campbell would take all of the heat for the Matiyek shooting. "I didn't feel I was doing something brave. . . . For me, it was the right thing to be doing because they [the accused] didn't deserve to be there. . . . I was ready, willing and able to do life. It wasn't all to protect them. It was just the right thing to do."

Campbell wore a suit and tie into court, as Affleck had suggested. It was the black suit he sometimes wore to weddings and funerals, the ones he didn't attend in his club colours. Aside from the clothing tip, there was no preparation for what would be Campbell's first and only time testifying in court. None of the rest of the defence lawyers gave him any clue about what type of questioning to expect or what traps could be set for him. Most importantly, he wasn't aware of the need for him to establish that Comeau had been shot that night. "When I was on the stand, I wasn't nervous. I really wasn't, and I wasn't coached. Nobody sat me down and said, 'These are the questions the Crown is going to ask.'" His previous training for dealing with the justice system had come from bikers. It was concise and easy to remember: don't point fingers at anyone, especially a one-percenter; and when in doubt, answer a question with another question.

The jury heard that Campbell was testifying under the Canada Evidence Act, which meant he couldn't be charged for any testimony he gave unless police could independently back it. The bikers already believed that some police were tampering with evidence and intimidating potential witnesses, so it wasn't a stretch for Campbell too to suspect there was a strong chance he would be wearing handcuffs shortly after he left the courtroom.

Campbell testified that he'd been wearing a green parka at the bar. Witnesses had described the shooter as wearing a green parka. Comeau all but lived in his black leather jacket, which he had also worn that night and which had gone missing after his arrest.

Under questioning from Affleck, Campbell said he had been drinking at the Choice clubhouse in Toronto with Gary Comeau and Larry Hurren the night he got the call about trouble in Port Hope. He felt okay mentioning their names in court because they'd given him permission to do so.

As Campbell told things, what happened after he approached Matiyek's table was very simple. "I pulled out my gun and I shot him . . . for my own protection. I didn't want to get shot."

"And where did you shoot him?" Affleck asked.

"In the head."

Campbell made it sound painfully understandable: someone was going to die as soon as Matiyek went for his gun, and Campbell didn't want that someone to be anyone with the Choice, including himself. "I do feel that if he had had a chance, I'd be dead right now," he told the court.

Sauvé's lawyer, Jack Grossman, used his examination of Campbell to attack the Crown's theory that there had been a murder conspiracy. Plenty of violence was rightly associated with the Satan's Choice, but meticulous planning was not the club's strong suit.

"Did you agree with anyone to kill Mr. Matiyek?" Grossman asked.

"No."

"And did you intend to kill Mr. Matiyek when you arrived at the hotel?"

"I had no such instructions."

"And did anyone suggest to you, sir, that Mr. Matiyek should be killed?"

"No."

Campbell told the court that he had carried a gun for about two years "because of propaganda about motorcycle clubs in the newspapers" and because "I didn't want to be next." This was his way of saying that he believed bikers had to worry about being shot by police as well as each other. What Campbell didn't volunteer was that guns were also handy things to carry when collecting drug debts. He lied when asked where he got the gun he used that night, saying he bought it from someone in Toronto. He wasn't about to point at whoever handed him the gun and drag someone else into the mess. Instead, he said that no one else knew he was carrying a gun. He also lied when he said he only recognized that Sonny Bronson and Fred Jones were Outlaws because of their distinctive skull-and-crossbones belts. Of course, Campbell didn't need to look at their waists to know who they were. Bronson and Jones had been Satan's Choice clubmates of Campbell's until they patched over to the Outlaws. Again, Campbell was following the one-percenter code. Even the hated Outlaws shouldn't be dragged into court cases.

Campbell lied again when he said he left the bar in Comeau's car. In reality, he left with someone else, but didn't want to give up that person's name to authorities.

He fumbled when asked about the distance of his arm from Matiyek when he shot him. Decades later, he still doesn't know the right answer to that question. "This thing happened so fast that I can't remember truthfully how far I was away. It's not like everything happened in five minutes. Everything happened in a split second."

Kerbel asked Campbell about his client, Nutty Comeau, immediately after the shooting. Campbell replied that Comeau had been hurt. That wasn't good enough for the judge to order the bullet removed from Comeau, so Kerbel pressed on.

"Well, what did you see?" Kerbel asked. "What is it that you saw?"

"Well, his coat had a hole in it and there was blood there."

With that, the defence lawyers finally had the answer they so desperately wanted. Now they could push to have the bullet extracted from Comeau and entered as evidence. Campbell recalls: "People were full of anxiety, from what I understand, before I entered the courtroom. They were very attentive when I was answering questions. The lawyers were extremely anxious because I wasn't answering the way they expected at first. I think a couple of them had to change their underwear when I was done."

Not surprisingly, Meinhardt's cross-examination was intense. When Campbell looked at him, he was reminded of a weasel in the Roger Rabbit cartoons, without the laughs. "He was pompous. Every time he'd ask me a question, he'd turn around and smile at the jury. That would make me mad."

Meinhardt had plenty of smiles for the jury as he asked Campbell about his old perjury conspiracy conviction. In court, the word "perjury" is never a pretty one, unless you're a Crown attorney cross-examining someone convicted of it.

"And so not only did you go into the box and tell a lie, you have somebody else go in for you to tell a lie?" Meinhardt asked.

"Yes."

"And this was for a driving offence?"

"Yes."

The implication was as clear as if Meinhardt had climbed up on a chair and screamed it into a megaphone: if Campbell would lie under oath about a driving offence, what might he do in a murder trial to save the skins of eight of his biker brothers?

Campbell recalls feeling calm on the witness stand, as he had stuck fast to the one-percenter code. That code hadn't been explained to the jury. Perhaps if they'd heard it, they would have understood what Campbell was *really* saying. He was confessing as fully and honestly as he could while trying to limit the damage to just himself. They might even have admired him, since he was stepping up and trying to absorb all of the blame. "I believe I basically told the truth. Even about the gun. I have bought guns from Toronto before. You have to look at the bigger picture."

When he was on the stand, none of the defence team had thought to remind the jury that Campbell was left-handed, just like the shooter described by Susan Foote and unlike any of the men in the prisoners' box.

After his testimony, Campbell and Affleck were riding the courthouse elevator together when the door opened to a group of defence lawyers standing outside. It was then that Affleck said something that troubled Campbell for years. "He said I was on Valium when I was on the stand. It really hurt."

At that point, it seemed to Campbell that Terry O'Hara, Blaker's lawyer, turned against him. This gnawed at Campbell. He had plenty of respect for O'Hara and felt badly about what he perceived as O'Hara's new, negative attitude. It was as though O'Hara were writing him off after hearing about it, even though he'd stepped up and confessed to the killing.

As a direct result of Campbell's testimony, something happened in the seventh week of the trial that was worthy of the old *Perry Mason* television series. Nutty Comeau was led into Victoria Hospital in London under armed guard and on a heavy-duty leash. Under the supervision of court officers, a medical operation was conducted that could prove, beyond any reasonable doubt, that he wasn't the shooter. A surgeon cut into Nutty's side and pulled out a tiny piece of metal. Forensic testing concluded that it was a bullet from the same .38 handgun that killed Matiyek. Further forensic testing provided an added bonus: a bit of cloth stuck to the bullet fragment was from the coat that Matiyek had been wearing at the time he was shot. It had obviously hit Matiyek first since it came to a stop inside Comeau long with a bit of Matiyek's coat. For the Crown's murder scenario to be true, Comeau somehow shot Matiyek with the same bullet that hit himself. That was too absurd even to consider. When Campbell heard the results of the tests, he felt that a storm had passed. "The feeling was relief, because in all of our minds now it was clear that the witnesses, for whatever reasons, were wrong. It was physically impossible for Nutty to be the shooter. Therefore, there goes the Crown's case."

With their backs against the wall, the Crown became more creative and argued the possibility that there were two shooters. It was also noted that the bullet did conclusively place Comeau at the scene of the crime. All that didn't get past the earlier testimony that there was only one gun. How—and why—two killers would shoot from the same gun within seconds was never explained. Nor was the fact that none of the witnesses had recalled two gunmen in the bar. And it was too late now for them to change their stories.

Campbell had been warned by his own lawyer, John Rosen, that he could be arrested after his courtroom confession, Canada Evidence Act or no Canada Evidence Act. The police just had to swear they were arresting him on *other* evidence than what he offered in the witness stand. For Campbell, it seemed that they had pulled witnesses out of thin air to implicate his brothers, so why would they not turn their sights on him now? That would take nine members of the Choice off the streets.

The Crown didn't appear to have established much more than the bikers' nasty images. In his closing arguments, Meinhardt claimed Campbell wasn't even at the scene of the crime, and noted that witnesses didn't place him in the bar. Meinhardt also asked the jury whether it was reasonable for grown men to run around with patches depicting Satan's head on their backs. It was an interesting question—but who in their right mind had ever suggested that outlaw biker life is based on reason? As Meinhardt explained it, the shooting of Bill Matiyek was staged as a cold-blooded public execution to send a loud message about what could happen if you defied the Satan's Choice. His comments about Campbell dripped with scorn. Nutty Comeau, Meinhardt claimed, matched the witnesses' description of the gunman, not Lorne Campbell.

"It is my respectful submission that you should treat him with all the contempt that he deserves. . . . There isn't an iota of evidence except from the lips of a convicted perjurer that the gunman was a dark-haired man with a goatee and an earring in his left ear. . . . All the evidence points to a blond-haired, blond-bearded gunman."

Justice Coulter Osbourne also undermined Campbell's testimony, albeit more subtly. The judge noted to the jury that he was testifying under the Canada Evidence Act, and also that Campbell had a criminal record that included a perjury conviction.

"That is for you to consider," the judge advised.

Years later, the judge described Campbell as the worst witness he had ever seen on the stand. Campbell, meanwhile, has no bad words for the judge: "He was the boss. I thought he was the most intelligent guy in the room. He was calmer. Asking with a curious voice. Not like the Crown was."

———

It was a complicated case involving multiple defendants, but the jury didn't take long in their deliberations. After huddling for just a day, the jury found Comeau and Sauvé each guilty of first-degree murder. This meant they would receive automatic life terms, with no eligibility for parole for twenty-five years.

McLeod, Hurren, Blaker and Hoffman were each convicted of second-degree murder and sentenced to ten years in prison. Gordon (Dog Map) Van Haarlem and Armand (In the Trunk) Sanguigni, the man with the roughest reputation of the bunch, were each found not guilty and immediately released from custody.

Campbell was stunned when he heard the verdicts, but says he didn't once second-guess his decision to come forward and testify. "I've always been old school. You always protect your brothers, and they didn't deserve to be there. Anybody with any sense would understand that."

Right after the verdicts were announced, Campbell felt the need to drop in on his father in Richmond Hill, north of Toronto, where he lived now with Doris.

His father had often been brutal in the past, but that day he was understanding and even gentle. "I read the papers and I don't care," his father said. "You don't have to explain anything. But if you need anything, come here."

Campbell took Charmaine with him when he went to visit his mother.

"I read the papers. What do you think my friends think?" she asked. "What do you think I'm going through?"

"You know what, Ma? I'm your son," Campbell replied. "Charmaine, put your shoes on. We're out of here."

There were more visits to his father. "He was thin. He didn't eat. It was terminal. Charmaine would rub his back when he was bedridden."

It was such a contrast to the fear he'd inspired, and the power he'd radiated, when Campbell was a child, when a smack from him would send Campbell reeling across the floor. There was nothing threatening about him now. The cancer spread quickly, and on July 23, 1980, Lorne Campbell Sr. died in Doris's home. "It wasn't a shock or a surprise. It still hit me hard. It hit the whole family hard. . . . He was the youngest of the thirteen kids [in his family] and he was the first to go."

Campbell had been working construction out of town and missed being with his father at his bedside during his final days. "I wasn't there when he died. A lot of people didn't forgive me for that."

Campbell was visiting his friend Joe Napolitano at his lodge near Port Carling, north of Toronto, in 1982 when he heard the news about the appeal application. Napolitano was now out of tattooing and making big money in the construction business and real estate. "He was a little crazy, in a good way, and his brother John was crazier. Loyal friends, the pair of them."

There was still the hope that the six Port Hope convictions would be overturned. The original decision seemed too crazy to remain intact, even if the jury discounted Campbell's confession. For instance, how did they explain away the bullet extracted from Nutty Comeau, with cloth fragments from Matiyek's coat on it?

At the time of the appeal, Campbell was lying low. He was wanted by the police for questioning after he put a severe beating on a man in an attempt to locate the man's brother, Gerry, who had previously escaped from Campbell after being hunted "just for speaking bad about us." Campbell recalls, "Gerry jumped off a third floor [balcony] to get away from me." He'd turned to the friend who was with him and said, "Holy fuck. Did you see that?"

They looked over the balcony and Gerry was nowhere to be seen. A little later, Gerry phoned to taunt them, saying he had been hiding behind the bushes, laughing and saying, "You didn't get me." So they decided to pound Gerry's location out of his brother. "I kept him up all night and beat him. Kept him all day and beat him. Then I dropped him off at the hospital because I liked him." In the end, Campbell bumped into Gerry at a booze can, but he spared him a beating because he heard Gerry's son had just died of a drug overdose. He even offered to drive Gerry to the funeral, but when he showed up to give him a ride, Gerry said he was too hungover. "It's your son, Gerry," Campbell said, and drove off.

Particularly since the London trial, Campbell needed good friends like the Napolitanos. He had been drinking hard, bypassing the seductive charms of whisky for the near-knockout stupor of 95-proof alcool, which could become a torch with the drop of a match. The alcool did its job, and also left him with daily stomach aches.

Try as he might, Campbell couldn't drink himself past the cruel irony of the case. He prided himself on being a club protector, and yet when he had stepped forward to sacrifice himself for the group, he failed miserably. He had followed the one-percenter code to a T while on the witness stand, and the result was a public disaster. The one time he testified in court was against himself, and he wasn't believed. For all of Campbell's noble intentions, a half-dozen of his clubmates were in prison for a crime he committed, while he remained a free man.

It would have been an easy time to quit the outlaw biker life, especially after he got news that the efforts to appeal the six guilty verdicts had quickly failed and his biker brothers could expect to remain in prison for a long, long time. He walked alone to the end of the wharf at Joe Napolitano's lodge, stared out onto the waters and wondered how things could have gone so wrong after he stepped forward to tell the truth.

"I don't mind telling you I cried over that one."

CHAPTER 13

Free and Uneasy

My name is Lorne. I'm a Satan's Choice. I'm not a coward.

LORNE CAMPBELL

I n the early 1980s, Campbell put his doubts aside and jumped with both boots back into the life of an outlaw biker. The Oshawa chapter of the Choice had folded after a spate of jailings and members quitting, and Campbell was a Toronto member now. His new home away from home was a two-storey red brick house on Kintyre Avenue near the corner of Broadview Avenue and Queen Street East. It looked like another comfortable family residence in South Riverdale, Toronto. No one, however, could remember when an actual family had last lived there. It had been an illegal booze can and the Vagabonds' clubhouse in previous incarnations. Now it was the Satan's Choice clubhouse.

At one club get-together, Campbell was in the backyard and saw Choice member Tony Valentine about to go inside.

"Grab me a drink when you're in there," he said.

"No."

Valentine didn't sound like he was kidding, but Campbell gave him another chance.

"Grab me a drink when you're inside."

Apparently Valentine thought he had risen above fetching drinks for fellow club members, but there was still a chance he was just joking. When he reappeared a few minutes later, though, he wasn't carrying a drink for Campbell. He had been asked just a small favour and he had denied it. Worse yet, he had done so in front of other members, who would be watching what Campbell did next.

Larry Vallentyne piped in first. "We should hang you," he said to Tony. Larry's last name sounded the same as Tony's, but they were very different men. Even on his gentlest day, Vallentyne was someone to take seriously.

The comment about stringing Tony up was an attempt to shock him into good manners, but he remained belligerent and unapologetic and refused to go back inside to fetch a drink. It was as though he was forcing them to take action. For all their outer rudeness and need to startle civilians, outlaw bikers are notoriously thin-skinned when it comes to insults against themselves and their sense of honour. There is logic to this. If you can be disrespected, then you can also be attacked; and if you can be attacked, then you can also be hurt; and if you can be hurt, then you can be killed. So you act quickly and stamp hard on any signs of disrespect. Besides, what's the point of being an outlaw biker if people are going to treat you like an anonymous piece of crap? You can get that any day in the outside world, without the hassle of earning a patch. So, after the hanging comment itself hung in the air for a couple of seconds, stringing up Tony Valentine sounded like a pretty good way to teach him some manners. Besides, Campbell already considered Tony a conniver. And hanging a conniver took only slightly more effort than it took to go inside and fetch himself a beer.

There was a strong tree in the backyard and plenty of rope in the clubhouse. Soon, despite some struggling, Tony was dangling by his neck in the backyard, his feet flapping in the air. The clubhouse sat in a densely settled downtown area, where one might expect an open-air lynching to attract some attention. But Tony couldn't say much once the rope drew tight, and neighbours generally knew enough to ignore odd happenings at the Choice's gathering spot. "We left him there for half a minute," Campbell recalls. "We weren't trying to kill him. We didn't care, though, if we did kill him."

Tony was still breathing when they lowered him to the earth.

"I'll never come to this clubhouse again," Tony said in a scratchy voice.

"Like we care," Campbell thought.

And that was the last they saw of Tony Valentine on Kintyre Avenue.

No one thought that much about him after that, until someone in the Los Bravos club of Winnipeg reported a sighting of Tony in their city a month or so later. The Los Bravo was curious to know why Tony had come all the way from Toronto and was wearing Choice colours in his club's city. It was a fair-enough question. The sight of the outsider flying his colours in Winnipeg upset the natural order of things on their turf, and so they made a call to the Choice in Toronto.

Campbell agreed to head west and deal with the problem. His approach was typically straightforward when he was finally reunited with Tony Valentine: "I beat him up and I took his colours." No one considered the banishment of Tony any great loss. If he was too rude to get a drink for a brother, he didn't deserve to hang around with them anyway.

One Sunday morning, Campbell was nursing a hangover. Every twitch brought him pain. He was reminded of Kris Kristofferson's lyrics for "Sunday Mornin' Comin' Down," and especially the line about having "no way to hold my head that didn't hurt." Then his buddy Larry Vallentyne walked in. "I hear him grab a drink. He comes up behind me. He's holding a pistol. He fires it right by my ear. It scares the fuck out of me. That's Larry's sense of humour. I jump and he's hysterical, laughing. I said, 'You know what, Larry? I have to catch up with you.' I ran to the bar and had a shot of whisky. I drink it. Within half a minute, my nerves settle down. He couldn't stop laughing."

Vallentyne was at the clubhouse another day when Choice officers approached him to say: "You're going to have to slow your partner down. He's getting out of hand." They were referring to Campbell. The Choice didn't officially have partners, but it seemed that Vallentyne and Campbell were always together.

Just then, Campbell arrived and opened the fridge. Jars of mustard and relish fell out and smashed on the floor. Campbell was convinced this was set up as a practical joke and he had a habit of taking all sorts of things personally, even falling condiments. So he scooped up mustard and relish and threw them around the room. "I threw everything all over the place. Then I got on my bike and rode away."

"You talk to him," Vallentyne replied.

The Hamilton clubhouse of the Choice was a steel-reinforced two-storey brick house in a grotty industrial stretch of Lottridge Street in the city's east end, about ten minutes' drive from Ivor Wynne Stadium, where the Tiger-Cats play football. During one visit with Vallentyne, Campbell found himself perched on the roof, lobbing eggs at bikers down below. When his supply was depleted, Campbell sent a striker to buy up all the eggs he could find.

A little later, Toronto chapter vice-president Michael John Everett rode in on his Harley, wearing a natty long fur coat. Everett was capable of putting on airs, like a rock star, and this day he was particularly insufferable as he squired about Hamilton with a new girlfriend. Sometimes when Everett got this way, Campbell took it as his club duty to let the air out of things. "I'd have to tell him to get down to earth with the rest of us," Campbell says.

Campbell looked down at him from atop the clubhouse roof and decided he would let his eggs do the talking.

"Watch this."

The first egg Campbell dropped hit Everett squarely on the top of his skull. Everett looked up and saw Campbell's grinning face where the sun should have been. Campbell was delighted. "He didn't have a clue what was going on. He hopped on his bike and took off. He was so fucking embarrassed. We almost got kicked out of the club."

It wasn't just the egg dropping that almost got Campbell expelled from the club. The real problem arose the next morning, when he, Mike (Jungle) McCullough and Larry Vallentyne thought it would be amusing to start a small, controlled fire in the Hamilton clubhouse. Everett had returned, presumably after washing the yolk out of his hair, and now Vallentyne siphoned some gas from the Toronto VP's bike. It was poured around somebody who was sleeping soundly, with the aid of drugs or alcohol or both, and lit. Campbell and McCullough were amazed at the amount of smoke this generated. It also amazed them that the Hamiltonians failed to see any humour in their prank. "We put it out within minutes. We didn't know there would be that much smoke. . . . We didn't set fire to the clubhouse—we set a fire in the club-house and we put it out. Fuck, were they ever mad."

It also didn't help that Campbell and Jungle were both stoned on mescaline and that they followed up the fire with tossing beer bottles around the property. Campbell's hijinks weren't totally without malice. Aside from the drugs, Campbell was fuelled by resentment for having to step in and provide muscle for the Hamilton chapter after they ran afoul of a local club called the Red Devils. The president of the Red Devils had been shot to death in his home and his club had blamed the Choice. Campbell was left to wonder: "Why didn't they look after their own problems? Would they do the same fucking thing for me if I had a problem?"

After the eggs and the clubhouse fire, it was tough for Everett to defend Campbell to the Hamiltonians. Further ratcheting up tensions was the fact that someone had recently attempted to torch the Hamilton clubhouse. "We did explain that we had no idea that two weeks before it was set on fire by an enemy."

Not surprisingly, at the next club meeting Campbell's fate was once again the topic of discussion.

"It was me too," Vallentyne piped up in a show of solidarity. For all his considerable wildness, he was loyal and unquestionably brave. Both men were demoted to striker for three months, while Jungle was spared any discipline at all, since the fire was considered solely another Campbell–Vallentyne caper. Despite the demotion, others in the club were wise enough not to give Campbell and Vallentyne a rough time.

Campbell had temporarily moved to Alberta in 1981 to work in construction in Redwater, north of Edmonton. He made the trip with a fellow ironworker who wasn't in the club. It wasn't uncommon for Choice members to work out of town for a stretch then get back into the routine of attending meetings once they returned home. During a break from work, Campbell headed into Edmonton for a house party, where he met up with Larry Vallentyne's younger brother Lyle, who wasn't in the club, and Gord Van Haarlem of the Peterborough Choice, one of the Port Hope Eight. Both of them were working construction jobs in Alberta.

"Where are you from?" another construction worker at the party asked Campbell.

"Ontario."

"You know any bikers there?"

"Yeah, I know some."

"Do you know any Choice?"

"Yeah."

He didn't expand, providing no names.

"Do you know Jungle? Mike Everett?"

"Yeah, I know those guys."

"Oh, I had them all against the wall one time with a shotgun." The man was clearly pleased with himself as he continued: "They just showed they're a bunch of cowards."

"Well, my name is Lorne. I'm a Satan's Choice. I'm not a coward."

Brotherhood meant sticking up for your clubmates, no matter what. It also meant sticking up for their reputations when they weren't there to do it themselves. And so Campbell pummelled the man. "I just beat the fuck out of him."

Campbell had brought a three-litre Texas mickey of whisky to the party and it was now clear he wasn't going to be able to enjoy it. The badly beaten construction worker had left the party looking like a freshly tenderized slice of round steak, and it was a safe bet that if he came back, he would be accompanied by friends. A little later in the evening, Lyle Vallentyne announced the inevitable: "They're coming."

Moments later, the beaten-up man and his friends barged in. They weren't bikers, just angry construction workers who thought they were sticking up for a buddy. Van Haarlem dropped one of them with a baseball bat.

"Get the fuck out of here," he shouted.

"I can't," the man whimpered from the floor. "My legs are broken."

Another of the men was Bill Yardley from around Keswick, north of Toronto. He was gripping a heavy chain.

"What are you going to do with that chain, buddy?" Campbell asked.

"I'm going to rip your face off."

"You have to come towards me, buddy. You have to make the first move."

Campbell was thankful that he had been working heavy construction and felt in good shape. He was also grateful for the baseball bat in his hands. "He took a swing and I broke his arm, collapsed his lung."

Campbell and his friends could hear a police siren coming their way and took off out the door. Campbell went up the street and then walked back, as if he were arriving at the party house for the first time.

"Who are you?" a police officer asked.

"I'm here because I was invited to a party."

It wasn't a lie, exactly. The cop looked at the blood on Campbell's cowboy boots.

"What's with the fucking boots?"

"I'm an ironworker. I must have hurt myself."

"What happened?"

The officer wasn't referring to the state of Campbell's footwear.

"I don't know. Ask the neighbours."

Campbell was driven to the police station, where his cowboy boots were confiscated as evidence. A few hours later, an officer arrived at his cell.

"We're cutting you loose."

It was winter in Edmonton and Campbell didn't know where the station was, but at least he had his cowboy boots back. "I don't know where I'm going. You want to give me a ride?"

The officer didn't feel like playing taxi driver.

"I said we're cutting you loose."

With that, Campbell walked away into the Edmonton winter.

Later, his friend Ken Goobie of the Choice heard about the fight and said he wished he had been there too. Goobie was good at that sort of thing, when the bats and chains and fists were flying. Campbell liked Goobie, but he was glad he missed the party. Goobie was the type of guy who preferred heroin to alcohol, and his presence that evening would only have made things bloodier. Even for an outlaw biker, Goobie had a hard reputation, although he would later leave the Choice for the Salvation Army, where he became an officer.

Bernie Guindon would one day have something to say about that fight too. He told Campbell that he wished he hadn't taken the baseball bat to Billy Yardley, since Yardley had served prison time with him and Guindon considered him a friend. Campbell understood. The bigmouth who started the brawl had likely lied to Yardley and claimed he was jumped by a group of men. Yardley probably thought he was just defending his friend, as a friend should. "I told people that if we had met under different circumstances, it would have probably turned out different. This guy went and told them that a bunch of guys jumped him and beat him up. He was trying to help out his friends. That was my code too."

One of Yardley's brothers told Vallentyne that the matter wasn't settled yet, and that Campbell should expect some people to deal with him. "Larry warned them, if you're going to go after Lorne, he'll shoot every one of you."

With that, Yardley's friends backed off. Campbell was able to save his bullets for other enemies.

Back in Ontario, Campbell fell into the stripper business. Now there are elaborate criminal operations in which women are transported from Asia and eastern Europe to dance and work as prostitutes, but this wasn't one of them. Campbell's plan was to work with his friend Joe Napolitano, supplying local dancers to strip clubs. "We weren't that serious. We were just dabbling. We'd book the girls and take a cut—that's how simple it was." For some bikers, the stripper business was a chance to make real money, but for Campbell it wasn't about dollars or even sex. He had enough money, and things were going well with Charmaine, who was also a dancer now. "It's the lifestyle. Bikers are outside of normal civilization and so are strippers. That's the actual bond between strippers and bikers." Aside from the bookings, Campbell and Napolitano offered security. "It has to be that way. You have girls out there without protection, they're open season. They have us and nobody fucks with them."

There was also plenty of club business on his mind around this time. After the Outlaws split, the Choice had a lot of rebuilding to do. It would have been nice to pull in more members, but it was important that they be the right members. All members in a chapter had to agree before they would permit someone new into their ranks with full brother status. One biker Campbell couldn't see himself ever voting for was Patrick (Tulip) Roberts, who rode a Harley with a pink tulip painted on the gas tank. For Campbell, there was just something unsettling about riding in a pack alongside a bike with a pink tulip, even if it was a roaring Harley. Tulip had problems with others in the Choice too, for other reasons. One night in 1982 he was punched in the head and ordered to leave the Gasworks rock club on Yonge Street by a Choice member who worked there as a bouncer. When they eventually left the bar that evening, the Choice members found their motorcycles had been damaged.

Hours later, a member of the Para-Dice Riders saw flames coming from the front of the Choice clubhouse on Kintyre Avenue. Sleeping inside were Larry Vallentyne and a biker Campbell knew only as Jamie. The Para-Dice Rider was a strong man and managed to run in through the smoke and drag them both outside to safety. It was no mystery to Campbell who was behind the attack that almost killed his best friend and destroyed his clubhouse. He had never wanted Tulip as a clubmate, and now Campbell reasoned that the damage to the bikes and the fire were Tulip's conniving revenge for the beating in the bar.

Tulip stupidly returned to the clubhouse a couple of days later, on October 21, 1982 around five in the afternoon, as if nothing had happened.

"That fucking guy's nuts," Toronto chapter president Larry McIlroy said. And McIlroy had seen plenty of nutty things, since he had been a Choice member longer than anyone else still on the street.

"Nuts? Watch this," Campbell replied.

Not long after McIlroy left for the evening, Campbell began hitting Tulip hard and often. For reasons even Campbell didn't understand, he also poured whisky down his throat.

Then Campbell ordered him to confess to the fire.

Tulip denied he was guilty.

Campbell put Tulip's hands on the bar. Larry Vallentyne made sure that Tulip couldn't squirm away as Campbell smashed each hand hard with a hammer.

Tulip screamed and cried and continued to deny he set the fire.

The beating continued. "I wasn't angry at all. It's called retaliation." Finally, Campbell began to march him away. "I was taking him out. Yes, that does mean killing him. He was probably hoping I was dropping him off."

Tulip had considerable difficulty making his way out the door, since Campbell had pounded on his feet with the hammer after he'd finished with his hands. Tulip also had cigarette burns, cuts on his knees, loose teeth and welts on his chest. He still hadn't confessed.

Everett rode up on his Harley as Campbell led Tulip out. He jumped in and stopped the execution, saying there had been enough violence that night. Campbell acceded to him, but didn't apologize for the blood-letting or bone-breaking. "If you're playing the game or if you're trying to harm me or mine, suffer the consequences. He could have killed one of my friends, including my best friend."

Some members still dared to suggest that perhaps Tulip was innocent, since he hadn't confessed in order to stop the beating. Campbell argued back that Tulip didn't admit to setting the fire because he knew it would surely seal his death.

"I never seen him after that."

CHAPTER 14

Short Honeymoon

Charmaine and I were married on Valentine's Day, and within three months I was in Millhaven Penitentiary.

LORNE CAMPBELL

W hen they were married on Valentine's Day in 1983, Campbell wore a grey Edwardian tuxedo and Charmaine a white and pink suit. If she wanted Campbell dressed that day in something more formal than Choice colours, that was a small concession he was happy to make. There was no doubt that Charmaine was a quality person; she had planned to stay by him even if he was hit with big prison time after coming forward about the Port Hope killing. They had been together eight years and had experienced plenty of highs and lows already, more than enough to assess each other's characters. Among their guests that day were his old friend Smutley and Smutley's new friend Dave. Like many bikers, Dave liked weightlifting. Unlike many of them, Dave had a ring through his nose that he wore every day, not just when his friends were getting married.

About three months after the wedding, Smutley disappeared from circulation for several weeks. It's not unusual for bikers to go away for a while, especially for out-of-town work on construction jobs. It is unusual that they just vanish, without saying a word. When Smutley finally resurfaced, Campbell saw him at a booze can and he was accompanied by two heavy-set men Campbell had never seen before.

He asked Smutley where he had been and Smutley's story reeked of a lie. In Campbell's world, you simply don't lie to a brother. "I just laid him out right on the floor," Campbell recalls.

Campbell glared at Smutley's new friends. "You want a part of this?"

They didn't, and stayed out of reach.

There were troubles at the time about an assault beef faced by Peter Rabbit and several members of the Para-Dice Riders. The Choice and PDR were getting along well, and both clubs were uneasy about a drug dealer named Billy who was apparently helping the Crown build its case against them. Not surprisingly, Billy was keeping a particularly low profile.

Campbell wasn't really hunting for him one night when he and Dave dropped in late on a woman named Muggins, who used to go out with Billy. Muggins seemed unusually jumpy as soon as they came in the door.

"What's wrong, Muggins?"

"Billy's here," she whispered.

"Where is he?"

"Behind the door to the stairs."

Campbell walked over to the door and swung it open.

"Hi, Billy. Come here."

Dave sat in the middle of the kitchen floor as Campbell started beating on Billy. This was something he could easily handle by himself. "He [Billy] was just shaking," Campbell says. "There was blood all over the walls."

Campbell asked Dave to go over to a booze can run by Muggins's sister to fetch some beer. "We're going to be here a while. Leave me alone with this guy."

After Dave returned, Campbell decided to bring the beating to an end. It was time for something decisive.

"You're coming with me, Billy. Get in the car."

Campbell was taking Billy into the country north of Oshawa. "He was history." As they pulled out of the driveway, Dave was at the steering wheel and Campbell sat in the front passenger seat, with Billy squished between them.

"Look behind you, Lorne," Dave said before they could get out of the driveway. Campbell recalls, "There was red. Like a dozen cruisers."

A cop leaned into the car with a shotgun. He was shaking. "Get out of the car!"

"Tell that guy to relax," Campbell told another cop. "I've been through this before, he hasn't."

As Campbell was led away in cuffs, he looked at Dave and saw that he wasn't under arrest. In that instant, Campbell realized that Dave, Smutley's friend with the ring through his nose, was an undercover cop.

Events of the past few months fell into harsh focus for Campbell. Smutley had turned on him to shake off new drug charges. One of Smutley's family members was also getting heat for gun-running. That explained Smutley's introduction of Dave to Campbell. He found himself angry at Smutley, not Dave, who had always seemed like a good guy. "Smutley, he's a piece of shit in my eyes. He was my friend." Dave was a different matter. Campbell had no qualms about lynching a biker for not fetching him a drink, but his code of honour didn't allow for any ill feelings against a cop who did his job so well. If you have to be arrested, it's best to be arrested by a smart and cool-headed cop, and Dave was certainly that. "Dave always wanted to be a cop. He can look at himself still in the mirror."

There were fifteen charges filed against Campbell from four different cities. They included possession of an explosive with intent to endanger life, after Dave had found boxes of dynamite while helping Campbell move. The dynamite was to be used to blow up the car and house of a Kitchener man, police said, although Campbell maintained he had no clue about the identity of the target. There were also three charges of forcible confinement and one of trafficking cocaine, for selling Dave an ounce of cocaine worth $3,200 on January 27, 1983. Campbell acknowledges that he was guilty of every one of them.

In the basement of the Whitby courthouse, a detective named Tolly Wozniak approached Campbell on his way to court.

"Can I talk to you for a minute, Lorne?"

Campbell was handcuffed and police blocked the entrance and exit.

"Are you ready for this, Lorne?" Wozniak continued. "You've got another charge."

"Yeah. What?"

"Attempted murder."

Campbell's eyes went to a water fountain behind the detective. "Holy smokes, Tolly. You really know how to make a guy's mouth go dry." Campbell collected his thoughts. "With who?"

"Does Pat Roberts ring a bell?"

It didn't initially. Then he remembered that Pat Roberts was the real name of Tulip, the biker with the flower painted on his Harley whom he had beaten and almost executed after the fire at the Choice clubhouse. "I had beaten up so many guys I didn't have a clue."

Once all the charges were packaged together, Campbell was facing the threat of at least fifteen years in custody. "Get it down to one digit," Campbell instructed his lawyer, Bruce Affleck.

After meeting with the Crown, Affleck came back to tell Campbell he could cut a deal that would mean five and a half years' prison for himself and five years for Larry Vallentyne. The judge was a military veteran and seemed sympathetic to arguments about the harsh things that are sometimes done in the name of brotherhood. It was almost too good to be true.

The most important thing about the deal Affleck had brokered was that Campbell wouldn't be charged with anything else arising from Dave's undercover operation. That was a relief, since the charge that Campbell was really worried about stemmed from his attempt to buy five hundred machine guns for Joe Napolitano. Campbell was the middleman in a deal that called for muscle, and what he had to gain was money. "A hundred or two hundred thousand I would have made." That meeting, in the basement of an Oshawa home, had almost gone awfully wrong, when one of the sellers, clearly drunk, objected to Campbell's presence, pointing a gun at his head and asking Napolitano, "What the fuck's he doing with you?" The man eventually lowered the gun, but the deal hadn't yet been completed at the time of Campbell's arrest.

Still, Campbell couldn't shake the fear that the machine-gun rap might mean some kind of treason conviction, which would carry a life term. It was easy to see why acquiring that many machine guns could be spun into an attempt to attack the state itself, although Campbell says that was never his intention.

There was a catch to the plea bargain offer that Affleck delivered: the judge was leaving soon, and if Campbell and Vallentyne wanted the deal, they both had to agree within a day.

"No fucking way," Vallentyne said.

"The deal isn't good after tomorrow," Campbell said.

"No fucking way."

When Vallentyne got like this, there wasn't much to do except sweat. Arguing would only make him dig in his heels. Finally, at the last moment, the penny dropped and Vallentyne agreed.

There was another snag when they appeared in court. The Crown attorney stood well under five feet. Vallentyne giggled at the sight of his courtroom booster seat. Campbell wondered if this Crown harboured an unhealthy dose of pent-up hostility towards big, bad bikers. But Vallentyne wasn't theorizing about Napoleon complexes. He just couldn't stop giggling.

"Don't laugh at him," Campbell whispered in the prisoners' dock. "Don't laugh at him." Campbell felt himself ready to start laughing too. "Larry. Stop it. I will burst out laughing and I will do fifteen years."

They managed to control themselves and the deal was cut, Campbell pleading guilty to wounding, selling dynamite, tampering with witnesses, assault causing bodily harm and trafficking cocaine. Toronto chapter vice-president Mike Everett, the one who stopped Campbell from killing Tulip, got two years for cocaine trafficking. This struck Campbell as odd and a bit unfair, since things would have gone far worse if Everett hadn't been present. "That's the irony. Mike talked me out of it and Mike ended up getting time."

Not surprisingly, Everett once again wasn't happy with Campbell. This was obviously far worse than yolk in his hair. A couple of years before, Everett had told him: "There's only one reason why you're in the club right now."

"Yeah, and don't you ever fucking forget it," Campbell replied. There would be hell to pay if anyone tried to pull his patch, but the "one reason" went much deeper than just his friendship with Guindon. There were no limits to how far Campbell would go to defend those close to him. "Maybe I'm willing to do more for me and mine."

Despite Campbell's relief at the reduced sentence, Charmaine fumed at the betrayal by Smutley and Dave. They had attended her wedding. She had cooked for them. They were supposed to be friends. She was still livid when she bumped into Dave almost a decade later at a friend's place, when he was back in uniform.

"You were in my house," Charmaine raged. "You came to our wedding."

Dave was with a young partner then, a big, strong-looking cop who didn't say a word.

"You stayed at our house," Charmaine continued. "You were at our house."

Dave seemed to respect Charmaine's anger, and Campbell appreciated that. "He just stood there. He said, 'Yes, I know, Charmaine.' He was polite. He let her vent."

A surprise visitor showed up at the Whitby jail one afternoon, as Campbell waited for the aftermath of Dave's undercover operation to work its way through the courts. Campbell had faced down drug dealers and gunmen and an assortment of bone-breakers while developing a reputation for toughness in an unforgiving environment. However, no one he had met up to that time made him sweat more than the sixteen-year-old girl who appeared unannounced at the jail that day. He hadn't seen his daughter, Janice, for seven years and here she was, right out of the blue, looking nervous on the other side of a Plexiglas wall. "It was really scary. I hadn't seen her since I burned the house down. She just showed up with friends. . . . You don't know what to say. I was actually sitting there sweating. I wasn't confident in myself about that. I didn't know how to act as a father."

Janice had put considerable thought into what to wear to jail that day. Years later, she can't remember the exact outfit, but she does remember the impression she was trying to create. She also remembers feeling afraid, since she knew she wouldn't likely see her father again for a long time. "I would have dressed like a lady. My mom always said you have respect for a lady."

Campbell didn't want her visiting him in a federal penitentiary, where he was sure to be headed next. "I didn't want my daughter seeing me in there. Letters and cards were enough. We were separated by Plexiglas. It was unnerving for both of us."

The guards gave them a couple of hours when they could have limited the visit to twenty minutes. It was a kind gesture, although it probably didn't hurt that Campbell had a reputation with staff for freaking out. He felt grateful that Janice still loved him, and he was also grateful that she had turned out to be the kind of young lady who makes a father proud. "I just thanked God that she loves her dad still, although I haven't been around a lot in her life." They didn't talk about how he'd set the fire to the family home, but he knew this must be on her mind. "I know she remembered. 'Why would my dad do that?' I never explained it. . . . Not that I understood either."

CHAPTER 15

Big House Crew

Guys that don't have anybody are preyed upon a lot.

LORNE CAMPBELL on prison life

t's not unusual for prisoners to shake or even break down and blubber like babies by the time they're fingerprinted at Millhaven super-maximum-security penitentiary. By this time, a prisoner has likely ridden for hours on a bus, with his hands cuffed together and his legs shackled to the floor. He has already passed along treeless lawns, through two nine-metre chain-link fences, each topped and linked in razor and barbed wire, and a metre-high "warning fence" that marks the outer limit of how far prisoners can walk from the exercise yard before deadly force can be used to stop them. He has also passed under guard towers, and if he looked up, he may have seen guards staring down at him, gripping machine guns.

Once he has been escorted into the mesh-lined holding cell where he's fingerprinted, the prisoner has become an unwilling member of a community comprising 525 of Canada's meanest, most dysfunctional men. Odds are, even if he was once the toughest kid in the class, he's not even close to the most feared convict on his new range. Millhaven, also known as "Thrill Haven," was Canada's highest-security prison, and a third of the inmates were serving life terms when Campbell arrived.

Some locals and inmates believed it was built on a Native burial ground, making it forever cursed. The prison itself certainly had a nasty birth. It opened prematurely in 1971 to accommodate prisoners from nearby Kingston Penitentiary, which required an extensive cleanup after a bloody four-day riot that year.

When he was there in 1972, Bernie Guindon saw a prisoner lead another inmate across the weight room, stop, and pull out a hidden shank (an improvised knife). It was so smooth and seemingly effortless that it looked somehow choreographed, and it took just seconds for the shank to be thrust into the inmate's chest a dozen times. "I went, 'Wow, quick.' It's just like watching television." Guindon saw another inmate get shanked in the exercise yard after demanding pharmaceuticals from fellow prisoners. That attacker also led his prey to a spot where he had hidden a shank.

"Are you going to help?" an inmate asked.

"No, he can die," Guindon replied. "He was stealing pills."

Like all new arrivals, Campbell first went to the assessment centre in E-Unit. He was slated for psychological and IQ testing and an audience with Dr. George Ducolon Scott. A jaunty, charismatic, terrier-like little man, Scott had the all-knowing air of someone who had borne witness at least once to almost every form of human depravity. He once told the *Ottawa Citizen* that he was fascinated as a boy growing up in Kingston by what he imagined lay inside the stone walls of the Kingston Prison for Women, which loomed within eyeshot of his childhood home. Somehow, the sight of the prison stirred "a deeper part of my soul," and tantalized him with a sense of mystery—"like running into the sun; you can't quite see what's there."

The doctor was in his early seventies when Campbell walked into his office, and by that time Scott had peered inside the minds of tens of thousands of prisoners. He hadn't just asked them questions from across a desk, either. He had overseen LSD experimentation on prisoners funded by the Canadian Department of National Defence, as well as testing on the effects of shock therapy, sensory deprivation and pain tolerance. When the press caught wind of this in the 1990s, he dismissed suggestions that such experimentation reduced patients to the status of mere guinea pigs. "It's a lot of bullshit," Scott told the *Ottawa Citizen*. "It was good research back then. It was good research with good motivation, with good supervision, and the government supplied the bucks for the whole thing." Pressed another time by the newspaper, he was even more to the point: "I am happy with myself. I don't give a shit."

Unfortunately for the doctor, some people in power did give a shit. A dozen years after he met Campbell, Scott was stripped of his licence to practise medicine for testing of a profoundly lurid sort: using Sodium Pentothal and electroshock to drop female patients into an almost comatose state. Then he would implant sexual suggestions and revive them with Ritalin.

But when Campbell met Scott that day in his office, the doctor still displayed the easy confidence of a man who enjoyed a secure, fascinating job for life, since there was little chance of prisons shutting down due to an outbreak of lawfulness. Every day, he could take a close-up view of varying degrees of deviance, and then stroll out again to have a quiet supper with his family in the comfort of his century-old hobby farm. "He took things in stride, like he was a movie star," Campbell says.

Given his decades of experience, perhaps it wasn't surprising that Scott seemed a little blasé as he scanned Campbell's lengthy rap sheet of assaults and other bikerish misdeeds.

"What are you here for?" the doctor asked.

Campbell was sure he must already know, but he answered anyway.

"Do you have any remorse for beating a man with a hammer?"

"Actually, no. He deserved what he got."

Campbell's reply didn't seem to faze Scott even a bit. Finally, the doctor looked up and said, "You're all right."

"I'll never forget him saying, 'You're all right,' after I was telling him about beating a guy with a hammer and selling dynamite," Campbell says.

Dr. Scott dropped his head again, the cue for Campbell to leave. With that, Campbell was dispatched to A-Unit, where he would spend half of each day in a cell measuring 3 metres by 2.1 metres. The other half of his new life was to be spent outside his cell, alongside inmates who were often happy, or at least indifferent, at the thought of slitting his throat.

The only other biker in A-Unit was Ken Logan of the Lobos Motorcycle Club in Windsor. Logan ran a sports betting enterprise in which the payoff was money and cigarettes. The rest of the penitentiary's bikers, including Rick Sauvé and Gary (Nutty) Comeau, were in J-Unit, Millhaven's other general population wing. They were all classified as part of the "Big House Crew" by their clubs, the biker term for members behind prison bars. None of the bikers in the prison were from the hated Outlaws.

Less than twelve hours after he arrived on the range, Campbell stood in the gymnasium with John Dunbar, also of the Lobos. Dunbar was a smallish, trim man whose appearance belied the enormity of his crime. He and fellow Lobo Ken Logan had gone into a house to kill a former Lobos president over a drug beef, and ended up also murdering another man and a woman when they showed up unexpectedly. Campbell and Dunbar had never met before, but as outlaw bikers they naturally gravitated to each other.

It was a little after nine in the morning when Campbell and Dunbar watched as an inmate picked up a baseball bat and walked briskly towards them.

"Stand here, Lorne," Dunbar said, and Campbell obeyed.

Seconds later, the man with the bat clubbed Michel Lafleur, a member of the Front de Libération du Québec, to death. Lafleur was thirty-three and he had been behind bars for fourteen years, sentenced to a term of more than forty-one years for an assortment of crimes relating to the Quebec separatist group, including armed robbery and discharging a firearm with intent to kill. His role with the FLQ was to raise money through robbery, and he was already an inmate when fellow terrorists kidnapped Quebec labour minister Pierre Laporte and British diplomat James Cross, eventually murdering Laporte.

Lafleur's murder was never solved, as no one in the gymnasium spoke with investigators, but it's doubtful there were any great political undertones to his death that morning in the exercise yard. Killings at Millhaven often happened for reasons that would seem petty to outsiders but which had a peculiar logic to someone inside the prison. "I was amazed that it happened so fast," Campbell says. "I heard he was a good guy. I never talked to him. I saw him a few minutes and then he was dead."

"Within six months, you'll have a sixth sense," Dunbar told him, describing a heightened awareness akin to how birds know to hightail it before a storm. "You'll know when something's going to go down," Dunbar continued. "It's a feeling. So you just clear out."

As Campbell settled in, he thought about something Mike Everett had said when he'd dropped by to see Campbell, alluding to a potential threat. Everett had said something cryptic to the effect of: "If you're classified for Millhaven, you have a problem with somebody there." He declined to expand, leaving the impression it was an inter-club problem in which he couldn't take sides.

There was a barbecue at the prison during Campbell's first week there, one of four held each year. It gave him a chance to look into Everett's warning, and so he walked up to Sauvé. "I saw him and Nutty for the first time in five years. They had been in jail for five years." Campbell had always confronted beefs head-on and that's what he planned to do right now. "I asked Rick and Nutty in the first half-hour, 'Who in this prison has a beef with me?' They didn't know. If anybody had a beef with me in Millhaven, they would have known about it."

Sauvé and Nutty talked about it between themselves later in the day. The next day, Sauvé told Campbell that they still didn't know of any real beef against him. Perhaps Everett was mistakenly referring to an old and false story that had circulated during the trial. There had been an unfounded rumour, started by one of the Port Hope Eight's lawyers, that Campbell had balked at the prospect of pleading guilty to the Bill Matiyek shooting. It wasn't true, but it was as dangerous as a shank to the ribs. Perhaps that's why Everett was so cryptic: he felt he was caught in a beef between brothers. Whatever the case, things were fine now. "That was the rumour," Campbell says. "They had found out the truth long before I got there, but it was never discussed again. There wasn't a beef."

Over time, Campbell learned there were shanks hidden throughout Millhaven. They were made out of anything that could be sharpened enough to cut into a human body, with pieces of metal from the machine shop, toothbrushes and hobby craft tools all fashioned into instruments of death and protection. "The nicest and largest shank I ever seen belonged to my close friend John Dunbar," Campbell recalls. "He had it machined to be part of his window frame so it was not detected during the frequent cell searches." Dunbar called it Excalibur, and he sometimes smuggled it from his cell by dropping it into his pant leg. "It was a beautiful piece of craftsmanship," Campbell says. "After work hours the odd day, John would retrieve it from his cell and before the doors closed for the count he would come to my cell and start swinging it within inches of my face while I was lying on my bed. As calmly as I could, I would ask, 'Is this John or the other guy?' This was insinuating that he had a split personality."

Both men found this a fine example of jailhouse humour. Even for a tough and relatively grounded inmate, Millhaven was a hard place to endure day in and day out, twenty-four hours a day. Inmates sometimes took a break by going "fishing" for seagulls. They'd put little bits of food on safety pins so a gull might swoop down and grab it. The payoff came when the gull reached the end of the line and its guts were suddenly ripped out. "That's the most humane thing that happened in Millhaven," Campbell says. He once watched as two inmates were shot by guards as they tried to scale the inner fence. It was like live theatre, as the shotgun pellets hit them and they went tumbling downwards, seemingly in slow motion. "It was like spiders falling," Campbell recalls.

A voice came over the loudspeakers: "Clear the yard!" One of the inmates who'd been hit wasn't about to give himself up and face charges for attempting to escape, so he ran back inside with the crowd. "He threw his coat down," Campbell says. "Somebody else gave him another coat." Once back in his cell, another prisoner treated his buckshot wounds. It was simple enough for guards to figure out what had happened, but they didn't press the matter. "They asked if he wanted to be treated. He said no. He didn't admit to it and was never charged. That was Millhaven."

Campbell didn't play hockey as a kid, but he was recruited as an assistant coach of a Millhaven inmates team anyway. He was replacing Nutty Comeau, who seemed on the verge of getting maimed or murdered by the Green Team's other coach, Gary Barnes, who was also a player. "This guy would eat Nutty," Campbell says. "I was asked to be coach in case he tried something."

As expected, things got ugly in a hurry. Behind the Green Team's bench, Campbell turned to Barnes and said, "I'm not Nutty, so go for it." What might have happened next could have taken hockey violence to a new low. "I had a skate in my hands. I was going to cut his throat. He still had his skates on. He could just kick me. He just wouldn't go."

Finally, Barnes eased up, saying, "Fuck it, I'll go to the Red Team."

The Green Team was a formidable bunch in the corners, and none of its players was more feared than its clean-cut defenceman John Drummond. He only weighed about 170 pounds and looked like a schoolteacher, but folks who knew him considered him a truly dangerous man, even for Millhaven.

Some one hundred inmates routinely gathered around the boards to watch games, and during one shift when Drummond was on the ice, a voice from the spectator section screamed out, "Kill the sonofabitch!" It may surprise habitués of mainstream hockey games, but there were unwritten rules about what you just didn't do at a Millhaven shinny game, where a large percentage of the players were convicted killers. Hollering "Kill the sonofabitch" was one of those things. "You don't scream that to a rink full of lifers, of killers," Campbell says. "You don't yell 'Kill 'em' in Millhaven."

The words hit Drummond like a hard slash across his back. Everyone went silent as he immediately skated to the boards and surveyed the spectators with cold eyes.

"Who the fuck said that?"

The moment couldn't have been more serious. The prisoners watching the game couldn't have gone more silent. It was a long-time inmate who finally dared to reply. "It's a guy who don't know better. I'll talk with him later. It's a fish. A new guy."

Drummond was still fuming as he skated away.

When the game was over, Drummond's mood wasn't any better. "Me and so-and-so and so-and-so are coming out tomorrow and we're bringing steel. The first guy that says anything is getting it."

Assistant coach Campbell found himself in the unaccustomed role of peacekeeper. "It's an expression," Campbell said to Drummond. "There ain't nobody going to die."

People who weren't familiar with prison hockey might have been surprised by the scarcity of fighting in the games. Things in Millhaven were too hard-core for the kind of brawling typical of how the game is often played in the free world. If violence anywhere in the prison were allowed to gradually escalate, people were killed. "In Millhaven, you don't often see a fight," Campbell says. "If there's a beef, somebody's died."

There were no disputes among Green Team members or coaches that resulted in murders—which was a victory of sorts. On the ice, success was more modest. In the three-team league, the Greens settled for bronze.

Christmas in Millhaven saw three drag queens in Campbell's unit slash themselves. These weren't superficial slashes, intended only to gain attention. They were deep, dangerous, potentially fatal cuts, which meant the three queens were carried from the unit on stretchers.

Campbell and Sauvé found themselves speculating about how it had happened. Did the drag queens decide on a particular order of who would be slashed first, second and third? Did one do it and the others thought it was a good idea and joined in? Campbell couldn't help but smile as he ran over his alternate theories with Sauvé, surprised that he could be so glib about something so grim, involving people who had never done anything to hurt him. Was it possible that prison was making him an even harder man? "We're not that fucking cruel, me and Rick."

Campbell had been behind bars plenty of times, but this was super maximum security and he was still a newcomer; there were plenty of things to absorb. He learned that he needed to be constantly on guard, especially in the mornings. The craziest, angriest inmates often stew about grievances all night, and by daybreak they're in a murderous rage, ready to bolt out of their cells to avenge some perceived slight that others have often forgotten. "You're on point as soon as your cell doors open," Campbell says. "Almost all murders there happen when the doors open. Even if you had only two hours' sleep, you're on point when the door opens, if you had any sense about you."

Campbell learned it was a dangerous thing to say hello to someone for ten consecutive mornings and then forget to do so on the eleventh. This could well be taken as a slight that must be avenged with violence. He learned that a 120-pound man can kill you just as dead as a 300-pounder, with a shank to your heart. Sometimes that 120-pound man will be more prone to using that shank than a bigger man, since he can't handle himself with his fists.

Campbell learned to walk with his eyes straight ahead and look slightly downwards and never peer into an open cell. Peeking into a prisoner's cell and catching him choking the chicken potentially invites a death sentence. Campbell recalls how one inmate warned another to control his wandering eyes. "Don't look in my cell," he ordered. The lesson didn't sink in. The next time the offending inmate looked into the cell, he witnessed a shank being rammed into his own heart.

Campbell learned that you do your time without complaining. Whining about a five-year term to someone serving life with no eligibility for parole for twenty-five years comes across as taunting, and taunting invites a violent response. You also don't ask anyone why they're in prison. They can tell you if they want, but there's a good chance you don't want to hear anyway. "It's doing your own time," Campbell says. "It's just none of your business." Once, he did venture to ask an inmate if he had any regrets about stabbing his wife seventeen times.

"Would you change anything?" Campbell asked.

"No, she was a fucking stool pigeon. I would do it all over again. She deserved every stab."

With that, the conversation ended. Campbell didn't want to hear another word about it.

Rather than pepper a prisoner with questions or random observations, Campbell understood that it was generally best simply to shut up. Prisoners were often one sharp glance or one clumsy word away from exploding. Campbell often felt like blowing up too, especially when he got the sense that someone figured his prison time was somehow easy because he didn't whine. "They'd think this was rolling off my back," Campbell says. "That it was not affecting me. Listen, I was doing every fucking minute. Think this doesn't bother me? That I don't have a life? That you're the only one that doesn't deserve to be in here? Go fuck yourself."

In prison, crazy was normal. A convict from the United States one day volunteered to Campbell why he was behind bars. Until that time Campbell had known him primarily as a guy who was good at making wooden flowerpots, a pleasant-enough way to pass the hours. Deciding to unburden himself, the flowerpot man told Campbell how he came home one day and caught his wife with another man.

"Oh yeah?" Campbell replied, not really wanting to know the details.

"She came after me with a pistol."

"Oh yeah?"

"I tried to get it from her and then it went off and then the trigger guard got stuck on my hand." He gesticulated wildly, trying to demonstrate how easy it was for a hand to get stuck in a pistol and how the stream of bullets that filled the air and ended the life of his cheating wife was a horrible—but totally understandable—accident that could have happened to anyone.

At this point, Campbell couldn't control his laughter. At first, he had thought the flowerpot man just had a dry sense of humour. When he realized he was deadly serious, somehow it got even funnier.

"Tell me that, but don't tell a judge," Campbell advised, leaving without a flowerpot.

Campbell was on the incline bench in the gym not long after his arrival at Millhaven when he got chatting with a prisoner from the Kitchener area. The prisoner, whom Campbell calls Bow, began explaining how his partner in the drug world was ratting on him, so he tricked his partner into believing he had a deal for them. They drove out into a wooded area and he directed his partner to walk ahead of him as he took his hunting bow out of his car's trunk. Campbell recalls, "As he was telling me all of this, he was getting angrier by the minute, calling his partner a stool pigeon."

Bow was soon totally lost in the moment of the murder. "I shot him in the back with the arrow and the fucker didn't die, so I had to run over with my knife and stab him till he died. That motherfucker, that cock-sucking rat. He deserved to die."

Campbell feigned outrage too and looked for the next possible exit point from the conversation.

Then Bow abruptly halted his rant. "Do you know how they got me?"

"No."

"So he proceeded to tell me," Campbell says. "He cut off his part-ner's head and buried it. His reasoning was that the bugs would eat away the flesh and he would be able to take the skull home and use it for an ashtray. I'm thinking, 'Of course, why didn't I think of that?' He kept going back to check on the skull, and—wouldn't you know it?—the police had him under their radar and the bastards followed him one day. Ain't life a bitch?"

"I gotta go back to my cell," Campbell told Bow.

"I had to tell the guy to get the fuck away from me a few times after that before he got the hint," says Campbell.

Campbell learned that inmates are safer with the right friends. "Guys that don't have anybody are preyed upon a lot." That said, it's often better to stick to yourself rather than get involved with just anyone, since you'll inherit all of your new friend's enemies. Anyone suspected of being an informant or a sexual offender, or someone who'd been convicted of crimes against children, was a prime target for a shank in the exercise room. So was anyone who looked like a friend to a diddler or a rat. There is a theory that convicts are so tough on sex criminals because they feel powerless to protect their own families on the outside from people like that. Whatever the reasons, rats and diddlers were for-ever targeted. Campbell's advice to a newbie inmate was simple: "Just stay to yourself and do your own time. Don't get involved with groups. If you do, see what they're up to."

Some inmates, such as a bodybuilder named Nick Nero, grated on Campbell's nerves because they acted somehow surprised and offended to be behind bars. "He was a wimpy motherfucker," Campbell says. "I liked Robert Blake's line [from the 1970s TV show *Baretta*], 'If you can't do the time, don't do the crime.' . . . You're a fucking drug dealer. Suck it up. Shut up and do your fucking time."

Sometimes there's just something about a prisoner that creeps others out. It's hard to define why they give off this vibe, but the creepiness is palpable. Any association with someone like that can be dangerous. Nutty Comeau couldn't abide the sight of a glue sniffer who sat down next to Campbell at an inmates baseball game. Prisoners could easily get glue to sniff from woodwork or leather craft hobby work, and when they did, they became a menace, or at best annoying. "Lorne, don't be fucking talking to that guy," Nutty cautioned.

At first, Campbell had no problems chatting with the man. Then Campbell saw what Nutty meant, when the man began babbling in verbal circles one day, making no sense to anyone but himself. That's when Campbell decided that Nutty, for all his own issues, was right: "The guy's nuts. A glue sniffer. Anybody that's on downers, glue sniffers, too fucked up when they do something, we'd stay away from in jail. He was too screwed up to hang around with. If you're sniffing glue, it's gluing your brain cells or something."

Keeping the company of glue sniffers was hardly on the same level as being friendly with a diddler, but Campbell quickly learned that seemingly little things in Millhaven could bring major and irreversible penalties. Bad personal hygiene was often enough for an attack. So was a sloppy cell. Potentially capital crimes behind bars also included stiffing someone on a gambling debt, failing to deliver drugs as promised, and theft. For the weaker inmates, it could be dangerous to snub sexual advances. And sometimes prisoners saw their time behind bars as an opportunity to avenge grudges from the outside.

Campbell was repeatedly reminded that it was often best just to keep his thoughts to himself. Prison drag queens weren't preyed upon or goaded, as they fashioned halter tops from boxer shorts and makeup from ash and food colouring. There was just nothing to gain in hassling them and provoking confrontations. One drag queen who was given a particularly wide berth by the other inmates was a solidly built, six-foot-five former army sergeant. Underneath the makeup and woman's clothing, he still had a soldier's strength and skills. He also had a chilling reputation, having landed in prison for stabbing his mother to death. Her crime was to call him a faggot.

Charmaine dropped by for visits religiously, reminding Campbell of the life that awaited him once his time was served. "She visited every week, rain or shine," Campbell says. "Bad weather or good, she was there."

Campbell had been running his stripper agency with Joe Napolitano when he was sent to prison, and Charmaine continued working as a dancer. Campbell was alarmed one day to hear that she was working at a bar in Windsor run by the Outlaws. It was easy to imagine them doing something terrible to her, just to punish him. "I said, 'Just go to the owner and get your pay. Don't work there. I just don't like the idea of some fucking wacko finding out you're my wife and doing harm on you.' I worried. Worried."

CHAPTER 16

Fighting Bitterness

I just wanted to come out and put a bullet between the eyes of some people.

LORNE CAMPBELL in Millhaven Penitentiary

I t was behind the walls of Millhaven that Campbell experienced runner's high for the first time, during a ten-mile jog. He belonged to the inmates' Olympic Jogging Club, which awarded round patches to runners who put in a hundred miles. Campbell earned his 100-mile award—just like he had earned his biker patches—and went on to earn patches for putting in 200 and 300 miles on the track. That afternoon in 1983 when he managed ten miles, Campbell rode a wave of endorphins into the auditorium, where "Bad to the Bone" by George Thorogood and the Destroyers was blasting through the speakers. It was a straight-ahead, unapologetic joyful sound, and Campbell bathed in feelings of calm and achievement that lifted him temporarily above his surroundings. Boom Boom McLeod took up running as well, dropping from 320 pounds down to 190. "I can't get rid of my child-bearing hips," he joked.

A wall of the common area in Millhaven's M2 range was painted like a biker saloon. It was the sort of place that encouraged conversation, and Campbell was in a chatty mood there when he asked inmate Steven Haudenschild about the progress of some artwork he'd been promised.

Campbell already had a silhouette of Doc Holliday and the Earp brothers that Haudenschild had painted. He liked looking at images of the Wild West's gun-fighting legends, and Haudenschild was currently painting a canvas for him of a biker riding into the wind, wearing no helmet, like a modern-day cowboy.

"Have you got that painting?" Campbell asked.

"I fucking told you, Lorne, I'd do that."

His mood was more than a little testy, so Campbell didn't push things.

When Haudenschild finally delivered the artwork, Campbell saw it bore the inscription "to the SC brother of the wind" and was signed "Steve Road Rash," slang for the burns a biker gets when he wipes out on gravel. There were also the letters "GRMC" in the corner. He knew Haudenschild was an outlaw biker from the west, and he also knew the Grim Reapers were a big deal out in Haudenschild's home province of Alberta.

"Are you a Grim Reaper?" Campbell asked.

It seemed an innocent-enough question, but Haudenschild looked like his mother had just been spat upon. "He lost it on me. He was really insulted."

"Sorry," was the best Campbell could say at the time. He didn't realize that Haudenschild was a Ghost Rider, a lesser-known western club that also used the initials GRMC. He also had no idea that the Ghost Riders hated the Grim Reapers as much as Campbell despised the Outlaws.

Later, Campbell would piece together part of Haudenschild's story. Like Campbell, he went to extremes in defence of his notion of brotherhood. Haudenschild landed in prison after confessing to murdering three Americans and dumping their bodies into a Lethbridge rendering plant, where the carcasses of dead animals are broken down into products such as lard. Haudenschild told police he killed them over an unpaid debt. In his version of events, he had lent the three Americans fifteen thousand dollars to come to Canada "because the heat was on them" and he later murdered them because they didn't repay him. That was all a lie.

Haudenschild's secret was that he wasn't a multiple murderer at all. He had falsely confessed to killing American Ghost Riders Kenneth Martin Solomon and Jeffrey Heath as well as Heath's wife, Kathy, as an act of good citizenship, as he saw things. In fact, they weren't dead, and his lie to police gave them a chance to start their lives anew in Canada, with blank slates and new identities, while shaking off a slew of American charges. The scheme was ruined when the Americans were discovered alive and well in Alberta a month after his bogus confession.

That didn't mean Haudenschild wasn't a cold-blooded killer. He was in prison for a verified murder, and had shown no agitation in court when he was called to account for the killing of Charles Drager, a former Lethbridge Ghost Rider president. He never told the court what Drager had done to anger him so profoundly that he killed him and dumped his remains into the rendering plant. Haudenschild simply said he felt "no regret or remorse for these acts—the only thing I regret is the adverse publicity this has brought on the Ghost Riders."

For the most part, long-standing biker club divisions didn't matter in a super-maximum-security penitentiary such as Millhaven. "That's all forgotten in there," Campbell says of club lines. The generally accepted view was that all bikers must look strong and united for their mutual benefit and security, because most often it was a small core of bikers against the rest of the inmates. Guindon, Dunbar and Logan had set the tone that way. Because of them, it was a received truth that you shouldn't fuck with an outlaw biker behind bars. "They paved the way for the rest of us. They wouldn't back down. There were anti-bikers there. They'll stab you in an instant, just because they don't like bikers. Maybe something had happened to them on the street."

That said, membership in a biker club wasn't a passport to easy living. "Just being in a club, that don't do anything. There's a beef, you've got to handle it. Some people that think that just because you're in a club, that'll handle it—it's the opposite. You earn it. It doesn't matter who you are. You must earn respect."

The idea that club tensions should be put on hold inside Millhaven didn't extend to everyone, as far as Campbell was concerned. Campbell heard that Dave Séguin, the Outlaw he'd once pummelled in the Montreal Choice clubhouse, was being hunted by police for slaughtering three men and wounding three more at the Chosen Few clubhouse on September 17, 1983, in the small community of Emeryville, east of Windsor. According to police, Séguin entered the clubhouse carrying a nine-millimetre semi-automatic handgun and emptied its bullets into the victims. Then he pulled out a knife and repeatedly stabbed them. One of those murder victims was Chosen Few club president Edward (Snake) Morris.

It only seemed a matter of time before Séguin and other Outlaws were arrested for the Emeryville slaughter and delivered to Millhaven. Campbell was primed to jump Séguin at the first opportunity, or any other Outlaw who got there before him. "The first Outlaw that comes in that strip, I'm waiting for him," Campbell announced.

Jeff McLeod urged him to hold back so that there wouldn't be retaliation by the Outlaws or their friends against Rick Sauvé and Gary Comeau. They were serving life terms, meaning they would be vulnerable for a long, long time. "You've got to think of Rick and Gary," McLeod told Campbell. "They're doing 'the book': life-twenty-five," meaning a life prison term with no possibility of parole for twenty-five years.

"I am thinking of them," Campbell replied. The idea was to send a loud message to the Outlaws to back off. "I figured I'd teach them a lesson right off the bat," Campbell says.

The debate turned out to be academic. In July 1985, Séguin was shot dead by police in Steger, Illinois, outside Chicago, the Outlaws' home-town. At the time, Séguin was on Canada's most-wanted list, living in Illinois under the bogus name George J. Johnson. Police surrounded his house after a neighbour said he had been abducted and bound by Séguin and then released ten hours later. The dead man's fingerprints were taken in the Cook County morgue, where they matched up with those of the fugitive Séguin. When police searched his home, they found nine-millimetre pistols like the one used in the Chosen Few massacre, as well as marijuana, cocaine, a machine gun, three other handguns, exploding ammunition, gunpowder, and a book on how to make bombs.

There were a few good memories from Millhaven for Campbell, such as the pleasant buzz he felt at Christmastime from some moonshine that had been stashed somewhere in the ceiling above the showers. There were numerous forms of prison moonshine, all vile and all effective. Prisoners gathered potato peelings, fruit peelings, prunes, peaches, vegetable scraps, sugar, yeast, cherries, ketchup, orange juice and even Cheerios to produce potent "shine" that was concocted in elaborate stills or simple garbage bags. The final brew could be ready in twenty-four hours, or it might take several days to produce a mix so potent it could burn.

Moonshine was highly valued in prison, and it was common for inmates to pay twenty or thirty cartons of cigarettes for two jars of 95-proof shine. It took skill, plenty of copper tubing and stealth to make a batch, and an inch of it in a jar could give even a veteran drinker a considerable buzz. "You can't sit and drink that stuff all night."

The shine Campbell consumed that Christmas was made by a prisoner in the cell next to Campbell's from hundreds of packets of ketchup, among other things. It wasn't smooth crossing the throat, but that Christmas it hit the spot nonetheless. To further enhance the festive mood, Campbell stole the crepe paper folding bell that was about the only decoration in the unit and hung it in his cell, where he was already displaying some one hundred cards from friends and family. The glow of his moonshine coursed through him as he called out, "How's life?" to the lifers walking past and wondered how much crazier his own life could get. "I was happy to be in my cell. I said to myself, 'I can't believe I'm happy to be here.'"

Most of the time in Millhaven, mob people didn't mingle with the other inmates. "The mob guys had young guys around them who were loyal to them. They stayed pretty much to themselves." Despite the general separation between groups, Campbell found himself on pleasant terms with Cosimo Elia Commisso from north of Toronto, who was in prison for an assortment of organized crime charges, including three for conspiracy to commit murder. Commisso could be gregarious and friendly, and Campbell became a personal trainer of sorts for him, introducing him to jogging and helping him shed roughly a hundred pounds.

A sore point with the mobsters was that Cecil Kirby, a former Satan's Choice member from Richmond Hill, had worked as a police agent to put Commisso and his brothers Rocco Remo and Michele behind bars. Kirby had been hired on to do dirty jobs for the mob, then turned police agent and disappeared into a witness protection programme. Campbell hadn't known Kirby well and didn't particularly like the little he saw of him. After his police agent work became known, Kirby was so reviled within the Choice that Larry Vallentyne ordered a rock musician whose stage name was Kirby Luke to go by a different name when he was around them.

One day in Millhaven, Campbell and the mobsters watched a television programme on Kirby, and Campbell felt Commisso's younger brother, Rocco Remo, glaring lasers at him.

"I said, 'Don't be fucking staring at me,'" Campbell recalls. "'Don't tell me you guys don't have problems with your members too.'"

Campbell felt it was the mobsters' fault if they placed too much trust in Kirby, whom he considered more hype than anything else. "Why would you trust a guy who wasn't true-tested? Kirby wasn't a hit man. He was just a guy who went around scaring people, knocking their mailboxes over."

Also sharing space with Campbell was Antonio (Tony) Musitano of Hamilton, who was serving a life sentence in connection with a series of bakery bombings which, in the late 1970s, had earned Hamilton the nickname "Bomb City." One afternoon during visiting hours, Charmaine arrived to see Campbell at the same time as Musitano was joined by his older brother Domenic, another mobster. Tony Musitano struck Campbell as a charming man, and he gave Charmaine a jovial hello before hunkering down to talk business with his brother.

Years later, Campbell read that the Musitanos' table at Millhaven was electronically bugged. The taped discussions from that day in the visitors' area suggest that Campbell's prison acquaintance Billy Rankin was about to begin enforcement work for their crime family. Rankin wasn't a biker, but rather a mob rounder, given to hanging around underworld characters. Campbell knew him as a serious guy inside prison, whose face was invariably knotted in a tight expression, as if he were permanently sucking on a lemon.

On Saturdays, the bikers would sit in the back row of the auditorium as movies were shown. "We always sat at the back. If somebody's going to be shanked, that's a good place to do it because it's dark. We'd be right against the wall, us bikers." Rankin would sit in the row in front of them, and Campbell would call him Bacon Hips because he pumped his legs and butt up doing heavy squats. "We'd say, 'Can't see, Bacon Hips. You're blocking the view.' He'd get pissed. There were no smiles."

Rankin was released from prison on December 7, 1983. It wasn't a shock to see that he quickly took up with Hamilton mobsters. It was surprising that Rankin abused drugs and bragged to strippers about his new job, which caused him to fall from grace with the mob. It was always a crapshoot to predict how an inmate would act once he was freed. "There are guys you see on the street who seem solid. When they get in the pen, they're fucking cowards. Tough guys on the street and then they just wimp out inside. That's when you see their true colours. There are guys who are comfortable and solid in the pen and outside they're totally different. They just short-circuit when they get out on the street. Drugs will do that to people. They turn into something they're not. Anybody's capable of anything, I think."

Campbell had things of his own to worry about. He and everyone else on his range were sent into solitary confinement for four and a half months. There had been a murder on the range and no one co-operated with investigators. For Campbell and the others, that meant time alone in a 1.83-by-3-metre cell, with only ten minutes a day to shower. He didn't have a television, but he did have a radio with five channels and reading privileges. There wasn't much to do besides ponder his situation and worry about the hurt he was causing others, especially his family. It was a scary trip, going inside his head to confront his bitterness, but it was worth the journey. "You get self-pity for a while."

He thought back to his time with the Durham psychologist who had helped him with relaxation therapy, and he concluded it was time to stop blaming others, even if he hadn't been dealt a great hand in life. Campbell started to appreciate that it takes more courage to love than to hate. "You get better. I got thinking about that saying, 'It's not the rest of the world, it's me.' I thought about that. I had been bitter. I just wanted to come out and put a bullet between the eyes of some people. I fought it, the bitterness."

CHAPTER 17

Disneyland

The only way to change your diet in prison was through health reasons or religion. I didn't have any health problems, so I became a Buddhist.

LORNE CAMPBELL

I f you drive by Collins Bay medium-security prison on Bath Road in Kingston and don't look too carefully, its bright red turreted roof makes it look like some enchanted castle from Disneyland. If you slow down and take another second or two, you'll also see the lookout towers and barbed wire and realize this elegant limestone structure wasn't built for fun. Those who see its hard, cold walls from the inside on a daily basis call it Gladiator School.

After fourteen months in ultra-maximum-security Millhaven, Campbell was bumped down to Gladiator School, and just two weeks after his arrival he was elected inmate representation for 3 Block. That's quite impressive for a newcomer. More impressive yet was his 88 percent approval rating from voters, most of whom Campbell hadn't met yet. It didn't hurt his campaign that Larry Vallentyne and two bikers known as Mule and Flex went cell to cell, saying words to the effect, "You're voting for Lorne, aren't you?"

Serving on inmate committees had become a tradition of sorts for bikers at Collins Bay. Bernie Guindon was a previous head of the inmate committee, enjoying the wide range of information the position offered about goings-on throughout the prison. For Campbell, it meant that at ten every Thursday morning he would sit down with prison officials, including warden Ken Payne, and prisoner representatives from each cellblock. It was a chance for both sides to air complaints. Sometimes the hostilities were between inmates, with staff relegated to the role of interested bystanders or referees.

One particularly contentious topic involved conjugal and family visits, during which prisoners could spend time with loved ones in a nicely equipped trailer, with a living room and a little yard for a barbecue. Prisoners who weren't expecting visits would often apply for them anyway, and then deal their credits for visits to other prisoners for the going price of ten rolling papers smeared with hash oil. It appeared everyone was happy with the arrangement, since prisoners with families got more visits while prisoners without families got the hash oil papers, and prisoners including Campbell and Larry Vallentyne made some spending money selling them. Guards who imported the hash oil also benefited from the trailer trade business, rounding out the circle of satisfaction.

So it seemed to be a perfectly symbiotic relationship, until an inmate representative known as O.J. spoke out loudly against it at one meeting. O.J.'s moral objection was hard to define, but he felt it strongly enough to risk the wrath of the pro-trade inmates and staff. Up to this point, Campbell had had plenty of respect for O.J., who was an outspoken advocate for black prisoners' rights. Until O.J. fought the good fight, black inmates had been unofficially barred from working in the Collins Bay kitchen, since it was understood that the white inmates would go on strike if blacks ever dared to handle their food. Kitchen work was a good clean job and the extra food it provided for workers was a perk. There was a sign outside the kitchen that was originally meant to refer to the cooks' uniforms, and which had read, "Whites only are to be worn." The sign had been altered to read, "Whites only." Through nerve and negotiation, O.J. managed to change all that, and got black inmates into the kitchen. "The guy's a drug addict on the street, but nobody else would fight for that. O.J. was the biggest fighter of blacks' rights in Ontario prisons back then, in my eyes. I respected him for it."

That morning at the meeting, however, Campbell's respect for O.J. was quickly forgotten when he spoke out against the conjugal visit trade. "It was cold," Campbell recalls. "The atmosphere was heavy. I'm looking right at O.J. You could cut the tension in the air with a knife at that point." In prison, that wasn't entirely a metaphor.

"Anybody that would begrudge another inmate extra visits with his family is less than a man in my eyes," Campbell said to O.J.

"Warden Payne and the head of security looked at each other and the warden ended the meeting." It could have got far uglier, but in the end O.J.'s attempts to stir things up over the visits went nowhere. "Everything stayed the same. His comment didn't ruin anything."

At another inmates' committee meeting, the warden noted a deadly cyanide threat inside the prison. Danny Spielchek, a First Nations hockey player who was captain of Campbell's Millhaven hockey team, had just died after overdosing on poison. It had been murder, not suicide. The warden told the committee that Spielchek's coffee had been spiked with cyanide, and that the threat wasn't over. More cyanide was believed to be in the hands of at least one unidentified prisoner.

"Just so you know, we believe it might have been brought over here recently by an inmate," the warden said. "A pinhead of cyanide. We can't help you. So watch what you're drinking. Be careful who you accept a cup of coffee from."

Prisoner Tommy (Retard) Horner wasn't a smart man, but he did know who had the cyanide. Retard had briefly been with the Choice, until Campbell kicked him out for being too much of an idiot. "He had the audacity to tell me, when we were in Millhaven, that he wanted to come back to the club. I reminded him who kicked him out. Duh." Making things worse, Retard had developed a serious Valium addiction since his ouster from the Choice. He had gulped down fistfuls of the drug at one point, rather than have them confiscated by guards. The results were repulsive. "He's shitting them out and eating them again because he's a Valium freak."

One day when Campbell was walking in the yard with an inmate named Phil, he heard a voice bellowing from the prisoners' sick bay.

"Lorne!"

Campbell looked around and couldn't see anyone.

"Lorne!"

"Keep walking," Phil said.

Campbell kept walking.

"Lorne! You know that fucking guard we're getting the Valiums from? He's putting it on us!"

"Keep walking," Phil said.

"Lorne! You know that cocksucker guard? He put it on us!"

The shouting was a reminder of how Retard got his nickname and why Campbell was right to boot him from the Choice in the first place.

After Spielchek's murder, Retard told the prisoners with the cyanide that he would hide it in his cell since no one suspected him. The poison was eventually discovered by guards and Retard was put in the hole until he fessed up about who had given it to him. "Eventually he put it on the other guys. He ratted on them."

Ratting on fellow inmates is a crime far worse than Valium addiction or idiocy. It's the worst possible breach of prison's unwritten rules, and it didn't matter if the cyanide had been used to kill a popular fellow inmate. Campbell lost sight of Retard after that, but it was clear he would now be forever shunned or worse by other inmates. "A rat is a rat is a rat."

Campbell's old friend Larry Vallentyne had been sent directly to Collins Bay upon conviction. By the time Campbell arrived, Vallentyne had already found himself a cherished spot as head of the inmates' grievance committee. But anyone who showed up expecting a warm shoulder to cry upon was in for a rude awakening. Prisoners who complained that they needed extra bed sheets or delivered up other snivelling grievances that bored Vallentyne were sent packing with words like, "Get the fuck out of here, you fucker!" One of Vallentyne's pearls of advice when approached by morose inmates who wanted to whine about their confinement was, "If you want to be a cowboy, you've got to learn to ride the range." He meant "prison range," of course. The message was simple: "You got caught, so shut up and serve your time."

Campbell asked Vallentyne for some advice when he was going to be sent for a few days to the medical unit inside the nearby Kingston Penitentiary to get his hemorrhoids treated. Kingston Penitentiary was the permanent home of the lowest of the low of prison society, the protective custody prisoners such as child molesters and convicted police officers. Some of them worked in the kitchen, and Campbell shuddered to think of such people handling his food. He wanted to get back to Collins Bay as quickly as possible.

"Larry said, 'When the food's delivered, fire it back at them.' I said, 'Okay, I'll do that.' . . . There's stool pigeons, child molesters. You don't take the chance to eat the food they're handling. I was on heavy medication. I thought the bed was going to rise up like a Frankenstein movie. It was like a dungeon."

Vallentyne's strategy might have worked, but Campbell was too high on medication to put it into practice. When a nurse arrived to talk about a meal, Campbell warned her, "If you give me that food, I'll fire it right back at you." The nurse just walked away. Campbell didn't get a meal or the chance to throw food, and wasn't transferred back to Collins Bay until the next day, which was when he was due back anyway.

While Vallentyne offered tips on food tossing, Rick Sauvé was definitely the man to consult about food eating. From the time of his transfer, Campbell was determined to focus on his mental and physical health. He had read some disturbing things that made him question the healthiness of his diet. "When I got to Collins Bay, I didn't want to eat any red meat or dairy products. I just wanted fresh vegetables and fruit. The only way you can change your diet is religion or health, and there was nothing wrong with me."

Sauvé impressed Campbell as extremely healthy, considering the circumstances. You might expect someone serving life with no chance of parole for twenty-five years for a murder he didn't commit to be a bitter man. Sauvé instead seemed to have risen above anger and self-pity to some higher plain of existence. Further, Campbell was struck by how Sauvé held no grudge against him, even though Campbell did the killing for which Sauvé had been imprisoned. Sauvé didn't seem to allow bitterness to pollute his soul. He also didn't want much in the way of material possessions. His cell was stripped down, with no television, radio, books or exercise equipment—nothing that was considered a prison luxury. He didn't even sleep on a bed, preferring to roll out his mattress on the hard floor at night and then roll it back up again in the morning. Sauvé practised Buddhism and transcendental meditation, and studied for his BA in psychology through correspondence, paying for the courses with money he earned behind bars. When that was done, he completed a masters in criminology, again paying for it with his prison earnings. He had broken up with his first wife, not out of anger but so that she could get on with her life.

Campbell wasn't the only one impressed with Sauvé. A guard once told Campbell: "Sauvé's a guy that can do time in a box."

Campbell didn't feel any special urge to join Sauvé in transcendental meditation, but he was impressed by Sauvé's steady supply of fresh fruits and vegetables.

"How do you have that diet?" Campbell asked.

"I get this because I'm a Buddhist now."

Campbell and Sauvé wrote to Toronto Buddhist temples until they found one whose leaders agreed to take Campbell on as a long-distance member of their congregation. Then Campbell and Sauvé started to talk about traditional Buddhist feasts they could order from behind bars.

"Rick told me once a year Zen Buddhists are allowed Himalayan yak. So I said, 'Let's go for it.' We were gonna, then we thought, 'No, we've fucked them enough.'"

Sauvé didn't just have what appeared to be the key to inner peace; he also had access to a secret stash of moonshine. The guards had the key to the enclosed plumbing unit, but Sauvé was able to open its panel with a piece of sheet metal, like a safecracker. The hooch was tucked away in the pipes, and odds were if you weren't looking you wouldn't find it. That was a particularly good spot, because it minimized the chances of guards smelling the foul concoction or seeing the fruit flies that tend to hover over jailhouse shine.

His occasional forays into moonshine aside, Sauvé was serious about yoga and meditation, and once said he was able to transport himself to another state of being. Campbell laughed that any journey Sauvé took was because of prison moonshine, not spiritual awareness. "He said, 'I can do transcendental mediation. I was outside my cell.' I said, 'No you didn't. I saw you puking on the floor.'"

With Sauvé's help, Campbell took up a self-help regimen that placed heavy emphasis on relaxation, with yoga and deep breathing exercises. There was also reading, including the self-help bestseller by Thomas A. Harris, *I'm OK—You're OK*.

Someone who definitely wasn't okay in anyone's books was Pigpen, the biker from Peterborough who had hid out for a time in the United States with the Outlaws under the alias "Garbage." Eventually, he was returned to serve out a sentence for violence in a Canadian cell. Pigpen carried about 245 pounds on his six-foot frame, and while his wasn't pretty, Muscle Beach muscle, he still possessed crazy, ill-defined "bug strength," hard to measure or oppose.

One day, Campbell was lying in his cell relaxing when he sensed someone close by. He looked up and there was Pigpen, blocking his doorway, his arms tightly crossed, staring at him.

"Scared you," Pigpen said.

Campbell denied he had been frightened, but the big crazy man with the tightly crossed arms could see that Campbell was rattled and seemed particularly pleased with himself.

Another time, Pigpen announced to Campbell that he had just seen the moon in the afternoon. "That's the first time that has ever happened," declared Pigpen.

"Howard, I've seen that dozens of times," Campbell replied.

Pigpen fumed at anyone daring to question his credentials in astronomy. "That's the first fucking time that's ever happened!"

Campbell didn't have a retort, and there was no point in getting Pigpen's dander up. Pigpen was unsettling enough when he was relaxed.

"You know what that means?" Pigpen continued.

Campbell had no quick reply. Pigpen leaned close to him, so close Campbell could feel the warmth of his breath. Campbell still said nothing. Then Pigpen leaned closer still.

"You know," Pigpen declared.

With that, he snapped his head back, gave Campbell a knowing look, turned quickly on his heels and walked out of the cell with a triumphant strut.

One day, Campbell and inmate Mike (Mule) Poisson had a disagreement about exactly what was going on between Pigpen's ears. Mule asserted that Pigpen was just playing crazy, albeit very well. Campbell argued that Pigpen was truly out of his mind.

"It's a big put-on," Mule said.

"What do you mean?" Campbell asked.

"He's not really insane."

"Yes he is."

At this point, Pigpen appeared and walked up to them.

"We were just talking about you," Campbell offered. "I say you're truly insane. Mike here is saying you're just putting it on."

"He just looked at us, turned around and walked out," recalls Campbell.

"That answers your question for you, Mike," he said.

One day, Campbell and another inmate were talking about Pigpen when a guard overheard them. "You have no idea how nuts he is," the guard said.

One of the prisoners Pigpen associated with was an Outlaw named Andy. Campbell advised Pigpen that it didn't look right for a member of the Choice to be talking with an Outlaw, even if Andy was a good-enough guy and married to one of Bernie Guindon's cousins. Campbell had already told Andy, "When you go by me, don't look at me." It wasn't personal; it was just the way things were. Members of the Choice weren't to mingle with the Outlaws in Ontario, just as members of the Hatfield and McCoy clans didn't share jugs of moonshine in Tug Fork, West Virginia. "He freaked out and then went out to Andy's cell," Campbell says. "Andy's sitting there doing his leather hobby craft. He punched the fuck out of Andy. He [Andy] had no idea why."

"I wasn't telling you to do that to Andy," Campbell told Pigpen.

"I believe he's insane," Campbell says. "He'd be a bad enemy."

Pigpen had his own notions about hygiene and personal health. He stayed away from showers, preferring to sponge-bathe his bulk in the privacy of his own cell. That way, other prisoners couldn't sneak up behind him and attack. Pigpen's strategy was tested after he ran afoul of Collins Bay's Caribbean population.

There were about fifteen Caribbean inmates in Collins Bay who were poorly educated and highly superstitious. For reasons known only to himself, Pigpen delighted in enthusiastically barging into their cells, spouting Bible passages. Whatever one might say about Pigpen, he did appear to know his Scripture. When he was done his oration, as a final crescendo, Pigpen would take his "whammy dust," made from crushed-up mirrors, and throw it into the air like a magician casting a spell.

"Serious? Who knows if he's serious?"

One day, after his Scripture rant and whammy-dust toss, one of the Caribbean prisoners was convinced that Pigpen had cast a curse upon him. He snuck up on Pigpen when Pigpen was having a sponge bath in his cell and shanked him. The shank didn't have the desired effect, and now Pigpen was even more dangerous, charging his attacker like a stuck wild boar.

Campbell caught sight of Pigpen hotly pursuing his would-be killer, with no clothes on and a shank in his hand. "What the fuck's he doing now?"

Guards let the black inmate run into a cell for safety, then moved him down into the hole and protective custody.

For all his unsettling and repugnant qualities, Pigpen was a biker brother, and so the hostilities with the Caribbean inmates became Campbell's concern as well. At this time, Campbell had a job on the range changing light bulbs. A perk of the job was that it meant he could wear a belt with a row of screwdrivers on it. In the absence of guns in holsters, screwdrivers on a tool belt were the next best thing.

Campbell's job allowed him to approach the Caribbean prisoner hiding out in the hole.

"Howard has no hard feelings," Campbell said.

Campbell's hands were on his tool belt, close to the screwdrivers, like a cowboy ready to draw a gun.

"Do you have a problem?" Campbell asked.

There was no reply. The prisoner still balked at coming out.

The next day in the yard, Campbell and Larry Vallentyne were just wearing T-shirts and shorts as the weather was too hot for anything heavier. Campbell noticed the curious clothing of more than a dozen Caribbean inmates in an area called Mosquito Alley, where there were a couple of benches. They wore winter coats and heavy boots, as if they were about to head out in a blizzard. They also had newspapers on their laps. "They're all carrying shanks," Campbell concluded as he and Vallentyne walked over to the Caribbeans' benches.

"Who's in charge here?" Campbell asked.

No one answered.

"Is this Stab-a-Biker Day?" Campbell continued. "So come to my cell—3A-10—and stab me."

By now, Campbell and Vallentyne were backed by Flex, Nutty Comeau, Rick Sauvé, Jeff McLeod and Paul Rogers, a karate black belt who joined the Choice in 1984, just before he was sentenced for armed robbery. They carried baseball bats from the recreation shack. The guards just stepped back and let events unfold. "They knew what was happening, but they didn't do anything. It was quite obvious. It was the day after Pigpen got stabbed."

None of the newspaper-toting men in winter wear appeared eager to take up the invitation. One of them denied that the prisoner who'd shanked Pigpen during his sponge bath was part of their group.

"Lorne, that guy's not with us."

Campbell wasn't satisfied. He let the others know that they had better keep that prisoner away from the bikers. The Caribbean inmates would still be responsible for his conduct. "Four months from now or six months from now, he's going to be with you."

The Caribbean prisoners stayed silent. Their eyes said that they didn't want things to go further. A baseball bat can do a lot of damage quickly, and the Choice controlled the recreation area, including the rack of baseball bats. "It just ended right there."

CHAPTER 18

Shaping Up

A lot of people are in there [prison] for a reason.

LORNE CAMPBELL

E ven in prisons, staff had to have some level of trust in the inmates. Prisoners were allowed to cut each other's hair with scissors and shave each other with old-fashioned straight razors, while prisoners who did leather craft were given sharp knives and glue that could get them high. Most of the time, prisoners lived up to the trust, but not always.

Campbell once saw an inmate with a nasty gash that ran across his throat from ear to ear. Campbell inquired of a friend how that had happened. He was told that the man with the gash had been sitting in a barber's chair, enjoying a soothing shave and chatting about a fellow inmate. The mellow man in the chair had said something to the effect of: "That guy's a stool pigeon." The last words he heard, before he was rushed to the infirmary across the hall, came from the barber behind him.

"That's my partner," the barber said, putting the blade in motion.

Much of Campbell's time in Collins Bay was spent in the weight room, where one of the stronger men was Jamie Scott Munro. He gave Campbell one of his first haircuts in Collins Bay. "He said, 'How do you want your hair done, Lorne?' I said, 'Make me look as much like Charles Bronson as you can. There are many big muscular guys in here.' It was jailhouse humour. From then on, Jamie cut my hair all the time I was in Collins Bay."

Munro's pleasant demeanour was at odds with his horrific backstory. He was just twenty-two in 1981 when he was sentenced to life in prison without eligibility for parole for twelve years. The judge who put him away, Mr. Justice Frank Callaghan, called Munro's crime "one of the most callous killings of a police officer this municipality has seen for many years." Munro and his older brother Craig were convicted of the murder of Toronto police constable Michael Sweet during a botched robbery at George's Bourbon Street tavern on Queen Street West on March 14, 1980. It was a breathtakingly stupid, cold crime. Jamie and Craig were robbing the tavern. They were trying to raise a thousand dollars to pay a fine against Craig for possession of a dangerous weapon. Sweet was thirty years old and the father of three daughters when he was patrolling in Toronto's downtown that night. Just after two in the morning, a restaurant employee flagged down Sweet and his partner, telling them there was an armed robbery under way and there had been hostages taken.

Sweet and his partner tried to sneak into the restaurant through the basement, but they were detected. Sweet was shot in the chest while his partner was able to escape and alert reinforcements. Sweet's injuries were serious, but there was still time to save him when the Emergency Task Force arrived quickly on the scene, led by Sergeant Edward (Eddie) Adamson. His paramilitary officers were ready to rush into the restaurant, but they were ordered to stand down as negotiations began. For the next ninety minutes, Adamson and his fellow officers heard Sweet plead to be set free so that his three little girls wouldn't grow up without a father. Eventually, as negotiations dragged on, Sweet's voice went quiet.

Eddie Adamson was the second casualty of that evening, but the bullet that killed him wouldn't be fired for another quarter century. Adamson couldn't stop thinking about Sweet and the Munro brothers and the sound of Sweet's voice as he died that morning. He couldn't outrun his sense of guilt for not risking his career and rushing into the restaurant sooner, despite the order to stand down from his senior officer. On October 5,

2005, eleven years after his retirement, Eddie Adamson gathered up some notebooks and press clippings about Sweet. He also took his handgun with him to a motel room in Simcoe County, where he ended his life.

Campbell didn't know any of this when Munro was cutting his hair that day in Collins Bay. He also didn't know that, on the day he was sentenced for killing Sweet, Jamie Munro softly told the court: "When people used to ask me, 'How do you feel about this incident?' I used to lower my eyes and drop my head in shame, because I felt there were no words that could express how very sorry I felt for the officer and his family, and mine. . . . I wish there was some way I could undo this whole thing, but unfortunately I can't."

Had he tried to explain, Munro might have mentioned his upbringing, and how eight of the Munro children had criminal records, as did their father. But Munro didn't talk about the murder while behind bars. He was considered a pleasant guy in the weight room and a friendly barber, who kept his thoughts to himself. "He was a good guy. I liked him. He worked out a lot."

Campbell was reunited in Collins Bay with his old mentor Bernie Guindon. Guindon hadn't mellowed much while serving his drug conviction. Between his boxing and his brawling, his nose had been broken eighteen times, to the point that it was difficult to breathe. He hoped that would be corrected through an operation that left his beak taped up and filled with gauze. He was in this painful state of recovery one day when a tall girl in her early teens came walking by as part of a group of Special Olympians who were at an event hosted by the inmate committee. It was considered a personal growth thing, with prisoners helping coordinate their events and awarding them medals.

The girl apparently had Tourette's syndrome, and made sudden jerky movements with her arms. When she was close to Guindon, one of her arms flew out wildly and smashed him directly on the nose. That gave the Frog his nineteenth broken nose.

"You do that again and I'll kill you," hissed Guindon, his eyes watering from the blow.

The Special Olympian marched away. "She knew what she was doing," Guindon recalls, without a trace of a smile.

One of the senior guards at Collins Bay had once been a striker for the Satan's Choice. He seemed to have a soft spot for the club, even if he was no longer part of it. Certainly, no guards under him objected, or even seemed to notice, when Guindon hosted a party of some eighteen inmates in his cell. Long gone were the days when Guindon threatened to take a baseball bat to anyone in his fold who dabbled with drugs. Now, Guindon was the master of "Frog Logs," his extra-strong hash oil cigarettes. His special recipe called for twenty-nine rolling papers, each saturated with oil that was heated up in a "hot plate" made of burning toilet paper stuffed around the rim of his metal toilet. They were powerful and they were consistent, just like a good biker in Guindon's road days. "One Frog Log will last you thirty-five minutes," Guindon boasts.

The guards knew about the Frog Logs, but didn't seem to care. They were far more concerned about prisoners cooking eggs in their cells than puffing mega-joints. Eggs in the prisoners' possession must have been stolen from the cafeteria. Cannabis, meanwhile, only made prisoners passive and less prone to violence. It was different for pills and moonshine, as they tended to make prisoners aggressive. "Valiums and booze are no-nos," says Guindon.

It was inside Collins Bay that Campbell smoked his first and only joint behind bars. It happened while listening to the music of blues man Stevie Ray Vaughan. Campbell played some guitar himself and that only helped him appreciate Vaughan's mastery of the instrument. He was so overwhelmed that he threw his earphones across the room, for a reason he still cannot explain. "I was so high. I thought he was playing three guitars at once."

When Campbell arrived in Collins Bay, some guards there still chuckled about a story from Guindon's boxing days back in the 1970s, when two guards from the prison took him to Windsor for a bout. After Guindon won his fight, they all retired to a party at the Choice clubhouse. "I wanted to get a broad down there," Guindon recalls. "I said to them, 'I'll get you one too.'" The guards thought this was a fine idea. "We partied at the clubhouse on a pass," Guindon says. When it was done, the guards were so partied out and exhausted that it was Guindon who drove them all back to Kingston.

Guindon took it upon himself to train Campbell. He told Campbell that hard abs were the key to protecting his kidneys from body blows. To toughen his core, Guindon coached Campbell to do plenty of hard calisthenics, including the tough core work the Cubans had so impressed him with back at the 1971 Pan Am Games. Then there was twenty minutes of skipping and a 6½-mile run. Guindon sometimes tried to spice things up during workouts. Once, he kicked Campbell hard when he was doing push-ups, just because he felt the urge. "Everybody backed away. They thought it was a fight. I couldn't stop laughing." Another time, Guindon smacked Campbell across the stomach with a board while he was doing leg raises. "I had him in the best shape of his life," Guindon says.

Campbell paid the experience forward, pushing a fellow Collins Bay resident, career thug and former pro boxer Joe Dinardo (a.k.a. Gabor Magaostovics and Joe Simon), to get back in shape. Dinardo was in his early forties and had packed on about twenty pounds since the 1960s, when he boxed under the nickname "Ironman" and enjoyed moderate success as a heavyweight out of Toronto's Lansdowne Athletic Club. He was described in the press during his ring days as "211 pounds, 6-foot-4 inches, wedge-shaped from shoulders to waist." His trainer, Vince Bagnato, was quoted as saying, "We're teaching him to keep his hands in his pockets when he doesn't have them in someone's kisser."

Dinardo was in prison this time for the robbery of a jewellery store in Toronto's swanky Yorkville neighbourhood, but his criminal record also included stretches for arson, forgery, assault, theft and weapons offences. His body bore the scars of an arson gone wrong, when he had to drive himself to hospital for treatment of burns. In the murder trial of Peter Demeter, a Mississauga millionaire developer, Dinardo told the court that in July 1973, Demeter's wife, Christina, a former model, offered him ten thousand dollars to kill her husband. A week after she allegedly made the offer, she was found in the garage of their home, bludgeoned to death with a crowbar.

It was part of prison lore how, back in the 1970s, Dinardo and Ken Goobie of the Choice had a bare-knuckle brawl worthy of John L. Sullivan.

Perhaps they were angry at each other, or perhaps they were just curious to know who was the better fighter, or perhaps it was a little of both. Whatever the case, it was a great fight. "The older white guys are probably still talking about it. The black guys didn't care. They fought to a draw. The guards just let them go. Apparently it was something. No rounds, no rules, no timekeeper, no winner. But I did hear it lasted half an hour or so. The thing that stands out in everybody's mind is that they fought to a draw. I believe they were friends after that."

Campbell got Dinardo running, along with bikers Paul Rogers and Tom Raimier. "I got him out there. [I told him,] 'You're out of shape.' The guys who run in jail run every day. It's an everyday thing."

Campbell pushed himself into shape to run a twenty-kilometre race on the track, and Larry Vallentyne was a trainer of sorts. Vallentyne had the duty of handing him water when necessary. Most of the time, Vallentyne lay on his back, swigging moonshine, enjoying the spectacle as Campbell pounded around the track. "At the halfway point, he goes, 'Well, you're downhill now.' I felt like kicking him in the head." Instead, Campbell shot his friend a dirty look. "He didn't catch the stare." Campbell finished the race in third.

There was also a chance to work off some aggression playing floor hockey. Fewer inmates at Collins Bay were killers than at Millhaven, so players could fight without worrying so much that it would necessarily lead to murder. "In floor hockey, that's where you'd see the fights, really nice fights. Just fights all over the place. Kicking each other in the head. The guards just let it go. I didn't play, but I was a good spectator. In the pen, guys take it very seriously." After one hard-fought 1-0 victory over 1 Block, Larry Vallentyne of 3 Block seized banners that read "1 block's #1" and set them ablaze. The guards let this go too.

There were two gyms on the same floor at Collins Bay. Campbell was skipping in one of them one afternoon when three inmates walked in. Campbell didn't pay them much attention as he was focusing on his workout regimen, which at that time consisted of the military 5BX Plan plus running and skipping. The three men were clearly serious, but Campbell wasn't about to be intimidated. He was doing his workout and just wanted to be left alone.

He started skipping towards a barbell bar that might make a handy club if things got ugly.

Larry Vallentyne came in another entrance, away from the three men and close to Campbell. "Lorne, you've got to leave," he said. "Lorne, you've got to leave," Vallentyne repeated.

Campbell kept skipping closer to the barbell.

"Lorne, there's a dead guy in the next room," Vallentyne said.

Suddenly it made sense, and Campbell almost ran back to his cell. The three strangers didn't want to do anything to him. They had just beaten someone to death with dumbbells in the adjoining gym and now they wanted a quiet place to talk.

Not long after that, the prison detective squad came by Campbell's cell to ask if he knew anything about the killing.

"Well, I know somebody was killed."

"Were you here when it happened?"

"I was in the other gym."

"Do you know anything about this?"

"Well, I know he was only nineteen and never should have been sent here in the first place."

Campbell later heard that the kid was killed because he told someone in a county jail to go fuck himself. That inmate made up a story about the kid and told it to other inmates. Thinking they were carrying out prison justice, the three men beat the kid to death. Campbell wasn't about to rat out the killers, but he couldn't help but feel bad for the kid who'd died.

Campbell was an organizer for the prison powerlifting competition. It was a serious event and spotters signed up in advance to help out, moving the barbells as needed and, if necessary, lifting them off the lifters.

There was one extremely powerful inmate who hadn't signed up as a competitor or as a spotter. He was in and out of shock therapy, and a hard man to understand or predict.

"I want to be a spotter," he told Campbell on the day of the event.

"We've already got our spotters."

"I want to be a spotter."

Campbell knew he had to be careful with his tone and words, but he wasn't about to be bullied either.

"Listen, if you had talked to us even as late as yesterday, you could be a spotter. But we've already got our spotters now."

"I don't care. I want to be a spotter."

There was no point extending the argument, and Campbell started to walk away. A couple of steps down the hall, he reminded himself that the matter hadn't really been settled. There are some wrongly accused people in prison, but there are plenty of others who truly must be separated from society. This man was clearly one of the latter. "A lot of people are in there for a reason," Campbell says.

Campbell wheeled around and glared at him, eye to eye.

"Don't even think about it. I will slit your throat."

CHAPTER 19

Freedom

You're suspected for twelve homicides.

CORRECTIONAL OFFICER to Lorne Campbell

C ampbell had a parole hearing scheduled for June 1985, but his classification officer told him not to get his hopes up. "I don't think you're getting it," he said. "I didn't recommend you. There are reasons why. Your record, and you're suspected for the homicides."

Campbell was shocked, and pressed to find out what he meant by "the homicides." He learned that his police file stated he was a suspect in twelve unsolved murders. "It wasn't fair. I was a violent guy, but I didn't commit twelve killings."

Years later, he would try to get his prison files through the Freedom of Information Act, only to be told that too much time had passed and they were unavailable. He was able to get a parole officer to give him a glimpse of his security record, but it showed no names of men he'd supposedly killed besides Matiyek. "It had no names on there. I was looking for them. It was upsetting when I read that. I said, 'I don't deserve that.'"

There was a certain whiff of irony here that Campbell didn't find amusing. Try as he might, he couldn't get sent to prison for shooting Matiyek to death. Now that he was inside prison anyway, it looked as if he couldn't get out because of other killings for which he had never even been charged and which he swore he hadn't committed.

At his parole hearing, Campbell was asked to talk about the night he took a hammer to Tulip at the Satan's Choice clubhouse on Kintyre Avenue. He wasn't about to fake contrition for what he thought was a righteous beating and what would have been a righteous execution, in his opinion. "I said I have lots of remorse in me but I can't have remorse for somebody burning the clubhouse down."

Members of the parole board weren't smiling as they looked down at files before them. "They told me that I was an enforcer for the Satan's Choice. I said, 'I know what you have in front of you because I have already been told, and it just isn't true.'"

Then they asked about Port Hope and the night Bill Matiyek's life ended.

"I'm not here for anything like that," Campbell replied.

At this point, Campbell got up from his chair and started out the door. Even in prison, some things were just a waste of time. To Campbell's surprise, they called him back before he made it out of the room. To his further surprise, he got his parole.

Charmaine picked him up from Collins Bay in her Chrysler K-car and drove him to a Peterborough halfway house.

"We didn't expect you for a couple hours," the house's director said. "Go to a restaurant."

They found a nice place by the highway, where Campbell put down most of the two bottles of wine they ordered. After prison hooch, whatever they ordered tasted full-bodied and satisfying. Finally, back at the halfway house, Campbell took a tipsy nosedive over a hedge before reporting in.

Campbell was ready to head off to another halfway house, in Gravenhurst, north of Toronto, which would put him close to Charmaine and the old stomping grounds of Larry Vallentyne. Just as he got his mind around the pleasant possibilities of the move to cottage country, that idea was nixed. The story, as he understood it, was that he wasn't wanted anywhere near the Gravenhurst cottage of Ontario premier Frank Miller. Campbell was told he would be moved to Peterborough instead. It was irritating, but at least he was out from behind bars.

Up in Peterborough, Campbell told his parole officer that he was eager to get down to the Ironworkers Local 721 hall on Queen Street West in Toronto so he could line up some work.

His parole officer balked. "Lorne, if you could read your record, you wouldn't let you out either. You're suspected for twelve homicides."

"I'm going down to the hall anyways."

At the Local 721 hiring hall, he was given a job even farther from Peterborough—1,900 kilometres to the east—on a two-month contract with his old chapter president Peter (Rabbit) Pillman of the Choice, who ran a construction company repairing smokestacks in Conception Bay, Newfoundland.

Once Campbell got to Newfoundland, he gave his parole officer a call. "I'm in Newfoundland and I start work tomorrow."

"You can't do that. They might pull your parole."

"If they do, they do."

His parole officer alluded to how outlaw bikers had been getting particularly bad publicity in eastern Canada ever since the decomposed bodies of five North charter Montreal Hells Angels were pulled from the St. Lawrence River, wrapped in sleeping bags along with weightlifting plates. They had been invited to a meeting at the Angels' Lennoxville clubhouse on March 24, 1985, where they were beaten to death with hammers. Their crime was being considered too wild and uncontrollable, even by Hells Angels standards. Their corpses were proof that if you're surrounded by tough people with loaded guns, you're either very safe or very threatened.

Campbell was heading out to the job one day when he passed some idle ironworkers.

"We're not going to work today."

"Why?" he asked.

No answer was given.

Campbell later got an ironworker drunk in a pub, and learned that the problem behind the work stoppage was tensions between the ironworkers' and boilermakers' unions. "One of the guys [a boilermaker] said, 'If you go on that stack, I'll shoot you off the stack' to another worker [an ironworker]. I got him to point the guy out to me."

Three hard punches to the head later, the offending boilermaker lay unconscious. A much larger man, accompanied by three semi-huge slices of humanity, stepped in front of Campbell.

"Who punched him out?" the huge man asked.

"I did."

He immediately stuck out his hand to Campbell. "Good for you. It's time somebody punched that guy out."

That settled, he bought Campbell a beer.

Once back in Ontario and free of the halfway house, with his sentence expired, Campbell fell fast and hard into the life of a cocaine dealer. There was plenty of money to be made selling coke, and members of all the clubs seemed to be cashing in. Since he had been sent away to prison, the Choice had set up an Oshawa chapter again and bought a clubhouse of its own: a squat red-and-white bungalow at 487 Ortono Avenue, near Wilson Road South and Highway 401. It had "S.C.M.C." boldly spelled out in black shingles on its red roof, lest anyone accuse them of hiding out. Campbell was its new president.

As Campbell moved back into the Choice fold, he was taken aback by how many of his old cronies and acquaintances seemed reluctant to approach him. Ultimately, he concluded that he shouldn't take offence, as this was a product of his fearsome reputation, not rejection. "I had punched out a lot of members."

At the same time, others who didn't know him at all pretended they were lifelong friends. When Campbell walked into a bar in Scarborough with Larry Vallentyne, he was stunned by how familiar some of the patrons acted towards him. "I was not used to guys sitting down and babbling on like they knew me for a hundred years."

Campbell met with suppliers to pick up kilos of cocaine at a time. They'd meet in parking lots for quick transactions, when he'd ride in on his Harley, not wearing club colours so that he wouldn't attract attention.

"He'd throw it to me. I'd put it in my pack. I'd say, 'See you later.' It would take ten seconds."

Once, he had seven ounces of cocaine in his vest when he was pulled over in Orillia at a speed trap. Three or four cruisers were there, and he had to reach around the Baggies of cocaine to extract his ID papers for a female cop. "I said, 'I haven't been pulled over for a speeding ticket for ten years.'" He rode away with the ticket and the cocaine.

The money was nice, but he couldn't help but worry, when he stopped to think about it, that drug money was changing life in biker clubs. Increasing numbers of members were missing club activities such as meetings and runs because they were in jail or too screwed up on drugs to take part. Maybe Guindon had been right back in the sixties when he threatened to take a baseball bat to anyone in the Choice who used drugs. Says Campbell, "When people are on drugs, there's no participation."

Campbell hadn't been on a Harley for three years, and now he made up for lost time by riding with a vengeance. Harley-Davidson had come out with its Evolution motor on its touring bikes, which used rubber to absorb road vibrations and smooth out the ride. "It was a pleasure after riding bikes that break down, rattle and leak oil for so many years." He and his associates bought seven new Harleys, worth between $15,000 and $20,000 each, within a two-week span from the same Toronto-area dealership, paying with cash. He expected the dealer to at least smile when they peeled back the bills to pay for the seventh bike, but he didn't. "I said, 'Have a sense of humour, buddy.' The implication was that we were drug dealers. He seemed to get it, as he smiled back a little bit."

Joking aside, he had a queasy feeling about the effects of all those drugs on people around him. "I've seen guys and women do things they would never do for cocaine. A lot of them don't come out of it. Some do. I like to see a happy ending." Although he was now a full bore drug trafficker, Campbell still prided himself on pulling a few girls off drugs. One was at a party and ready to stick a needle in her arm. "She was going to do a hit and she could not find the vein. I threw her down on the floor, grabbed the fix and hid it."

———

Throughout the 1980s, the Choice got along well with the Lobos from Windsor and the Vagabonds from Toronto. During Campbell's prison stay, the Vagabonds had sent him Christmas cards, which counted for something in his books. For all their outward gruffness, outlaw bikers are nothing if not sentimental. Anniversaries of special days in club history—such as the formation of chapters—are dutifully marked with parties that all members are required to attend. Alliances between friendly clubs were also something close to sacred. That was part of what rankled Campbell about the 1977 split, when half of the Choice patched over to the Outlaws. The Choice and the Outlaws had an alliance before that split, and they went so far as to create a special brotherhood patch, with a crossed piston and sceptre. So when some members of the Choice connived with the Outlaws behind the backs of members like Campbell, it was worse than disrespectful. It was treasonous.

The Vagabonds only had one Canadian chapter, but they were also in a brotherhood with the Scorpions Motorcycle Club in the States, which made them more than just another local Toronto club. In effect, if you were a Vagabond, you were a Scorpion, and vice versa. As a novel twist, the "Vags" wore patches with *100%* on their vests, rather than the *1%er* patches other outlaw clubs wore. It was a declaration that they considered themselves 100 percent biker.

Campbell was riding to Windsor for a party with about a hundred other bikers in the mid-1980s, where they planned to meet up with the Vagabonds and Lobos, among others. Bikers in packs ride at clips of a hundred kilometres an hour, with just a bike length between them. Many of the bikes didn't have front brakes and there was no room for mechanical errors, stupidity or bad luck, or there'd be broken bones and grated skin—or worse. "One cop was trying to pull us all over. He was in a cruiser, going up and down, trying to pull us over. It's very dangerous doing that. Experienced cops know how to do it. They go up to the front of the pack and signal for everyone to turn off somewhere, like a truckers' weigh station. This guy obviously wasn't that experienced and it was really dangerous what he was doing. Once we were pulled over, this guy's fucking trying to get IDs. He's screaming and yelling. He shouts at [Choice member] Dougie Hoyle, 'Who the fuck's in charge here?' Dougie said, 'You,' and tapped the cop's hand.

"One cop went into a truck and pulled out a shotgun. Tee Hee Hoffman was back with us then. He was let out of prison after four and a half years because a police wiretap showed he was in Kitchener the night of the Port Hope shooting. Tee shouted at the cop, 'Put that fucking shotgun back in the truck or I'll shove it up your ass.' All of us were shocked. Tee Hee never shouted at anyone before that.

"All of a sudden, here come the Vagabonds. The cop who tried to pull us over at first ran in front of them. Snorko [Vagabond president Ralph "Snorko" Melanson] just kept ploughing through and hit the cop. They [police] jumped him and started giving it to him. They beat the shit out of him. Put him in the cruiser and arrested him.

"Then finally a sergeant showed up and ordered the cop who had been in charge, 'Get these fucking guys off the road.'"

That was one of the last times Campbell saw Snorko, who could be a one-man spectacle even on a quiet day. Snorko got his nickname for his nose, and his propensity for hoovering up long lines of cocaine through it. He was also good at buying large amounts of cocaine on credit. He wasn't so good at selling it off so that he could repay his debt. That perhaps explained why someone shot Snorko to death in September 1987 in a Toronto hotel room. By the time of Snorko's murder, Campbell had noticed a sea change in biker attitudes towards drugs, as businesspeople started to squeeze out party people. "It turned good guys into greedy people. I've seen friendships fall on the wayside."

Through all his hard riding and partying, Campbell continued to be followed by the unresolved matter of Port Hope. He couldn't get it off his mind that Gary Comeau and Rick Sauvé were both still serving life terms for a crime he had committed. Campbell needed the legal establishment to believe that he was the real shooter. In 1988, he talked about his crime to a University of Ottawa law school class that studied miscarriages of justice and wrongful convictions. It was their first and last lecture by a chapter president of the Satan's Choice.

After the class, Campbell rode his Harley down to Port Hope with a female law student on the back. It was his first trip to the Queen's since the shooting, and he was still on parole. "Nobody recognized me. I introduced myself under a different name. A guy walked over and asked me if I wanted to play pool. Two or three guys who were there in '78 [the night of the shooting] were there. I recognized them. They didn't recognize me. . . . I played as bad as usual. A pool player I'm not."

By the time he turned forty, in 1988, the clean eating and spirituality that had been inspired by Sauvé were but a memory, as was the fitness derived from workouts with Guindon and long jogs around the prison yard. In their place were junk food, cocaine and whisky. There hadn't been parties for his tenth or twentieth or thirtieth birthdays, but his fortieth was different. His September 2 birthday coincided with the Labour Day weekend that year, and the two events collided to make a monster event at a big dance hall in cottage country north of Huntsville. "I had just done a big line of cocaine. We had a good band. Somebody said, 'Go sing, Lorne.' My fingers weren't working when I was playing one of their guitars. It was probably 'House of the Rising Sun.'" His playing and singing that night weren't his best, and when he left the stage a friend advised: "Lorne, don't quit your day job."

In 1989, he was riding his Harley down the QEW to St. Catharines to see and hold Jemelie, his first grandchild, who had been born on August 6, when he felt something wrong in his chest. It didn't ease up when he tried the deep breathing exercises he'd learned in prison. Campbell eased his bike through the heavy traffic, which couldn't have been going more than fifteen miles an hour, towards the right lane. It wasn't a sharp pain, but it was a serious, crushing one, and it wouldn't go away. "It's like a thousand pounds on your chest. I was just in so much pain, I have my eyes wide open and I still couldn't see anything."

He rode on to St. Catharines, where he described the experience to his daughter. "You just had a heart attack," Janice said. She was right, although a stress test showed there was no heart damage.

Campbell resolved to cut out the drugs and stay away from junk food. The temptations of freedom were threatening to cut short his life. "I was partying, let myself go. It didn't take long."

———

By the end of the 1980s, newspapers were often branding outlaw motor-cycle clubs as organized crime syndicates, second in power only to the Italian Mafia. The dire warnings in the press about the threat posed by outlaw bikers were never shriller than when police were trying to pump up their funding at budget time. Such reports often grossly overesti-mated the level of planning in outlaw biker camps. While biker crimi-nality was a constant, the amount of thought involved was often darkly comical. One needed look no further than Campbell's Oshawa chapter of the Choice for proof.

At the end of summer 1989, Campbell's friend Stan was looking for a place to hide an M1 carbine near the clubhouse when he had a brain-wave that struck him as both simple and effective. He tucked the assault rifle into the branches of a tree in the clubhouse backyard. All was well for the last few weeks of the summer, but then the leaves started falling. Meanwhile, the stashed rifle had faded to the back of Stan's mind. In October, police raided the Choice clubhouse and Stan found himself charged with possession of an illegal firearm—the M1 carbine.

"How the fuck did he find that?" Stan asked, genuinely baffled.

"He just looked up," Campbell told him.

Lorne Campbell at age 4.

Lorne Campbell Sr.

Grandparents, Matthew and Mary Campbell.

Young Lorne with his surviving sisters, Loretta and Lyne.

18 years old with daughter, Janice.

Christmas with Elinor and Janice.

Morning wake-up call, Satan's Choice style.

Outside the Oshawa clubhouse on SCMC's tenth anniversary.

Campbell and SCMC founder, Bernie Guindon.

Captured colours. The club dominated central Canada in the sixties and seventies.

Larry Vallentyne, 1980.

Campbell's partner in debt collection, John Foote.

Campbell was a feared man in the seventies, but even he had a soft spot—Janice, growing up.

One of several Oshawa SCMC clubhouses.

Hot dog race at SCMC field day.

1980. Carrying the weight of the world.

Vallentyne, at the clubhouse.

With club mates at Collins Bay Penitentiary: (back) Larry Vallentyne, left, Jeff McLeod, second from left, and Gary Comeau, right; (front) Campbell and Rick Sauvé (centre).

Campbell and Charmaine during a visit at Collins Bay Penitentiary.

Painting by Ghost Rider Steven Haudenschild.

Friends in tough places: (l. to r.) Ken Goobie, Rick Sauvé and Brian Beaucage at Collins Bay.

Patching over the Loners to SCMC: "You're not president any more. I am."

Balloon race at a field day.

Leg wrestling with Hamilton Choice member and professional wrestler Johnny K-9.

Jeff Peck of Los Bravos and Doug Hoyle of Satan's Choice belly up to the bar during one of Campbell's trips to Winnipeg.

Meeting Ruben (Hurricane) Carter, whose Association in Defence of the Wrongly Convicted supported the cause of the Port Hope Eight.

William (Mr. Bill) Lavoie gets his 25-year plaque from Satan's Choice.

Above: In the last days of Satan's Choice, Campbell (second from l.) prepares to ride out with Bernie Guindon (second from r.) and friends.

Left: Rocker Steve Earle with Evelyn and Campbell. His song "Justice in Ontario" has shared the story of the Port Hope Eight far and wide.

Newly married, Campbell joins the Hells Angels and is soon president of the Sudbury chapter.

Andre Watteel, president of the Kitchener Choice, joins the Angels with Campbell and 166 other Ontario bikers.

Becoming a Hells Angel opens the world to Campbell. Partying with the Dutch Angels.

Visiting the Paris clubhouse (third from l.), along with old friend from the Choice Tony Biancofiore (second from r.).

Mamas, don't let your babies grow up to be bikers. Campbell and his mother.

Olympian and Hells Angel Phil Boudreault with "Dad"—one of the few who ever called Campbell by that nickname.

Campbell and Biancofiore (left, top and bottom) meet Sonny Barger, the world's most famous biker.

On a Hells Angels World Run in France.

CHAPTER 20

Bo

I couldn't keep a guy and break his fingers all night. Things were done more diplomatically.

LORNE CAMPBELL

Campbell had heard of Brian (Bo) Beaucage long before 1985, when he met him at the tiny Choice clubhouse on downtown Weber Street in Kitchener. Beaucage's name came up whenever convicts or prison staff discussed the Kingston Penitentiary riots of 1971, back when he was in the third year of an eight-year prison term for manslaughter. And police in his hometown of London, Ontario, knew of him long before then. He was about fourteen when he was pinched for a break and enter, but the crimes that stood out were the violent ones. "You always knew Brian wasn't going to die a natural death," retired London police superintendent Don Andrews once told a reporter.

The defining day of Beaucage's long criminal career came on April 18, 1971, or what prisoners called Bloody Sunday. That's the day Beaucage and other inmates known as the "Dirty Dozen" forced fifteen convicts—including child molesters—to sit in a circle, tied up, with sheets over their heads, and face judgment by a kangaroo court as other prisoners screamed, "Kill the baby molesters! Give them a taste of their own medicine!" Then they executed two of them with sticks that had nails hammered through them. That done, Beaucage assumed another role with the rioters. "Of all the guys, he was designated to protect the guards. That [killing a guard] would be too serious. All they wanted was better food, and they didn't want the bell to be ringing all of the time. That wasn't worth a first-degree beef." His role in the brutality added just twenty months to Beaucage's prison term.

As a biker, Beaucage showed a flair for making passionate enemies, especially when he was revved up on speed. He moved on from the Holocaust Motorcycle Club, which was run by sociopathic hillbilly Wayne (Weiner) Kellestine of tiny Iona Station, west of London. Kellestine later attained infamy as architect of the Bandido Massacre, when he led the slaughter of eight of his clubmates and associates. Beaucage graduated to the Satan's Choice, where he adopted the Choice's hatred of the Outlaws with the fervour of a true zealot.

He disrespected the London Outlaws in any way he could, from running strippers and selling drugs on their turf to trying to rip down the Outlaws sign from their clubhouse. On that occasion, he was shot before he could get the sign down but escaped unbloodied because he was wearing a bulletproof vest. The Outlaws had a separate policy for dealing with Beaucage. Rather than waste time on hand-to-hand combat with him, they were simply to "take him out."

That was easier said than done. No man is unkillable, but Beaucage was certainly a challenge. He had been shot in the heart by an Outlaw with a .45 calibre automatic pistol outside an east end London bar on January 16, 1987, but lucked out: a heart surgeon happened to be on duty when he was rushed to Victoria Hospital.

In 1988—twenty years after his original prison term began—Beaucage was in the Kitchener Satan's Choice clubhouse, snorting cocaine with Campbell. He had found work as an enforcer for the Montreal mob and that evening Beaucage had plenty to say to Campbell about his Satan's Choice clubmates. None of it was good. They argued in the upstairs washroom where they were doing lines, but only briefly. "It didn't last too long. We didn't dwell on it."

Around this time, a friend of Campbell's named Danny told Beaucage that he wasn't afraid of him. "I know I could take you," Danny said.

Nothing came of it at the time, and Campbell later took Danny aside. "Danny, you might be able to do that, but you don't have the meanness. If you beat him up, he will likely come back and put one in your head. That's the meanness that you don't got."

Danny took the advice and lived for another year, when he died of a motorcycle accident near Kitchener.

Campbell and Beaucage met again at a party later in 1988 with Charmaine and Beaucage's wife, Val, in the Kawarthas near Lindsay, where a mutual friend had built a sprawling log cabin. Since their last meeting, Beaucage had left the Kitchener chapter, where he just didn't fit in, and been given a full patch with Oshawa. Campbell was Oshawa president and didn't realize the depth of hostility between Beaucage and the Kitchener members. "We just thought he'd be a good asset, and then I saw how mad they were. I didn't realize they'd be so mad. It put me in a spin because they were so mad."

Again, Beaucage was quick to disparage the club, and again he quickly grated on Campbell's nerves. "I'm extremely loyal, so it's an argument. He was really running things down. I had been Choice since I was seventeen. That's just not done around me." They didn't exchange blows that evening, but as the get-together ended, they both said words to the effect of: "I don't want to see you again. When I see you again, it's going to be heavier than an argument."

Campbell stewed about it overnight, and when he got up the next morning there seemed only one way to solve the problem. "I went home. I got a gun. I told Charmaine I'd probably be gone for a couple of weeks. Brian was a dangerous guy and I knew it. I told her, 'Don't worry about it.' She knew enough not to ask."

His plan was to visit people and places Beaucage frequented until he finally found Beaucage himself. This wouldn't be easy, since Beaucage didn't have predictable haunts. Once Beaucage was found, Campbell would kill him. Campbell was sitting on his couch, ready to head off on this mission in his own private war, when Charmaine picked up the phone. "It was Brian. He apologized to me. He said, 'I'm sorry. I shouldn't have said the things I said.'"

The apology didn't cause Campbell to lose respect for Beaucage. Quite the opposite. It takes a big man to admit a mistake, and in

Campbell's eyes Beaucage had just proven he was a big man. "Brian wasn't apologizing through fear. He knew he was wrong. I was relieved that he phoned, because he was my friend."

Police raids were a part of outlaw biker life; grovelling to police wasn't. Campbell made it known to clubmates that they were to remain standing even if ordered to do otherwise by police during a raid: "Anybody gets down on his knees, I'll kick him in the face."

In January 1989, police raided the club's Scarborough clubhouse.

"Everybody get on your knees," shouted an officer who was carrying a rifle.

"Nobody gets on their knees," Campbell responded. "Anybody who wants me on my knees has to put me there."

This wasn't well received by the officer who'd made the order. "And this cocksucker hits me with his gun right below the solar plexus."

Campbell stayed on his feet, struggling to deny the officer the satisfaction of knowing how hard he had hit him. When he regained his breath, he managed to say: "I guess you don't know we do stomach exercises."

Campbell had no stomach for a new breed of biker who hopped on a plane and shipped his bike to his destination unless there was an overwhelmingly compelling reason to do otherwise. Life has its mysteries, but some things are very simple in Lorne Campbell's universe, and one of them is that bikers ride bikes.

Campbell rode his Harley west in 1989 for a "mud run"—or ride on rough roads—from Winnipeg to The Pas, a burg 630 kilometres to the northwest. There was a lot that he liked about the western bikers. He had been impressed by the Los Bravos of Winnipeg when he went there to hunt down Tony Valentine and retrieve his Choice patch in the early 1980s. Campbell noted how everyone had seemed to come to attention when a member of the Los Bravos walked up to the bar. "Everyone in a second stopped talking."

The health kick Campbell had begun after his heart attack was cooling considerably, and they dropped lots of acid while at The Pas. The next morning, as he climbed back on his 1989 Harley Classic, Campbell couldn't believe how much the front end of the bike was shaking. The road was bad, but not enough to explain the vibration of his handlebars.

He pointed this out to Bernie Guindon, who was finally out of prison. The Frog sounded skeptical, so Campbell told him to try to ride the bike himself if he needed proof. Guindon turned the throttle, rode a ways, and then pronounced a typically blunt judgment. "You're still fucking high, Lorne," he shouted.

Campbell and Guindon rode out of The Pas to Alberta to meet with the Grim Reapers, and somewhere along the road the acid wore off and Campbell's Harley got less shaky.

While in Calgary, Campbell met Gerry (Gentleman Gerry) Tobin of the Grim Reapers, whose murder two decades later in England would make international headlines. "He was a gentleman. A big guy. A quiet guy. A responsible guy. Well spoken. Polite."

Campbell and Guindon rode on to visit a friend in the Grim Reapers in Lethbridge, Alberta, named Jimmy. Jimmy had founded the club and was its national president. He owned no phone or television and didn't want them. He did know how to show Campbell a good time. "There were the nicest-looking girls and pure cocaine."

Campbell wasn't the only Reapers guest around this time. A decade later, a photo would surface of then Calgary mayor Ralph Klein having a drink with members of the club. That photo became public at the time when Klein was premier and talking of allocating more money to fight organized crime—including outlaw biker clubs.

As Campbell rode out on his way home, Jimmy waved at him. "Stay Canadian, guys," Jimmy said.

There had been a time when the Satan's Choice was fiercely Canadian, but by the winter of 1990, Campbell and some others wondered if the American-born Hells Angels might be a better fit. By now even Guindon was unhappy with what had become of the club he had helped build. There had been a whole new generation of leadership since Campbell and six of the Port Hope Eight went off to prison. New members often seemed too soft, and it felt as though some people thought it was okay to take liberties with the Choice. "There were some violent things that happened. Nothing was done [to retaliate]. . . . I'm a person who retaliates."

That new-found conciliatory tone in the Choice was a far cry from the time, a decade earlier, when Campbell took a hammer to Tulip for suspicions he'd torched the Choice's clubhouse. Campbell did that crime and then hard prison time for it without a word of apology, and made it clear he would do it again and again and again if necessary. Newer members didn't seem to understand what this was all about. "I couldn't keep a guy and break his fingers all night. Things were done more diplomatically."

No one took liberties with the Hells Angels in Quebec. They protected their brand as jealously as any major corporation, and were prepared to kill even their own members and dump them in the St. Lawrence if that's what it took to keep the club in line. Making the Angels even more attractive in Campbell's eyes was the fact that they had never got along with the Outlaws, the club of Campbell's enemies Mother McEwan and Dave Seguin.

A half-dozen Satan's Choice, including Campbell, Guindon and Wayne Kelly, rode east to visit the Angels at their Sorel clubhouse, about ninety kilometres north of Montreal. The Sorel charter was the first for the Angels in Canada, and it had at one time been the home base for founding president Yves (Le Boss) Buteau and Maurice (Mom) Boucher.

The feud with the Outlaws dated back to 1969, when an Outlaw raped the wife of an American Hells Angel. As the story went, her husband and fellow club members beat the Outlaw to death. Not long after that, American Outlaws began frequently using the word "Adios," for "Angels die in Outlaw states."

Guindon asked a polite postman in French for directions to the clubhouse. He had grown up in a francophone family, but his command of his mother language was mangled and it took the letter carrier a few minutes to understand the question. "Anybody there would have known. They're beside the biggest church in Sorel. They had a sign on top of the building saying 'Hells Angels.'"

Campbell, Guindon and the other Choice members rode through the gate, past the motion detectors and up to the three-storey bunker. Then they walked through the steel-reinforced doors to see about setting up an Angels charter of their own. There was a security room with one-way bulletproof glass that faced the yard, and it was always manned. Inside it was a wall of TV monitors that showed every inch of the surrounding area. Rumour had it that even if a pane of glass was broken in a member's home, it would show up on one of the monitors. Another wall was lined with rifles and shotguns, all registered. There were also a number of guard dogs in the yard. "How's that for organized?" Campbell says.

If accepted into the club, the Satan's Choice members would have the first charter of Les Hells in Ontario. It would infuriate the Outlaws, which was always a good thing in Campbell's books. During the visit, the Angels noted that they had had a similar visit from three bikers from Ireland, who were part of a new Angels charter and who rode rundown bikes. They sent the Irishmen away with three new Harleys and words of encouragement.

Within an hour of the arrival of Campbell and his crew, representatives of the Angels from across the province joined them. The Quebecers were respectful, something that always impressed Campbell. "They listened to us. Even though they had the reputation for being dangerous, there was no confrontation. There was no pulling heavies. They were perfect gentlemen."

When they left, there was no promise made about patches, but they weren't rejected either. Campbell found himself wanting to be part of an Angels charter even more.

That year, Campbell heard a story that Andrew (Teach) Simmons, the national president of the Outlaws from London, Ontario, was planning to head north of Toronto to kill him. Simmons was the son of a British military sergeant major, and in previous incarnations Teach had served as a schoolteacher and a youth church choir leader. That day, Teach had a court appearance in Barrie, and Campbell confronted him as he left the courthouse and told him what he had heard.

"If you do, I'm ready," Campbell recalls saying. "If you come to my house, Teach, you will die in my driveway."

"That's not true," Teach replied. "Who told you?"

"He really denied it," Campbell says. "He was a gentleman. Obviously nervous about what I was saying to him. Every night I sat with a high-powered rifle, waiting for them."

CHAPTER 21

The Hard Way

Just because you're paranoid doesn't mean they aren't out to get you.

old Kingston Satan's Choice saying

I t was also in 1990 that Campbell got a call from journalist Mick Lowe that chart-topping alt-country singer-songwriter Steve Earle wanted to meet him. Earle was riding high from his critical and commercial hit albums *Guitar Town* and *Copperhead Road*, while Lowe had written *Conspiracy of Brothers*, a book that raised serious doubts about the Port Hope convictions. Earle first learned of the book and the Port Hope story from Wally High, an original Kingston Satan's Choice member, who liked to say, "Just because you're paranoid doesn't mean they aren't out to get you." The musician was impressed by the courage and brotherhood in the story, and especially by how Campbell had tried to take the rap for the killing.

The meeting was to take place at the bar of L'Hotel, the upscale Toronto hotel where Earle was staying while promoting his album *The Hard Way*. When Campbell and Charmaine got there, Earle was nowhere to be found. That wasn't surprising, as Earle hadn't yet gone into rehab to clean up his heroin and booze addictions, which had started back during his early teens in Texas. After several minutes Campbell and Charmaine went to the front desk, and the clerk called up to his room. A few minutes later

Earle stepped out of the elevator, looking as if he hadn't slept for three days or so, which may have been the case.

"Lorne, I think you're overdressed," Charmaine said to Campbell, who had worn his dress garb of clean jeans and a red Satan's Choice T-shirt.

The meeting went well when it finally began. Earle's an anti-war, anti-handgun, anti–death penalty peacenik, but he took a liking to Campbell, whom nobody has ever accused of being a pacifist. "He was really nice," recalls Earle. "Actually, he was the quietest of those guys. Larry Vallentyne, you always knew he's in the room when he's in the room."

Both men understood the transformative power of stories, and both men had plenty of life experience to draw on when they told theirs. Earle hadn't been in a club himself, but he understood what it meant to be an outlaw biker. He had spent much of his childhood in Texas, close to a clubhouse of the Bandidos Motorcycle Club. The Bandidos had been set up in the 1960s in the Texas Gulf by returning Vietnam veterans, and working-class kids there knew there was a good chance they would end up fighting in Vietnam, unlike middle- and upper-class hippies, who could get draft deferments by enrolling in university. "Peace and love didn't make much sense [to them]. . . . There was still the class distinction."

Much of Earle's early performing was done inside the Bandidos club-house. "I grew up with bikes. I grew up with scooter trash. . . . I carried guns for years. I don't carry them anymore. . . . I'm a different person than I was when I was hanging out." Earle didn't have to be told there was plenty of crime in biker clubs, but he also saw it was simplistic and inaccurate to dismiss clubs such as the Satan's Choice as nothing more than organized crime units. That sort of judgment totally missed the point of men like Campbell. "It was really more about live and let live, defending everybody's right to do whatever the fuck they wanted to do."

Earle also realized there were subtle but real cultural differences between clubs such as the Hells Angels and the Choice and the Outlaws, even if they all might look the same to outsiders and sound the same as they roared by on their Harleys. Memorials to dead club members in Choice clubhouses showed photos of the fallen men in their prime, smiling and alive. Not so with the Outlaws. "When you went to an

Outlaws clubhouse, you saw pictures of them in their coffins and at their funerals. It was a little creepy."

Earle was an avid history buff, and Campbell particularly enjoyed "The Devil's Right Hand," a song about a gun-toting juvenile delinquent in the Civil War era whose mother calls his handgun "the devil's right hand." Earle saw a historical parallel between Campbell's attempt to take the fall in court for the Matiyek shooting and General John Buford's actions in the Battle of Gettysburg. Buford, who headed a Union cavalry unit, chose to dismount and confront the enemy at close quarters, despite being heavily outmanned and ultimately doomed. Buford's battlefield decision gave Union forces time to occupy a ring of hills around Gettysburg and win the battle, so his cavalry's sacrifice ultimately saved their brothers' lives. Earle respected how Campbell was willing to step up in court and try to protect his biker brothers, despite daunting odds. "He nutted up, man. He saw those guys were all going to go down for something he did. He didn't just do it, he did it knowing it might not do any good, and he did it anyways. . . . I've got a lot of respect for Lorne. . . . Being honest didn't get him very far. That should never happen. Being honest should count for something, and in Lorne's case it didn't."

Earle's involvement in the drug world taught him that notions of honour among thieves are most often just fantasies. Still, there was something solid there, in the way Campbell conducted himself. "Lorne's that rare guy that I don't think ever gave a piece of information on anybody but himself. I don't think he has it in him."

There had been a time when Earle kept loaded guns, including a pistol under his mattress. But he realized that the very presence of a gun changes the dynamic and possibilities of interactions. "I didn't see anything incongruous with being a peacenik. . . . I'm pretty non-violent and I'm getting more so every day, and he's the only person I know for sure who killed someone." As their improbable friendship grew, Earle realized that Campbell suffered personally over ending Matiyek's life. "I think he thought about Bill Matiyek all of the time. . . . It has more than bugged him. It has followed him."

Campbell became a regular at Earle's concerts in Ontario, and made a point of always requesting "The Devil's Right Hand," while Earle began dedicating his song "The Other Kind" to Campbell. It includes the lines:

> *And I'm damn sure not suffering from a lack of love*
> *There's plenty more where that came from*
> *Ah—but leave it up to me to say something wrong and hurt someone*
> *before I'm done.*

Other lines included:

> *There are those that break and bend*
> *I'm the other kind ,,,*

Back in Kingston, Rick Sauvé and Gary Comeau were still behind bars serving life terms, but there was some room for optimism. In January 1990, Sauvé married a 22-year-old University of Ottawa graduate, who was just ten years old and growing up in a middle-class family when he was convicted.

Michele wasn't how one might imagine a woman who marries a man serving a life term. She wasn't desperate. She wasn't tattooed. She wasn't one of those women who send lurid letters—and full-frontal Polaroids—to convicts. She first met him when her criminology class visited Millhaven as part of their study of "lifers." Their dating consisted of two-hour visits, several times a week, for almost five years. In a sense, the physical distance imposed by their extended engagement gave the relationship an oddly chaste, traditional feel—if you could somehow imagine prison guards as chaperones.

Sauvé had filed a court challenge to a provision in the Canada Elections Act that barred convicts from voting. Sauvé kept fighting until eventually prisoners were given the right to vote. The fight to win his own freedom, however, was far from over.

Earle played a benefit show in an Ottawa nightclub on June 30, 1991, to raise awareness of the Port Hope case. That night, he was invited into the Ottawa clubhouse of the Outlaws but said he wouldn't go unless

Campbell was invited too. Campbell said he was game, but also ready for trouble. "I said, 'If there's one derogatory statement, then it's a go.'"

Campbell and Earle entered through the side door with Wally High, who was close to Campbell and Earle but also managed to stay on friendly terms with members of the Outlaws who had once been Satan's Choice. There was music playing on the ground floor—the usual biker mix of artists including Led Zeppelin, Grand Funk Railroad, George Thorogood and the Destroyers, and Bob Seger—and other guests that evening included some Outlaws up from the States.

The Outlaws president gestured towards photos on a memorial wall of Satan's Choice members who had died before the 1977 split, along with memorial photos of fallen Outlaws. It harkened back to when Outlaws and Choice members actually got along and shared a brotherhood. "I thought that was respectful," Campbell says.

The Outlaws were on their best behaviour, as Campbell wore his Choice colours, but one friend of the club looked at his vest and snapped at him, "What the fuck's this?"

"Before I could get a chance to get to him, they got him and beat the snot out of him and threw him out. Then they beat him up again and told him never to come back again. It was all before I got a chance to hit him, and I was pretty fast."

Campbell and the president went upstairs to talk in an office for about three hours. The president was curious about what was happening in prison, where Outlaws were being beaten by Satan's Choice with baseball bats. "We were comfortable, but I was ready for anything," Campbell says. "I didn't feel tense because I don't feel tense." He told the Outlaws president that he had turned down another biker's offer of a pistol to bring into the Outlaws clubhouse, in case things went sour.

"Well, look around you," the Outlaws president said, referring to the numerous potentially dangerous Outlaws in the building. "It wouldn't have done you any good."

Campbell nodded at the point well taken.

When it was time to leave, Wally High said he considered the evening a success. "He always felt he could be the peacemaker," Earle says of High. "I think it was the only time a Choice member was in an Outlaws clubhouse anywhere." Earle considered High "the most peacenik biker you ever met," and High radiated particularly good vibrations as he left the clubhouse.

"We made a lot of peace tonight," High said as he walked out of the party.

"No we didn't," Campbell replied.

"I wasn't there for that," Campbell remembers. "That wasn't my goal. I just went because they invited Steve."

There were a few more drinks back at their hotel before Earle fell asleep on the phone talking long-distance to his wife. The next day, Canada Day, Campbell rode Earle on the back of his Harley up to Parliament Hill. "I rode right up on the lawn." There, Earle sang "Justice in Ontario" before telling the crowd: "These guys have been locked up for pushing thirteen years, and I really truly believe that they're innocent. . . . The thing that irritates me is not a matter of someone else's differing opinion, it's their complete and total indifference to the situation."

Bill (Mr. Bill) Lavoie of the Choice had ideas of his own about how to spring Sauvé and Comeau from custody. A visit to Mr. Bill's place in the village of Warsaw, near Peterborough, was always an adventure, but the day he discussed freeing the imprisoned bikers was odd even by the standards of Mr. Bill.

To get into Mr. Bill–land, you always had to call in advance and let him know you were coming. Otherwise, odds were high he would be in a surly mood in his laneway, with a loaded shotgun in each hand. Back before the Port Hope convictions, Merv (Indian) Blaker had once neglected to call ahead, which explained the shotgun damage to the side of his car. Before you went to Mr. Bill's, you were also advised to use a washroom, as his facilities didn't include a toilet that actually flushed. Sometimes, new arrivals to Mr. Bill's would assume things couldn't be as bad as others claimed and ventured into his washroom despite the warnings. "They'd go in and they'd come out green." Also at Mr. Bill's, visitors were expected to take their shoes off at the door. Even though it appeared he hadn't moved things inside the house for decades, and that he didn't care in the least about the paint-peeling devil's brew in his toilet, Campbell and his friends pretended Mr. Bill was fiercely protective of his floors and made visitors remove their footwear.

Mr. Bill had been in the Choice since 1967 and was president of the Oshawa chapter between the Peter Rabbit and Campbell terms. He knew his way around a Harley to the point that he could stand up on the seat of his bike while riding down the road, though most of the time he was a safe rider.

Mr. Bill was also a paranoid's paranoid. When planes flew over his property, he would invariably look up and earnestly proclaim, "Look, it's the police."

Recreation at Mr. Bill's often involved shooting guns in his backyard. Once, Mr. Bill levelled a pistol at Campbell and pulled the trigger.

Bang.

Campbell was wise to Mr. Bill's antics and knew it was just a starter's pistol.

"Did I scare you?" Mr. Bill asked.

"No, but look at her," Campbell said, gesturing towards Charmaine. "Charmaine just about had a heart attack."

Mr. Bill had a disarming way of looking deadly serious while saying ridiculous things. Once, while punching out a couple of men he found irritating, Mr. Bill barked out: "You guys are jerk-offs. I've jerked off better men than you." Campbell and Fat Frog couldn't stop laughing, trying to figure out what he was really trying to say.

Another time, in Windsor, a biker slipped Mr. Bill dried horseshit wrapped in a rolling paper, and watched him take a long hard drag on it, thinking it was marijuana. "Fuck, this is good shit," Mr. Bill pronounced. During a meeting in Hamilton, Mr. Bill snuck up behind Campbell and kicked his legs out from under him. Campbell was wearing a buck knife and thought seriously of burying it in him. "The only thing that stopped me was seeing that [Satan's Choice] crest on his back. He had enough respect [that] he didn't do it in front of anybody. If he had, I probably would have stabbed him."

Mr. Bill talked fondly and often of his weapons collection. Bikers liked to remember the day Mr. Bill went to a police station to retrieve a shotgun that had been seized during a raid. "He loaded it and fired it right in the cop's desk. He said, 'You have never seen so many cops run so fast.' He got three months [in jail] for it."

Campbell arrived one day at Mr. Bill's home only to find him stretched out naked on his bed, wearing nothing but a neck brace and a pained expression. He needed the brace to help him cope with pains from a bike accident of years before. The pained expression came from his thinking about what could be done to help his imprisoned clubmates, Sauvé and Comeau. His first question was about the daily routine at Millhaven.

"Lorne, do they still have everybody go out in the yard?" he asked.

"Yeah."

"Do the guys go out?"

"Yeah."

Next, Mr. Bill directed the conversation to the old tank *Conqueror* that was parked in front of the Oshawa armouries, across Simcoe Street from Campbell's boyhood apartment.

"We can get that going," Mr. Bill said. "We could get it transported down to there. We'll go through the fence. We'll have a boat waiting. They won't know what hit them."

"Are you aware the Canadian army is nearby?" Campbell asked.

"By the time they get there, we'll be gone."

"Okay, I'll think about it," Campbell replied, not wanting to excite Mr. Bill further.

Campbell was drunk when he arrived one night at the Oshawa clubhouse. The only person inside was member Stan, who had on his back a tattoo of the body of Jesus with Stan's face on top, wearing a crown of thorns. Apparently, no one ever asked Stan what the tattoo signified, perhaps fearing that he might explain it.

Stan was dead asleep in an upstairs bedroom. Campbell shouted for him to come down and join him for a nightcap.

"No, I'm sleeping."

"Come down and have a drink with me."

"No, I'm sleeping."

"Go on, have a drink with me."

"No."

"Well, you're coming down."

"No."

Campbell started to climb the stairs and Stan didn't want to be bothered anymore. It was so dark that Campbell didn't see the armchair Stan pushed down the stairs until it was on top of him. Stan then fired a shot down with his Walther PPK 7.65, the same snazzy pistol used by Agent 007 in the James Bond movies. He wasn't trying to kill Campbell, just make a point.

"Oh, you want to play that way?" Campbell thought. He went behind the bar and pulled out the much more substantial .30-06 rifle that was stored there, and fired a round up through the ceiling.

Campbell could hear Stan make a break for it across the top of the stairs. Campbell squeezed off several shots, and they all went between Stan's legs. Campbell had thought he was firing somewhere else, farther from his friend.

Clink, clink, clink.

Stan pushed his Walther down the stairs, signalling surrender.

"Have a drink with me."

He did.

Another night at the Oshawa clubhouse, a young biker named Danny caught Campbell's attention with a boastful comment.

"If I ever fought you, I'd punch your fucking head in," Danny announced. "You're forty-something and I'm twenty-something. I know what moves you make, what you do. I won't tell you, but you've only got three or four moves."

"Tell me what you'd do."

"I won't tell you, but you've only got three or four moves."

"Tell me what you'd do."

"No, I won't."

The conversation was getting repetitive, so Campbell punched it up by giving Danny a short, sharp hook to the head. Danny responded with a shot of his own that didn't come close to dropping Campbell, but which made Danny oddly proud anyway.

A moment later, Stan walked into the clubhouse just in time to see Danny hit the floor.

"I'm out of here," Stan said, and retreated back outside.

Out of prison for a little while now, Bernie Guindon became a partner in a 120-acre campground called Shangri-La in cottage country near Huntsville. There, they staged outdoor shows with name acts. One memorable appearance was by John Kay, whose classic open-road freedom song, "Born to Be Wild," was part of the iconic 1969 biker film *Easy Rider*. What biker didn't want to hear him live, singing "I like smoke and lightning/Heavy metal thunder" and "We can climb so high/I never wanna die"?

"We build the stage by ourselves for him," Campbell recalls of Kay's show. "He said, 'I'm not playing on that stage.' Wayne Kelly said, 'If you won't play on that stage, we're taking all of your equipment and your vehicles and you're walking or hitchhiking home.' He played. It was an excellent show. They go through all of the songs exactly like what's on the albums in the 1960s."

Guindon's impresario career ended shortly afterwards, when an investor pulled a knife on him and Guindon responded with his fists. That meant another six months behind bars and the closure of Shangri-La. "He filled him in," Campbell says. "Bernie doesn't hit softly."

CHAPTER 22

Rock Bottom

*If you want to shoot somebody, walk up and shoot him. Don't spray a
house. That doesn't make you tough. That doesn't make you solid. That
doesn't make you stable. It does tell everybody that you will kill someone.*

LORNE CAMPBELL

Campbell had an associate around this time named Stephen James
Readhead, but everyone in Campbell's circle called him Close-Up.
He was a grim and intense man who got his nickname for his
unsettling habit of standing extremely close to people while talking—so
close they could feel the heat of his breath as he gave his high-octane
views on life. Even more disturbing was the story about why he was
missing the ring finger on his left hand. Close-Up parted with that finger
after he became disillusioned with the concept of matrimony in general
and his own marriage in particular. Simply removing his wedding ring
didn't seem nearly dramatic enough for the force of the anti-wedlock
emotions coursing through him, and so Close-Up did the only thing he
considered appropriate: he blasted the offending wedding band off with
a pistol shot, removing his ring finger as well.

Close-Up wasn't to be confused with Campbell's friend Sean (9
Fingers) McLay, who killed his parents with a shotgun at age nine
because of extreme abuse. It was easy to believe 9 Fingers's story after

a glance at his nose, which had obviously been broken several times. Campbell was never told how 9 Fingers lost his digit, and he didn't think it proper to ask. Despite the scary backstory, 9 Fingers struck him as a nice and respectful guy.

On November 29, 1989, a police wiretap picked up Campbell talking with Charmaine in the early afternoon. Campbell was on the road with Close-Up, while Charmaine was at their home in Orillia, putting away groceries. It started as a typical domestic conversation, as they talked a little about the money they owed on their Canadian Tire credit card. They joked a little about Christmas, and Charmaine said she had already bought his gift.

Then Charmaine teased him a little, saying, "You wouldn't believe what I'm expecting."

"It's too bad," Campbell joked back. "I don't like that kind of pressure."

The conversation shifted to their dog Oddie, a Yorkshire terrier ("The toughest dog in the world, pound for pound, I'm told"). Campbell said he would be home in a couple of days. Then he teased her a little himself, talking of a new car.

"The one you're getting me?" Charmaine asked.

"No, I'll see about that one next week. That's what I mean about Christmas presents. Like I gotta get this car, so don't worry about Christmas presents."

"Um."

"Ya know, don't worry about Christmas presents until January. You know what I mean?"

"Umm."

"It don't have to be Christmas when you get a gift."

Charmaine wasn't aware of his plans to buy a used Chevrolet for $1,200 as a joint Christmas gift for both of them. Campbell wasn't aware that others in his circle, including Close-Up, were using car names as code in a drug deal. "The phones were tapped. I didn't know that."

The 1991 trial that followed in Newmarket, north of Toronto, was short and unsweet. "One of the jurors fell asleep during the trial. That was disheartening. I thought that it was important." He was found guilty of conspiracy to traffic cocaine, as the jury didn't buy his story that he was talking about buying a used Chevrolet. The jury concluded that he knowingly drove another man to Montreal to pick up cocaine. "That's the only one [conviction] that I was truly innocent in."

With that conviction, Campbell found himself back in the Millhaven Penitentiary assessment centre at age forty-two, facing a 3½-year term, or 1,280 more days behind bars, if he didn't get parole. Bob Anderson, one of the prisoners on the maintenance crew, was working in the reception centre and decided to make a strong impression. Anderson weighed well over 350 pounds and was one of the few inmates anywhere in the country with a 500-pound bench press, about double what a large, strong man can lift. "Reception is double bunked, and Bob took a monkey wrench and broke the chain on the top bunk in my cell so I wouldn't have to put up with anyone. Bob knew who I was through other people."

The prison hadn't been a pleasant place the first time Campbell was housed there, but it had declined considerably in his absence, Anderson's gesture notwithstanding. Prisoners were no longer allowed to use common rooms for eating, like back in 1983. There weren't any more hockey games in the winter. There had been drastic changes to the yard, which had previously held two baseball diamonds, a miniature golf course, a weight pit, three handball walls, a running track and the outdoor rink. Now it was split into three separate yards and there were only short periods of time when prisoners from each range could go there. Black, white and Asian prisoners were generally kept apart, as gang tensions had grown worse. All in all, it was clear the old neighbourhood had gone downhill. "As far as prisons go, Millhaven was a far better place the first time I did time there." There were still familiar faces from his first visit. "Career criminals usually have the same MO [modus operandi] and the cops know it. MO goes a long way [towards catching them]."

The worst part about his return was how he found that attitudes of fellow inmates had also worsened. Prisoners now did previously unthinkable things such as stealing each other's shoes. "They're called cell or box thieves, and they're the lowest of the low. In the eighties, they'd never get away with that. They'd get jumped. Jail etiquette, protocol, that's just gone out the window." Even Anderson, the behemoth who gave him the welcome, would prove a disappointment. He was suspected of pilfering money from the prison canteen, which was a taboo since canteen funds were used to buy sports equipment.

For his part, Campbell was determined to stay as positive as possible as he settled into another prison term, even though he maintained he hadn't been part of Close-Up's drug conspiracy. He told himself, "I guess I'll make up for the stuff I didn't get caught for."

It was in the Millhaven assessment area that Campbell heard startling news regarding his old friend and would-be murder target Brian (Bo) Beaucage. It had always seemed as if Beaucage was on borrowed time. Beaucage had a long-standing problem with heroin, and he had accumulated a dangerous list of enemies. Campbell personally knew of plans for a hit against Beaucage, since he had been approached to carry it out. "Wayne Kelly told me that he wanted Brian Beaucage killed. He wanted me to do it. I liked Beaucage. I went and told him. I didn't like Wayne Kelly. Wayne Kelly was a very smart guy. He read a lot of books on brainwashing, things like that. In the end, he turned out to be someone not to be trusted. He was a manipulator."

Beaucage wasn't one to leave a grudge—let alone a murder contract against him—unattended. However, before he could do anything about Kelly, his own fate was determined by someone he considered a friend. Frank Passarelli of the Loners Motorcycle Club killed him in a rooming house on Lansdowne Avenue in west end Toronto after a night of drugs and pornography and an argument over a woman. Brian Beaucage, perhaps the most feared of the Dirty Dozen of the Kingston prison riots, died because he had a woman in his room and asked Passarelli to leave. "No one is going to ask me to leave for some girl," Passarelli allegedly said, according to the prosecutor who got him convicted of second-degree murder for bludgeoning Beaucage to death.

By the time police found Beaucage's body on March 4, 1991, his remains had been chewed over by Bouvier dogs owned by another tenant in the rooming house. Beaucage had made it to age forty-three. Seventeen of those years were spent behind bars. Aside from the damage done by the dogs, his head was almost totally severed from his body, an event that became known in the biker world as "Fifty Whacks with an

Axe." After all the hard situations he had survived, he had been killed over a few words, just as Campbell had almost killed him over words a half-dozen years earlier.

As Campbell lay on his cell bunk and heard of the murder on television, he felt a wave of disgust towards Beaucage's killer. "He must have been asleep," Campbell says. "He had to give it to him in his sleep. Brian wasn't no slouch. . . . My thoughts, when I first heard that, was to think, 'What a coward. He couldn't do it when he wasn't sleeping.'"

Campbell was still housed in the Millhaven assessment area when Close-Up rushed into his cell.

"Guess who got killed?" Close-Up was obviously in a good mood.

"Who?"

"Wayne Kelly."

Campbell recalls, "It didn't excite me, but he [Close-Up] was excited. He [Kelly] was known as NG. No Good. Not to be trusted."

Kelly, who had floated the contract to have Beaucage killed, was shot to death in a Richmond Hill basement by David (Skinny) Nelson. As Campbell heard the story, Kelly had been using heroin when Nelson walked in on him. It's never safe to walk in on a drug user who has been awake for a couple of days, especially when he has a loaded gun. Skinny Nelson hadn't been considered a violent guy, which led Campbell to conclude that Kelly must have fired first. "I was kind of surprised that that happened. He nailed him right in the head with the first shot. That's what I heard."

Nelson was charged with first-degree murder after he sought help at Richmond Hill's York Central Hospital for gunshot wounds to his stomach. Murder's always at least a little unsettling, even in Campbell's world, but it was never totally shocking when serious drug users met unnatural ends. So it also wasn't surprising when Skinny Nelson died of a drug overdose not so long after that in Collins Bay. "This was a heavy crew."

Campbell's conditions improved markedly when he was transferred from the Millhaven assessment centre to the low-security Bath detention camp. It would take only a few minutes to walk from Millhaven to

Bath—if you could somehow make it past the armed guards and the double gates and the razor-wired fences—but the two institutions are in fact worlds apart. Millhaven is designed to hide you away and severely restrict your every movement, while Bath is preparation for life on the outside. Bath is ringed by a fence and barbed wire, but inside that fence men live in trailers or houses and often barbecue their own meals.

An official Campbell knew at the Millhaven assessment centre made sure that prisoners he liked—or who would pay him two thousand dollars—were sent to Bath and not to a heavy institution such as Collins Bay. The official was a fat, often drunk man who liked to belly-fight bikers and steal chocolate bars from their cells. His wife was dying of cancer and he was clearly becoming unhinged by stress and loss. Once, a prisoner tied a string to a Mars chocolate bar and placed it in the hallway. When the portly guard bent over to pick it up, the prisoner yanked on the string. It took several more tries before the official caught on that the prisoner was fishing for him.

"Fuck you," he finally snorted before waddling off.

Other times, the fat official announced that he was taking prisoners off to a work detail. Then it was down to the kitchen, where they would dine on pilfered steak. The official was eventually fired for corruption.

Not long after arriving back in custody, Campbell got *Class of 91* tattooed onto his chest, using the high E-string of a guitar and the small motor of a transistor radio. He was given a job as clerk, ordering clothing and supplies for a couple of hours a day. A prison official noted in his file that he "works well in a difficult area and has learned the job quickly with little supervision." Much of the rest of his time was spent working out. As prison stays went, it was relatively comfortable. One counsellor wrote in his file: "Lorne appears to have a positive attitude and is a very pleasant individual." In one psychological test, Campbell was asked if he thought of himself as a worthless person. "Not at all," he replied. He gave the same answer when asked if he felt that life wasn't worth living. Asked if thoughts of suicide kept coming into his mind, Campbell replied: "Definitely not."

He was classed as a multiple recidivist with a maladaptive lifestyle, but staff also concluded that Campbell wasn't out of control and lacking impulse control. To the contrary, he appeared very much in command of himself, however wild his actions might appear to an outsider. In the world of freelance debt collection, beating someone with a hammer was a logical method of enforcing verbal contracts. "Violence was planned and designed for effect rather than impulsive + uncontrolled," his file states.

There was also a certain order to his personal interactions, staff concluded. He told a psychologist that he deeply loved his wife, Charmaine, whom he had been with for seventeen years. That said, he also didn't feel any guilt over a string of one-night stands during his married life. This was simply part of the biker lifestyle, as he told things, and he gave no hint of ever wanting to leave that lifestyle or the Satan's Choice. His case management officer wrote: "Still member of Satan's Choice. Very 'solid' with his club."

For Charmaine, this was the second time she'd had to deal with her husband doing federal prison time. Since quitting school as a young teen, she had always managed to support herself, working in an office and at the Mitsubishi plant in Midland that made colour television tubes, and then dancing in strip clubs across the province. Through it all, even while dancing, she remained a loyal and loving wife. "She was always there for me. She visited without fail. She was doing everything for me."

Campbell was proud of how Charmaine always managed to hold things together, even though life had never been easy. Oshawa in the 1960s and 1970s had a reputation as a city with lots of good unionized jobs, and perhaps that's why her parents moved the family there from Nova Scotia. Her parents split after the move, and Charmaine learned early on to stay positive in difficult times. "She never had an enemy in the world. Everybody loved her."

Among her friends was a former co-worker at Mitsubishi named Evelyn Hughes. Charmaine and Evelyn had met in 1986, when they were both taking a weekend course at Georgian College in Barrie to obtain their motorcycle licences. Evelyn was impressed with Charmaine's no-crap attitude towards an instructor who didn't seem to think women should ride motorcycles, and who went out of his way to make the course difficult for Charmaine and Evelyn in particular. In the end, they both got their licences. "We were the only two girls that passed," Evelyn says. "There were five or six of us." Soon they were enjoying regular potato pancake breakfasts together as friends.

Evelyn hit the roads on a maroon 750 Suzuki while Charmaine rode a black one. Getting a Harley to fit a smallish woman simply wasn't in the cards, but the Suzuki frame was a manageable size for Evelyn. "I could reach the ground on it," Evelyn recalls. "We could leave the guys in the dust, and we often did."

Evelyn was a comfort to Charmaine when Charmaine went into hospital for a hysterectomy. It was during this operation that doctors discovered Charmaine had advanced cancer. She was transferred to hospital in Kingston, where medical treatment was better. Evelyn and another friend, Jacquie Ross, had stayed with her for the last seven weeks, providing whatever comfort they could, but it was clear their friend's health wouldn't be getting better. Campbell was allowed out on day passes to visit her and given permission to sleep in a cot by her hospital bed in the cancer ward. The cancer had hit Charmaine's lymph nodes, so they all knew the end wasn't far away. Without a morphine derivative, the final months would have been unbearable for her. "It hurt her even to blink," Campbell says. She would alternate between seeming to be worlds away and being totally focused and in the moment. "She'd be not there, then she'd be sharp as a pin."

On April 14, 1993, ten months after Campbell got the news that Charmaine had cancer, she died in his arms at home. "She was coherent right to the day she died. She had cancer everywhere but her brain. She was a beautiful woman. Beautiful personality." Jacquie had stayed with her for the last seven weeks, and she and Evelyn lovingly bathed her, washed her hair and did her makeup before anyone from the funeral home arrived.

Among those who sent their condolences was Dave, the undercover cop who had attended their wedding, eaten at their table and weathered Charmaine's verbal blast after she learned he was really a cop working against her husband. "He wanted to come to her funeral. His captain told him he couldn't."

Campbell was on parole at the time of her death. He moved in with his friend Larry Vallentyne so that he wouldn't be alone. "I don't think I was right for a long time. I was devastated, just devastated."

CHAPTER 23

Smugglers' Alley

We were making money hand over fist.

LORNE CAMPBELL

I t didn't take long after Campbell's release from prison in March 1993 for a friend to call with an employment offer. It wasn't parole-board approved. Campbell was asked to provide security for smugglers moving cigarettes from the United States to Canada via the St. Regis Mohawk Reservation/Akwesasne Reserve that spanned upstate New York and eastern Ontario on the St. Lawrence River. He would be working for two white guys from the Cornwall area with ties to Mohawk smugglers, and organized criminals of various ethnic groups in Ontario and Quebec. About a dozen such groups operated in the area, and smugglers needed protection from their underworld rivals. Campbell picked three helpers from the Oshawa Satan's Choice and started accepting jobs that paid him as much as $3,000 or $4,000 a day. In what seemed like no time, Campbell was so flush with money that he gave a hundred dollars to a panhandler in Cornwall while leaving a Mexican restaurant. "He was just elated. I thought about it later. I thought, I probably killed the bugger. If he goes around anybody out there with a hundred-dollar bill, they'd kill him."

His parole officer sensed something was afoot. "What have you been up to?" he asked during one meeting.

"Not too much. Sitting in the backyard."

"How many trucks do you have?" the parole officer asked.

"I've just got a car."

"That's not what I hear."

"What do you hear?"

"You haven't got a few trucks?"

"No. Why?"

The parole officer didn't answer.

"Why would you say that?"

The parole officer didn't say why he would say that.

It was early morning work, as Campbell stood guard while smugglers picked up cases of cigarettes on the American side of the St. Lawrence River. One pickup spot was a warehouse with visible stacks of bills, which he estimates ran well into the millions of dollars. Campbell often sat waiting in a boat laden with eighty cases of cigarettes, holding a massive firearm. He kept his eye on hijackers who prowled the shore in speedboats, ready to pounce and steal Campbell's cargo. "They'd see you with a machine gun and just go, 'Fuck that.'

"There's nothing like going down the river at eighty miles an hour on a flat-bottom boat with a bunch of cigarettes. You have a machine gun on your lap and you don't trust the guy with you and he doesn't trust you."

It was about a forty-minute trip on the St. Lawrence River, and Campbell only had to make one trip a night. Each boat held about eighty cases, each of which contained fifty cartons of cigarettes. Once on the Canadian side of the river, Campbell and his cronies moved the cigarettes to safe houses, where they could be stored temporarily. "They had houses all along the river. They were paying people just to use their houses."

Cigarettes bound for Quebec were then loaded onto bogus Purolator vans, ambulances or even a limousine, complete with a driver in a suit and black cap. Earlier smugglers had used transport trucks, but police caught on to them, forcing them into more discreet vehicles. Smaller trucks were often bought at a gas station/car lot north of Toronto, whose owners had invariably purchased them at auctions. They were fitted with special switches to allow all their lights to be shut off instantly, making them hard to see when parked at night. The vehicles were further modified with ultra-hard suspensions so they would ride high off the road even when carrying heavy loads. "The cops see a low truck, they pull it over," Campbell says.

Ontario was safer ground for the smugglers than Quebec. Getting caught only meant losing the load for a first offence, losing the vehicle for a second, and the possibility of imprisonment for a third. Since the trucks were registered under a multitude of names, the odds of anyone being nabbed for multiple offences were minimal. The smugglers didn't bother to disguise the vans heading to Toronto; it wasn't worth the bother.

The smugglers' level of planning impressed Campbell. Guards were stationed on highway overpasses to watch for police both on the roads and in the air. Night-vision goggles allowed them to see high in the sky, to detect police surveillance aircraft that couldn't be heard or seen from the road. They also had jumbo-sized cellphones that looked like something out of the North African conflict in World War II. "It was so fucking organized I couldn't believe it."

Smugglers had to budget for boats, trucks, safe house storage, security and drivers. That said, the profits were staggering. The wholesale value of each boatload was about $56,000, depending on the brand of cigarettes, while the retail value for consumers was roughly $320,000.

There were money-counting machines that could quickly detect counterfeit bills. The few times bogus bills were found, the culprits acted mortified and quickly offered proper currency—as well as a generous tip—to mollify Campbell's business partners. Cash was stuffed into duffle bags, to the tune of $500,000 a bag, and it was the job of Campbell and his crew to protect and move that money. "Every day, there was at least a half-million dollars we'd take over to the island to pay for the cigarettes."

His crew included Musclehead and Stan from the Oshawa Choice. They each received a thousand dollars a week as base pay, plus extras for running errands, delivering money or doing extra security work. On Stan's first day on the job, his task was to bring $500,000 in a duffle bag to the water's edge, where he was to give it to a man who would come by in a boat.

"His name's going to be Bob," Stan was told.

A man came by in a boat and stopped in front of Stan.

"Are you Bob?" Stan asked.

"No, I'm Jack. Bob's sick today."

Stan was armed with a .38 revolver, which was nothing to snicker at, but Jack was packing a machine gun, which could have cut Stan in half. "He [Stan] didn't want to be on the boat with him." As is often the case, the man with the bigger gun and the most bullets won out, and so Stan stepped into the boat with the $500,000 and headed out to the middle of the waters with Jack. The middle of the St. Lawrence isn't a comforting place to be in the middle of the night when you're carrying $500,000 in cash and sitting across from a stranger with a loaded machine gun. Stan stared at Jack and his gun. Jack stared back at Stan and his .38. The only sound was the whir of the motor. As Campbell tells it, "There was only smugglers and lakers [commercial vessels] on the water at night. They were just looking at each other."

To Stan's great relief, Jack turned out to be telling the truth. Stan's first job didn't end with him shot and dumped overboard. Later that day, Stan told Campbell, "Lorne, if it was anybody else but you, I'd have been gone."

Mornings often meant breakfast in the dining room of a Cornwall hotel, where they could expect to see RCMP officers eating a few tables over, close to members of the military. As a professional courtesy, smugglers and police generally left each other alone while getting ready for their workdays, except to perhaps say hi.

Sometimes, Campbell's party was joined by Dwayne, a Mohawk who would carry on an entire conversation using only different inflections and combinations of "huh." Dwayne seemed to assume he could behave with total impunity, and from what Campbell saw, he was correct, as he was generally surrounded by four or five other Mohawk men who gave the impression they would proudly die for him. On occasion, Dwayne placed a big bowl of cocaine on the table, in plain view of other diners, and snorted a long line, as if this were a normal part of anyone's breakfast.

Like the operators of many a thriving business, the smugglers threw a company Christmas party, with a live band and presents and prizes under a tree. First prize at the "Smugglers' Ball" was a four-by-four truck, while the runner-up received a high-speed cigarette boat.

That night at the banquet, a blond woman came on to another woman at Campbell's table. When a love connection wasn't made with her, the blonde made a pass at Campbell, who also rejected her. It's not pleasant when your partner publicly tries to stray from you. It adds insult to injury when your partner attempts to stray—with both genders—and is rejected by both right in front of you while your peers watch in amusement. So it wasn't surprising that the husband of the blond woman didn't react well when Campbell told her to cut it out. "They were swingers," Campbell says.

No sooner had Campbell brushed her off than the husband sucker-punched him in the nose. Campbell responded with a stiff left, then threw him down the stairs. There, the husband found himself questioned by Stan from the Oshawa Choice, who was working security for the soiree.

"What happened to you?" Stan asked.

"I got into a fight with Lorne."

Out of loyalty to his friend, Stan caught him hard in the head with a karate-style roundhouse kick. They were on slushy ground and both fell over, which embarrassed Stan.

The brawling aside, it was an enjoyable evening, even though Campbell didn't win the truck or the speedboat and someone stole envelopes of cash from a hotel room that were intended as gifts for attendees. "That was a good party."

If Campbell had known the identities of some of his partners in the smuggling enterprise, the level of organization wouldn't have been so surprising. Working alongside the bikers, Mafiosi, Native gangsters and Asian gang members were top-level executives of the tobacco industry. In an effort to exploit the high taxes on cigarettes, tobacco executives were selling large caches of contraband smokes to smugglers through middlemen. This allowed the businesspeople to work both the legitimate and the illegal ends of the multi-billion-dollar tobacco market. In December 1998, executives in the Northern Brands International unit of the RJR Nabisco Holdings Corporation pleaded guilty in Federal District Court in Binghamton, New York, to criminal charges stemming from a scheme to smuggle cigarettes into Canada through the Akwesasne Reserve and avoid both Canadian and American taxes.

Sometimes Campbell rode shotgun on loads bound for Chinese- and Vietnamese-born criminals in upscale Toronto neighbourhoods. He arrived at dawn, and the people receiving the loads were precise about the time; showing up a little early or a little late wasn't permitted, and often Campbell had to cool his heals at a nearby McDonald's restaurant while waiting for his time. Then the truck would be backed into a lane-way. Some of those lanes were so narrow he had to retract the truck's mirrors so it would fit. Someone dropped a tarp in front and in back of the truck and Campbell remained inside in the dark as it was unloaded. No words were exchanged with whoever was picking up the cigarettes, and within fifteen minutes—not much longer than it takes to drive through a car wash—he was back on the road.

Campbell also acted as a bodyguard when money was exchanged, making sure there were no rip-offs when cash was laid out on the table. For two weeks in October 1993, he was paid to stay in the west end of Toronto, watching television in a Holiday Inn bar near Highway 401 as the Blue Jays tried for their second straight World Series title. Campbell wasn't a big baseball fan, but he still got caught up in the excitement when Joe Carter homered for his series-winning run.

A few problems cropped up when some junior members of Campbell's side routinely came up a couple of hundred dollars short. A former Vietnamese soldier who was receiving the money suggested Campbell help one of the offending men improve his counting. "You take one of them. You take him and snip his finger off," he said, sounding as if he were giving tips on how to prune a rose bush. He wanted the offender to confess that he had been skimming money. "If he don't talk, you snip off his other finger," the former soldier continued. If there was still no confession, he advised, "You snip off his wrist."

This was too much even for Campbell. He knew they shouldn't steal, but he had got to know them on ironworking jobs and didn't think they were bad guys.

"Slow down," he said. "They don't need that."

It was clear the former soldier was speaking from personal experience.

"He's serious," Campbell says. "He ain't trying to scare me. This guy's done it. He wants me to do it. He was not excited. He was saying, 'This is how you do it.'"

Throughout the summer, the atmosphere in Akwesasne smuggling circles took on an increasingly Wild West flavour. Once, on-reserve gangsters who were standing just a few feet from Campbell opened fire with machine guns at an army helicopter overhead. The pilot clearly didn't see or hear what was happening, as he hovered dangerously nearby. Campbell exploded at the gunmen.

"If you shoot this down, they will bomb us," he warned.

Some of the Natives got too familiar for his liking and started calling him Harley Man. Campbell had never been big on nicknames and wasn't starting now, especially with people from outside the club. "I said the next time you call me Harley Man, I'll stab you in the throat."

Just the sight of a Mountie sitting in his cruiser was enough to enrage Dwayne one day. "Cookie, go down there and beat him up," he ordered a Blackfoot from out west.

Cookie seemed eager to begin his assignment, but Dwayne called him back for a few minutes. "Hey, wear your war paint," Dwayne ordered.

"It wasn't a joke," Campbell recalls. "Cookie goes down with his war paint, drug him out of the car and beat him, and nothing was done about it."

One afternoon in the summer of 1993, Campbell was on the reserve with two of his Native contacts as they talked about selling guns to a couple of white strangers. Campbell had a bad feeling about the strangers, and sent one of the Choice members to follow them. He reported back that they had driven to a fast food restaurant, where several police cars soon appeared.

There had been increased heat from the police after someone threatened the life of Cornwall's mayor—twice—and opened fire with an automatic rifle on a city building. Tensions were stoked by the shooting of a Québécois smuggler in the stomach for refusing to hire Natives to work with him. "I was on parole and my instincts told me it was time to move on. They hated to see me go, but understood and are still friends. I just wish I could have been there a year earlier."

The money was great, but Campbell didn't second-guess his decision to leave. He didn't fancy any more prison time and he had already made enough to buy a new Harley and a nice headstone for Charmaine's grave. He hired a stoneworker to chisel into the granite the image of an owl gracefully landing "Charmaine collected owls, stuffed owls. Always. I just started getting her owls. She'd buy them everywhere she went."

CHAPTER 24

Mostly Happy Trails

Larry, you just about shot my dick off.

LORNE CAMPBELL on things almost going horribly wrong at a party

The May Two-Four long weekend is always a big one for Canadian bikers, as they're expected to have their motorcycles up and running by then. It marks the official start of riding season, just as Sarasota Springs mark the full stride of race season for horse-happy bluebloods in the American South.

"Do you want to go to a party with me?" Campbell asked Charmaine's friend Evelyn in 1993, before the May 24 weekend.

Evelyn balked.

"Come on. Come on. You're going."

Evelyn was a petite, pretty blonde with a natural smile who grew up on a farm near the Georgian Bay community of Midland. She ran track and played basketball at school and taught gymnastics at the YWCA. Perhaps her best sport was barrel racing in rodeos, a difficult test of horsemanship in which a rider directs her mount around a cloverleaf pattern of plastic or metal barrels in the fastest possible time. Evelyn was a strong rider. She could ride horses on the farm with no saddle or bridle. Campbell was particularly impressed by how she could get a horse to rear up on command, like a movie cowgirl, and expresses his admiration in a way befitting his past: "She does wheelies with the horses."

When she was fifteen, a photographer at the local paper took a shine to her and made her "Girl of the Week." She wasn't an eager subject. In the photo, her expression is somewhere between annoyed and threatened, and it appears she's almost being stalked as she wraps herself in a denim jacket and turns away from the prying lens.

As an adult, Evelyn was a volunteer for Child Find of Canada and Meals on Wheels and worked as a shift manager at Mitsubishi Electronics in Midland. She was also a sucker for any kind of stray or mistreated animal, and was rejected as a Humane Society volunteer when she voiced her strong opposition to euthanizing animals, saying she would take strays home with her instead. Campbell took to calling her Evie May—a nickname Vallentyne's wife, Brenda, had already coined for her—after Elly May Clampett, the animal-loving beauty on the *Beverly Hillbillies* sitcom.

Eventually, Evelyn stopped balking at Campbell's invitation to attend the May 24 party. "I wanted him. I was just reeling him in. I had him all the time. I just made him work for it."

Campbell packed his guitar and collected Evelyn. They stopped for a beer at one of his old haunts, the biker-friendly Atherley Arms hotel outside Orillia. The Arms could have been renamed the Armpit, as it reeked of stale cigarettes and ten-cent draft from generations past. There was a stage for strippers, who also provided private lap and couch dances for a fee. Campbell and Evelyn headed far back from the stage area—or "Perverts' Row"—to enjoy their beer.

A stripper's head snapped up when they sat down. She stopped mid-dance to wave at Campbell. Then, when her set was over, she pulled on a see-through housecoat and joined them, her back to Evelyn. Soon, their visitor went back onstage and resumed her show. "Oh, I know her from years ago," Campbell told Evelyn.

If not for her friendship with Charmaine, Evelyn would likely never have been drawn into Campbell's circle. It didn't take her long to learn that dating a biker wasn't like going out with a stamp collector or curler or anyone with a more regular passion. Campbell was old school and wore his club colours whenever he rode his Harley. In the winter of 1994, he was with Evelyn, wearing his Satan's Choice vest at the Highwayman Hotel in Orillia, when three men clearly felt the need to provoke him rather than just enjoy the hockey game on television. They kept bumping into Evelyn and her chair, as if begging for a response. "I just had enough of that," Campbell recalls. "Said, 'What the fuck do you think you're doing?' . . . Where there's a lot of people, I always picked out the biggest guy. That's my technique."

Campbell didn't wait for an answer. "I knocked him off his chair. There's blood all over the place. He's crying."

Campbell looked down at the man blubbering on the floor. "Look at you, you baby." Then Campbell turned to the other two men and said, "Do you really want a part of this?"

They didn't. Not long after that, the police arrived. The waitress stuck up for Campbell, while the bloodied man continued to cry. The police left without pressing charges, and the three men bought Campbell and Evelyn drinks.

On another excursion, they rode northwest to Thunder Bay, where they stopped for an oil change and a visit to the Choice clubhouse. It should have taken just half a day. They found the clubhouse empty, and when they tried to leave, the door wouldn't open. Campbell yanked it hard and it still didn't move. They were locked inside and he realized they would need a key to get out.

Evelyn contemplated jumping off the balcony, but it was a major fall even for a former gymnast. Had she survived that, she'd still need to scale a steel wall surrounding the premises. They were marooned for a day and a half with nothing to eat but a few chips and other munchies, until Campbell saw a man on the street and yelled at him to go to one of the members' houses and send someone back.

Larry Vallentyne had left the Choice in good standing in 1987 and remained a particularly good friend of the club. But a bullet fired in jest by a friend is just as dangerous as one from an enemy. So Campbell wasn't too happy when Vallentyne brought a loaded .38 revolver and a .22 semi-automatic pistol to a party at his house in 1994.

Evelyn was sitting on Campbell's knee and Vallentyne was seated at the other side of the table. "All of a sudden it went off. Right through the chair."

Campbell couldn't help but worry that the shooting wasn't over. "It was a semi-automatic. The next shot is ready to go."

"Larry, do you realize what you did? You just about shot my dick off, Larry."

Vallentyne had the .22 in his hand and the .38 tucked in his belt.

"Give me the gun, Larry."

Vallentyne wasn't quick to respond, most likely because he wasn't even close to sober.

Campbell pressed his point. "Larry, you almost shot my dick off. I don't want you to do that again, bro."

To a sober man, that would have sounded more than reasonable, but Vallentyne was nowhere near reasonable at the time. He paused for a few seconds, although it felt much longer to Campbell.

"Yeah, okay," he said finally.

Another time, Campbell and Evelyn were at the home of Vallentyne and his wife, Brenda, along with Choice member Doug Hoyle and a striker. The striker remained outside with the wives on the deck as Campbell, Vallentyne and Hoyle went into the garage to talk. There, they sat around a small round table.

"Put the pistols down," Campbell ordered.

They were all good friends, but it was generally better to discuss things without loaded guns, especially when there was booze around.

Three guns were placed on the table.

Campbell emptied them all into the baseboard of the garage, firing almost two dozen shots. "Now we're even. We can sit here and talk."

The striker had no way of knowing what was going on inside the garage. It was also forbidden for a striker to question the actions of senior members. He could only imagine what Campbell was doing to his old friend as he heard the bursts of gunfire. "He was just white," Evelyn recalls. "It was over for twenty minutes and he still hadn't got his colour back. He looked like he wanted to run."

Evelyn tried to lighten things up by noting that she had just bought new tires for her Firebird. "All I could say was, 'He better not put a hole in those tires or he's paying for them.'"

The striker didn't laugh.

Despite the happiness of his new relationship, Campbell couldn't stop thinking about Comeau and Sauvé, still serving their life terms. Sauvé was now spending some of his time visiting schools, warning students to stay clear of a life of crime. He paid the $300-a-course tuition for psychology and criminology classes with the $5.10 a day he was paid for working in the store at Frontenac minimum-security institution in Kingston. He also sold wooden figures he carved in prison. Earning his tuition was tough, and so were the lockdowns that followed stabbings or other disturbances when he was trying to study.

By February 1994, there were signs that people on the outside were listening to Comeau and Sauvé. They had been in prison almost fifteen years, and now had the support of the Association in Defence of the Wrongly Convicted, whose director was Rubin (Hurricane) Carter, a top contender for the world middleweight boxing crown who served nineteen years in prison in the United States for a triple murder he did not commit.

Campbell attended an AIDWYC conference in Toronto where Comeau's and Sauvé's stories were told to assembled lawyers and activists. That night, Campbell shared drinks in his room with Subway Elvis (a.k.a. Michael McTaggart), an Elvis impersonator who had once been a fixture of sorts at the Yonge and Bloor subway stop in Toronto. Subway Elvis was wrongly convicted and jailed for twenty months for armed robbery, and his life had spiralled downwards into substance abuse, not unlike his idol. That night, Subway Elvis helped Campbell drain the hotel mini-bar.

There was room for hope in March 1994, when Comeau was granted a judicial review aimed at winning an early parole hearing. The review heard from a psychologist who called him a "very, very low risk to society." The next month, Comeau's parole eligibility was cut from twenty-five to seventeen years. He had already served fifteen years and four months, which made him eligible for full parole in less than two years.

He was also able to apply immediately for unescorted day passes from Warkworth Institution, east of Peterborough.

Good news arrived for Sauvé as well, in May 1994. A jury ruled that he was eligible for an immediate parole hearing, after hearing that he had been a model inmate. He was the first prisoner at Collins Bay to be awarded a degree from Queen's University, earning his BA in psychology in 1987. He was working on a master's degree in criminology at the time of the jury's ruling.

One way of following the relationships between bikers is by their tattoos. Another is by murder plots. In 1995, Campbell and Evelyn rode with Brian Beaucage's widow, Valerie, and Valerie's common-law husband, Ollie Nelson. Ollie was the brother of Skinny Nelson, the man who shot Wayne Kelly between the eyes. Wayne Kelly was the biker who had tried to enlist Campbell to murder Beaucage while in prison. Now, Campbell and Evelyn were on good terms with Valerie, even though Campbell had briefly plotted to murder her late spouse. Aside from his short-lived bid to murder the man, Campbell had considered Beaucage a valued friend.

The two couples rode up to a bar near Sault Ste. Marie and ordered a round of drinks. Three Outlaws were there, including Randy Robitaille, who was also connected to the group through a murder plot. Robitaille had been charged with trying to shoot Beaucage outside a strip club in London.

"They were obviously packing," Campbell says. An Outlaw behind Campbell had his leg on a stool and kept pulling back his long coat so that they could clearly see the pistol stuffed into his waistband. Ollie and Valerie quickly recognized the Outlaws, and Ollie followed Campbell into a washroom.

"We've got to leave," Ollie said.

"I ain't leaving," Campbell replied. "I just ordered a tray of beer."

Leaving in a hurry would have been humiliating and a profound show of weakness, and any display of weakness is a dangerous thing in the biker world. Aside from that, an early exit really would be a waste of good beer.

The Outlaw behind Campbell kept patting his pistol, an annoying habit in any situation.

"Sit down at the fucking table. Don't stand behind me like that."

The Outlaw sat down.

When the tray of beer was emptied, Campbell and his group got up and left. Valerie was riding her own Harley Low Rider with "In memory of Bo" painted on the gas tank, while Evelyn rode on the back of Campbell's Harley.

The Outlaws had got into a pickup truck, and on a remote stretch of road it pulled ahead of Campbell's party. There were no street lights, and everything around them was darkness, except for their headlights, the truck's tail lights in the distance ahead, and the stars and moon above. If anything happened out here, the only witnesses would be owls and chipmunks. Just ahead of the bikes, gunfire flashed from the back of the pickup.

"Did you see that?" Ollie yelled.

"Yeah, I see them."

Some of Campbell's party had to pee because of the beer.

"What do we do if they come shooting?" Ollie asked.

"Run," Evelyn offered.

"See those trees?" Campbell said. "That's where I'm going."

Evelyn recalls: "All I could think of was, 'If he's hit, I'll drag him off the road. Which side should I drag him to?'"

Campbell pretended to talk on a cellphone, hoping this would signal that reinforcements were on the way and push the Outlaws to back off. Hopefully, the men in the truck wouldn't realize there was no cellphone reception in the area. That done, there didn't seem to be a better option than to ride ahead into the darkness. Says Evelyn: "You couldn't just stop because then you're a sitting duck. But you don't know if they're waiting down the road."

Campbell's party stopped at a motel in the remote town of Wawa, where Campbell slept well while Ollie spent the night at the window.

"They aren't going to attack us in a public place," Campbell said.

"I didn't know if they were shooting to kill us. They didn't know if we were carrying weapons. I was known to carry a weapon at the time." That day, however, he was carrying just a knife. Every biker has heard the saying that you don't bring a knife to a gunfight, even if it was

Campbell's military replica model with "One shot, one kill" engraved on its seven-inch blade.

In 1995, the Outlaws weren't the only concern. That summer was one of serious tensions between the Satan's Choice and the Loners, who had a club north of Toronto that included several former members of the Choice. Frank (Cisco) Lenti, a long-time biker and tow truck operator, was at the core of the tensions. Lenti had left the Loners for Italy in the wake of bitter club infighting. It was also a good time to leave because of a police probe of the underworld after former Satan's Choice member Cecil Kirby decided to turn police agent.

Upon his return to Canada, Lenti formed a group called the Diabolos, who were quickly absorbed into the Choice. This infuriated the Loners, and the summer of 1995 saw a half-dozen bombings directed at biker businesses—including a bar, a shop specializing in motorcycle repairs and a tattoo parlour—and a rocket launcher attack on the Toronto Choice's Kintyre Avenue clubhouse. Three Loners were shot but not seriously injured in Woodbridge, and the home of a Choice member in Kitchener was hit with two Molotov cocktails.

Then, around ten in the morning on August 25, Lenti put his key in the ignition of his midnight blue Ford Explorer, parked in the laneway of his red brick house. He lived just across the street from a Montessori elementary school and just a hundred metres down Kipling Avenue from the Loners' clubhouse. The noise of the explosion that followed startled people for blocks. Lenti survived the attack, but just barely, as parts of his back, legs and buttocks were gone forever. Some cops started calling him a half-assed biker, but never to his face.

Campbell and Evelyn were entertaining a visitor from the Loners and his wife in their home when they received a phone call informing him that the Choice was now at war with the Loners. Campbell turned to his guest and announced, "Sorry, Rob, but you've got to go." Evelyn gave the Loner's wife a sweater, as it was a cold day, and they left with a smile, not bitterness. "I was laughing. I said, 'Fuck, sorry, I can't have you here.'"

Campbell had discussed a "no-war zone" north of Highway 7 in York Region with local Loners, to keep the violence from getting too personal or close to home. He also instructed Evelyn to take a flashlight and check under her car from now on before starting it up. "I was always security-wise about Ev. At that time, any enemy that showed up unannounced at my home would have died where they stood." Knowing Campbell's frame of mind, Evelyn was jolted when a half-dozen Keswick Loners rode up to their home. She didn't know he had reached a deal to patch them over to the Satan's Choice.

The initial phase of the patch-over took place in his garage. "They all came there with Loners patches that night and we made them Satan's Choice." Then Campbell turned to their chapter president and said, "You're not president anymore. I am." He remembers, "There was the party in my garage and it moved over to the clubhouse in Keswick. It continued on for many months, with booze in our stomachs and telltale white powder on our noses."

There were disputes with other clubs at the time, but nothing that involved bullets, bombs or rocket launchers. Campbell spotted riders wearing a patch for something called the Eagle Riders MC, and also Straights Inc-1995 M.C., Lakeshore Area, Clean & Sober. The patch for the latter was done in turquoise and baby blue, with a graphic of playing cards, and looked like something for a seniors' Wednesday night bowling league, not an outlaw bike club. He stopped them and confiscated their offending patches. It wasn't like the 1960s, when a sound beating often accompanied a patch-pulling. Now it was a polite, if terse, transaction, as if the soft-core bikers should have known better and Campbell was a bylaw officer merely doing his job. "They'd say nothing."

CHAPTER 25

Milestones

There were two guys snorting cocaine right beside a [police] cruiser. It was unmarked.

LORNE CAMPBELL describing his wedding reception

Bernie (The Frog) Guindon retired from the Choice in 1996 at age fifty-four. He exited in good standing, ushered out by a growling quarter-mile run of chrome and leather that snaked north from Oshawa into the quaint lakeside town of Port Perry for a two-day camp-out and field day. It was a no-bottles-or-pets event, with French toast, Polish hot dogs, hamburgers, chili and beef on kaiser buns for sale, and donations accepted for a local food bank. Campbell was riding alongside Guindon at the head of the pack, and at one point he turned to him and said, "Check it out, Frog. Stand up on your bike and look around."

"What? What?" the Frog said.

"Check it out."

Guindon had always been the one to tell Campbell to look in his mirrors when he was riding so that he could fully enjoy the scenery. "He got me doing that once for a sunset. 'Look in your mirror to see how beautiful it is.'" This time it was Campbell's chance to return the favour, as he asked Guindon to look out over the club he had revived back in the

1960s. "It was nice, happy. Everybody had to stop. He could just check them all out. Soak it in."

The next summer, it was Campbell's turn to retire in good standing from the Satan's Choice, after nine straight years as Oshawa chapter president. There was no dramatic or even specific reason for his departure. It was just his acknowledgement that something had faded away. He realized he wasn't putting in 100 percent anymore, and in his world you had to be 100 percent 1 percent. As someone who left in good standing, he was still allowed to attend parties, but he and Guindon weren't obligated to attend meetings and events. Since each of them left in good standing and had a quarter-century with the club, they were also permitted to keep their club colours; they just weren't permitted to wear them anymore.

To mark Campbell's retirement, there was a party planned called A Run of Memories. All of the outlaw clubs in Ontario—except, of course, the Outlaws—attended. To get there, Campbell led a procession of club members and friends on his brand new 1997 Harley Classic. They first rode up Simcoe Street through Oshawa, a massive re-enactment of the Simcoe Street parades by the Phantom Riders that had so impressed him as a child. Then they wound through Durham Region and west to their eventual destination of Brown Hill in East Gwillimbury, north of Toronto. The pack grew as they rode along, pulling in current and former members of the Vagabonds, Para-Dice Riders, Red Devils, Last Chance and other clubs, as well as friends and supporters. Some 150 Harley riders finally arrived at the field day site, under the eyes of officers circling in an OPP helicopter.

Mae Boardman, a local fortune teller who read tea leaves and tarot cards, was duly impressed. She had a special connection to the event, as her son Tim had been a Choice member known as "Grizzly," and was buried with his Harley after he was killed in a car accident in 1979.

"Isn't that nice, Lorne?" Mae said. "They even gave you a helicopter escort."

"I didn't have the heart to tell her it wasn't a nice escort."

———

Campbell's fiftieth birthday on September 2, 1998, was another chance to get together with members, past members and friends. There were country and rock bands present, and speakers were set up around his and Evelyn's property in Port Bolster. Campbell himself got onstage to sing something—probably "House of the Rising Sun" again. "There were more people on our property than lived in Port Bolster," Evelyn recalls. "It went all night and the next day."

There was one unpleasant incident when a guest flashed a handgun and Campbell was too into party mode to sort things out himself. "I said, 'You guys go and look after that, please.' So Larry Vallentyne went out and knocked him out. There might have been other guns there, but I would have known about them. As long as I know about it, it's okay."

Among those attending was Bill (Scotty) Dunn from the Para-Dice Riders. Scotty used to joke to Campbell that he was going to take him to Scotland someday so he could show him pubs with "No Campbells Allowed" signs over their front doors. Dunn belonged to the MacDonald clan, and some of the MacDonalds apparently still hadn't got past an ugly incident in 1692 called the Massacre of Glencoe. That's when seventy-eight unarmed MacDonalds were slaughtered by soldiers led by Captain Robert Campbell of Glenlyon. What made it worse was the abuse of hospitality involved in the preamble to the slaughter. The victims were wined and dined for a week until their guard was suitably lowered. It didn't lessen the hatred felt by Clan MacDonald that only seven actual Campbells (none of whom were named Lorne) were involved in the bloodbath.

When Dunn made these offers, Campbell would reply, "Sure as hell, after a few drinks you would be saying, 'Lorne, tell them your last name.'"

It was a joke between them that seemed to improve with age, like good Scotch whisky. And so it was with a great deal of pain that Campbell heard that Scotty had crashed his bike and suffered severe brain damage in an accident near Sudbury, riding home from Campbell's birthday party. His girlfriend was badly injured as well.

Scotty was strapped to a hospital bed in Sudbury when Campbell arrived to see him.

"I want a drink," Scotty said.

"I can't give you a drink," Campbell replied.

"Untie my hands."

"I can't."

"Untie my hands."

"Scotty, I'm sorry, I can't."

Scotty noticed a door in the corner of his room. His tone was now conspiratorial, like that of a gangster in an old movie. "Lorne, where does that door go to?"

"I don't know."

"Check it out for me."

Campbell checked it out. "It's a set of stairs."

"We're out of here tonight."

"Okay, Scotty."

Campbell left his friend in the care of the hospital. He was eventually untied and allowed to leave the bed, but Scotty was never the same.

Psssh.

Psssh.

Campbell was intrigued by the soft hissing sound at a party at "Hells Half Acre," the waterfront property at Caesarea, west of Toronto, in 1999. "I'm looking at a half-dozen Hells Angels. They've all got balloons. I'm thinking they're going to hang them up. Decorating. Half an hour later they've still got them. Nurget [senior Hells Angel Walter Stadnick] comes over and says, 'It's nitrous oxide.'"

Nitrous oxide isn't to be confused with helium, which can make an imbiber sound like Donald Duck. Nitrous oxide's also known as "laughing gas" or "sweet air," and it's used in surgery and dentistry, as well as for boosting the power of rockets and engines. It wasn't a new or novel way of getting high, having been a mainstay of naughty British upper-class parties in the late eighteenth century. The bikers liked it because it gave them a powerful buzz that only lasted a couple of minutes. "That was the first time I tried it, and I didn't get anything out of it. Didn't do it right, I guess. I've never heard of it except at parties. All you hear is *pssh pssh*. A lot of guys don't like to drink and drive. Half an hour later you can drive."

Campbell and Evelyn decided to make it official and get married on May 27, 2000. There wasn't anything sentimental about the date, just that it was after the May Two-Four weekend, when every club in the province had a run. At first they planned a small, relatively quiet affair, but somewhere along the way it took on a life of its own. "Every time Lorne came back from a party, there was another chapter invited," Evelyn recalls.

They chose to have the wedding in Baysville, in Muskoka cottage country north of Toronto, where they could find cottages for some two hundred guests. There was a minor hiccup when they realized that the banquet hall they had rented was in the same building as the local Ontario Provincial Police detachment, but there wasn't much choice in the area, and OPP surveillance was a given anyway. At least this way they would save the taxpayers gas money. In the end, the police weren't a problem. "They were good. There were two guys snorting cocaine right beside a cruiser. It was unmarked."

There were tuxes and club colours, and Campbell sang "Today I Started Loving You Again" by country stars Merle Haggard and Bonnie Owens. Among the invited guests were plenty of Satan's Choice and Vagabonds, but no Hells Angels, since the Satan's Choice had a non-association rule regarding them at the time, stemming from a drug debt dispute in Thunder Bay. To celebrate Campbell's nuptials, his old Oshawa clubmate Stan rode north from Durham Region with his gift flung over his Harley, wrapped in a blanket.

"Guess what this is?" asked Stan.

Stan was the same member who had unsuccessfully tried to hide an M1 assault rifle in a tree behind the Oshawa clubhouse and who worked with Campbell in security at Akwesasne.

"It's a fucking rifle," Campbell replied.

"How the fuck did you know?" asked Stan, genuinely surprised that another of his firearms had been detected.

There was a minor glitch when Evelyn tossed her garter into the crowd as part of a good-luck ritual. The garter had bullets tucked into it and the biker who caught it was on parole stipulations, banning him from possession of weapons or ammunition. Fortunately, police surveying the event let it pass.

In September 2000, Gary (Nutty) Comeau finally walked free of prison after twenty-one years inside. Comeau was forty-eight years old and the last of the Port Hope Eight to be released, as Rick Sauvé had been granted his parole the previous year. They had both maintained their innocence from the time they were led into prison until the day they walked out; but, in true one-percenter fashion, neither pointed a finger at Campbell or anyone else, even if he'd been publicly pointing one at himself.

By this time, their former co-accused Armand (In the Trunk) Sanguigni had been dead for close to two decades. Sanguigni was found in October 1984 in his semi-detached home in a working-class neighbourhood of west Toronto, alongside his common-law wife, Katalin Dobrovolszky. A hypodermic needle lay nearby. "It could be murder-suicide, a double suicide, a drug overdose—we don't know at this point," a police spokesperson said. No one was ever charged with the deaths and bikers assumed it was a misadventure with heroin, the drug Sanguigni was so confident he could control.

Another of the Port Hope co-accused, Campbell's long-time friend Larry (Beaver) Hurren, died in a motorcycle accident in 1996. He was riding towards a dead end, which left him a choice of going either left or right. He often travelled on that road, but for some reason Beaver shot straight ahead, dying when his bike crashed into a tree. On the gas tank of Beaver's crashed Harley were the words "Justice in Ontario," the title of the Steve Earle song about the Matiyek trial and the nineteenth-century massacre of the Donnelly family.

In the fall of 2000, Campbell got a phone call from Mark Stephenson, the millwright who had succeeded him as president of the Oshawa

Satan's Choice chapter. Stephenson gave Campbell the news that the Hells Angels had offered his chapter full membership in their club. It was part of a mass patch-over that would absorb the Choice into the Angels, if the Choice agreed. Stephenson wasn't sure how Campbell would take this. It was a chance to be part of something global, since the Angels had more than 3,600 members on five continents. It also meant the end of the road for the once fiercely proud, all-Canadian Satan's Choice Motorcycle Club.

Campbell liked the idea. He had tried to get the Angels into Ontario a decade earlier, when he and Guindon and others rode out to Sorel to make their pitch. In Campbell's view, it helped that the Hells Angels still hadn't made peace with the Outlaws.

"Go for it," Campbell told Stephenson. "It's the biggest and best club in all of the world."

Not long after he got the call from Stephenson, Campbell too got a call from the Angels, along with his old Satan's Choice mentor Bernie (The Frog) Guindon. They were both still part of the Choice brotherhood, even if they weren't still members. Campbell and Guindon talked about it on the phone. Once, they had both been particularly against American-based clubs, but the world had changed and they didn't want to be left behind. "It's a club with charters anywhere in the world," says Campbell. Guindon felt some obligation to accept an Angels patch. It would be a signal to others in smaller clubs that joining the Angels was the way of the future. "We had to follow," says Guindon. "We had no other alternative in a sense. You are trying to keep your guys together."

There could be severe health risks if current Choice members simply blew off invitations to join the Angels. The president of a Winnipeg club who didn't want to join the Angels had recently been murdered. There weren't any convictions for the killing, but it was only natural to wonder if he was killed because he opposed assimilation.

The move meant there would be no Satan's Choice left from the club that had given Guindon so much pride. "It was sad, but like everything else, it's progress," Guindon says. "You think you're moving in the right direction, but in a sense you're not because you're taking on somebody else's battle."

In December 2000, Campbell was back inside the Hells Angels' fortress-like bunker in Sorel, northeast of Montreal, this time standing with 167 other Ontario bikers. The Sorel charter was the first for the Angels in the country. It was here that they planted their flag when they moved into Canada in December 1977, building from the membership of the old Popeye club. Campbell had ridden there on a new blue Classic Harley for an event that would change his life.

Eight industrial-strength sewing machines were hauled into the club-house to stitch the winged death head patches onto the new members' vests. For Campbell, it was the chance to see the world, not prestige, that pulled him out of retirement. "The club was in every country. You can travel."

Bikers lined up and waited their turns to receive their vests with the bright new patches on the back. Each man's name was tucked in a pocket of his vest. While most bikers gave black leather vests to the sewing crews, Campbell had handed in a denim one, a tip of the hat to his old Choice days, when denim was the style. All the new members were also given brass death head pins of a winged skull as a final touch. Campbell celebrated inside the clubhouse with whisky, then went outside to catch a ride in an Angels van back to his hotel. By mistake he stepped into the wrong van.

"Hi, Lorne," said a man inside. It was Guy Ouellette, Sûreté du Québec biker specialist.

"What the fuck are you doing?" shouted a Hells Angel from outside the van.

The Angel was hollering at Campbell, who didn't yet realize he had entered a police surveillance van by mistake. The other SQ officers were as stunned as Campbell. He climbed back out of the police van and returned to the Angels' fold for more partying.

Soon, Campbell found himself overseeing the Road Warriors in eastern Ontario. They were an Angels support club built on the remnants of the Demon Keepers, which had been run in the mid-1990s by an enigmatic biker named Dany Kane. Kane's life and death remained a source of mystery inside biker and police circles. He ran a gay singles magazine in Montreal in the late 1990s, which was secretly funded by the Royal Canadian Mounted Police as part of his undercover work against the Hells Angels. Over six years, on and off as secret agent for the RCMP and the SQ, Kane helped justice officials gather information needed to charge some 120 Hells Angels with more than a dozen murders and an assortment of other crimes. He also helped dismantle a drug network that netted $1 billion a year as part of a $2-million deal with the police to rat on his friends. Along the way, he carried out at least two biker hits. Kane's motivations weren't just money. He had never been awarded an Angels patch and was apparently bitter that his bisexual lifestyle inhibited his promotion within biker ranks.

Campbell and others wondered if Kane was behind the blast that accidentally killed eleven-year-old Montrealer Daniel Desrochers on tree-lined rue Adam in Montreal's east end in 1995. For Campbell, it was impossible to swallow that a true club member could do something so sloppy and callous as to detonate a bomb near a school. Angels like Campbell also doubted whether Kane really died of suicide on August 6, 2000, as authorities stated. They're not the only skeptics. Author Daniel Sanger asks in his excellent book *Hell's Witness* why Kane's family members were not allowed to see his body. It was also curious that samples from his body were destroyed before they could be tested by scientists hired by biker defence lawyers, who wanted to verify the cause of death.

Some Angels speculated that Kane had been killed by police and not by his own hand. Others thought he hadn't died at all, and was instead secretly relocated by authorities. Campbell says he was told by former Demon Keepers that they believed he received ten million dollars to move far away, after his death was faked: "They swear to me he ain't dead." Kane's former clubmates can't believe that he was suicidal. "He was not like that," Campbell says.

One of Campbell's new contacts was a man heavily into the porn and adult sex toy business, who was trying to divine how to make money off the Internet. During one meeting, Campbell joked that he was having trouble finding a suitable penis enlarger. His contact gestured towards a woman, who disappeared into another room. "She brings two out. How do I say, 'I was just joking'? I didn't." His new contacts also gave him a thousand Viagra pills to sell. Campbell declined the penis enlarger but took the Viagra, which he gave for free to his friends, spawning obvious jokes about hardened criminals.

Campbell was set up with a stripper agency as well, a business he had tried to run back in the early 1980s. The dancers from Quebec were beautiful professionals, and Campbell was also provided with a business manager. The enterprise seemed like a slam dunk. Providing protection for them was certainly no problem. "We were Hells Angels. Nobody would fuck with us. That's the protection."

The general business arrangement seemed simple. "They [dancers] would just pay us so much a week. They wouldn't pay us by the lap dance. How would we know how many lap dances someone does? They had a place to stay at the storefront. We had beds for them." However, the matter got more complicated when the manager sent from Quebec fell hard off the wagon and began drinking heavily and non-stop. Dancers weren't getting to jobs and money intended for them was going for booze instead. Whenever Campbell dropped by to check on things, there seemed no end to the complaining. What Campbell had hoped would be a fun way to make money was now the source of a string of headaches. Strippers complained of rashes from dirty floors and that their colleagues were stealing their hair products and dance moves and favourite songs. "They'd say, 'You stole my moves. That was my song.' They'd fight over anything." There also was plenty of strong competition in the ever-expanding pole-dance community. Campbell and Evelyn were still living in the Orillia area, and not eager to move down to eastern Ontario to referee stripper cat fights and double-check accounting. Within months, the business withered on the vine.

CHAPTER 26

World Run

We're apolitical. Hells Angels have always been that way. Once you get political, you're going to lose.

LORNE CAMPBELL

Being a Hells Angel meant a chance for Campbell to get out of Canada occasionally and see the world, but there were limits. Club members were barred from entering the United States, Australia and New Zealand. The Angels had charters in dozens of other countries, though, where he was still free to visit. "In South Africa, it's way different. It's like the Wild West. I heard of a member who was met at the airport there by a guy with a gun on his back and an ammo belt."

In May 2001, Campbell visited Amsterdam for the first time. His plan was to carry on to Paris, Nice and then the Côte d'Azur on the French Riviera, site of a new Angels charter and a World Run that would draw some 1,500 international club members. First on his agenda was a stopover at the Amsterdam clubhouse. A Dutch member with a face full of stubble who looked a bit like the Ancient Mariner excitedly told him that they were about to be visited by a Canadian who had been involved in the "Conspiracy of Brothers" case. Campbell realized he meant the shooting of Bill Matiyek and the trials of the Port Hope Eight.

"The guy's going to be here," the Angel told Campbell. "He's here for the France thing in Côte d'Azur."

The case was recognized by outlaw bikers far beyond Canada's borders as an example of extreme brotherhood. Bikers around the globe loved to hear how the Satan's Choice members had refused to testify against each other, even with the looming threat of prison time, while the real shooter tried to take the rap.

"It's me," Campbell said.

"The guy's going to be here," the excited Angel repeated.

Again, Campbell said that he was the guy from the case.

This repeated itself a couple more times, until the Dutch biker finally caught on to what Campbell was telling him. "He just gave me a hug and we talked the rest of the afternoon."

During his Paris stopover, Campbell was in a van with the wife of a German charter president. She looked at the swastika tattoo on his arm and said something to her husband in German. Campbell asked for a translation and was told, "If you come to Germany with that tattoo or lightning bolts, your ass goes to jail." He thought of how his father had fought overseas in World War II and how that sort of tattoo on Canadian bikers was meant just for shock value and not as a political statement. "That's what bikers would do. Part of their facade. Freak out the citizenry." It was at that point that he decided to cover the tattoo on his right forearm with psychedelic artwork.

Campbell and fellow Simcoe County charter members Ian Watson and Tony Biancofiore tried to take a cab from Nice to the Côte d'Azur. The driver spoke no English and they spoke no French. All they could do was say "We're looking for the clubhouse" repeatedly and hope it would somehow sink in. The confused cabbie mistakenly drove them to a country club before finally making it to the World Run site.

The Côte d'Azur charter was less than a year old, but by the time Campbell arrived the clubhouse already had a 1.5-metre hole in the ground inside its outer wall from a bomb lobbed over it by an enemy. The crater notwithstanding, the walled compound was a pleasant spot, just a five-minute walk from the ocean.

One day at the seashore, Campbell got chatting with three English

Hells Angels, one of whom was the president of his charter. The Englishmen produced a packet of white powder, which Campbell assumed was cocaine.

"Want to do a line?" one of them asked.

The package had an odd glow in the Mediterranean sun.

"Want to do some, Lorne?"

"All right," Campbell replied, then snorted about four centimetres of the powder.

"Hey mate, where's that package?" another of the Englishmen asked.

"What do you mean? I did it all."

"Hey mate, that was for all of us!"

Campbell's nose felt as if someone had crawled up inside it with a blowtorch. The Englishmen were laughing. They had plenty more of the potent powder for themselves.

"What was it?"

"Crystal meth, mate."

"Holy fuck, no wonder it shines."

Campbell noted that the European Angels weren't as immersed in criminality as their Canadian counterparts. "Those English guys work for a living. They're tough individuals, very tough guys, but they're not criminals. Most countries are not Hells Angels like we are here. You fuck with them, they'll kill you, I think. Guys from Germany would say, 'Instead of drugs, why don't you start businesses?' They have hotels. In the Netherlands, they have businesses too. They don't understand that in Canada, if you start a hotel or a car business, they're [police, government] right on you. It's not easy. They have their own wine. Their own spirits: Route 81. They have their own cigarettes. It's actually legal. They own whole fucking blocks there. In the Netherlands, they own coffee shops and bars that sell pot. They own whorehouses that are legal. In Canada, we can't do that."

Campbell was in the Côte d'Azur shortly after 9/11, and he didn't get any grief from police, who were bent on stopping terrorists. "The cops don't give you a second look."

It was in France that he was introduced by Angel Rick Ciarnello of B.C. to outlaw biker icon Sonny Barger, the man alternately credited with or blamed for organizing the modern-day Hells Angels' worldwide expansion. Barger was a legend in the Angels' world. In one of many stories about him, he once put a man's hands in a vise and horse-whipped him for stealing his Harley, which he had named *Sweet Cocaine*. He was also something of a marketing phenomenon, with a full range of signature products, including American Legend sunglasses, beanies and Cabernet Sauvignon. Campbell's meeting with Barger was brief, as other bikers were crowding around and one drunken member kept cutting in.

Barger signed a couple of copies of his autobiography for Campbell, one for himself and one for an Angel friend who was about to get married. He was alert and personable, although it was an effort for him to speak after a bout with cancer, since he had to press a valve in his throat whenever he wanted to say something. "He's quite the gentleman. . . . The man's earned his respect big time. Partly for the organizer he is. He doesn't take any shit. *If you fuck with me, I'll fuck back.*"

A year after the patch-over, a tattoo artist came down from Barrie to the Simcoe County clubhouse near Georgian Bay to ink the copyrighted Angels death head onto Campbell and his clubmates. There's a Canadian rule that Angels can only get club tattoos a year after membership, once they have proven themselves worthy. For Campbell, it would be the first of five Angels tattoos.

The one-year anniversary of the patch-over was marked by a provincial Angels convention in Toronto's entertainment district. Bikers were warned by senior club officers to be on their best behaviour. When they went to restaurants wearing their colours, they were told to be pleasant and to tip large. People would be talking and the club wanted the public saying good things.

Campbell was in charge of security for the Simcoe County charter and wasn't surprised when police told Hells Angels spokesman Donny Petersen just before the convention began that there had been a bomb threat in the hotel and that they'd have to immediately leave the building. "Well, that would solve your problems for you, wouldn't it?" Petersen said, suspecting it was just a ploy so that police could plant recording devices in their rooms and throughout the hotel. "No go. Nice try, boys."

No bombs exploded that week at the hotel. There was a media bombshell, however, when Toronto mayor Mel Lastman popped in for a surprise visit, shaking the hand of Simcoe County member Tony Biancofiore. Biancofiore was finance manager for a General Motors dealership, and suspected that Lastman recognized his face from community events. He doubted that Lastman knew before that day that he was also an outlaw biker.

"He walked in and he came towards me," remembers Biancofiore. "I ran towards him. I think we both stuck our hands out at the same time. I was sort of stunned that he was even there. He had that look on his face: almost stunned or in fear. . . . I don't know what he expected."

The mayor accepted a souvenir T-shirt from Biancofiore. The next day, a photo of the handshake was in newspapers across the country, with headlines such as MAYOR HAS DEVIL TO PAY FOR SHAKING HANDS WITH ANGEL; MEL, IT'S TIME TO GO; and HANDSHAKE FROM HELL.

In an effort to quell the shitstorm of bad publicity, Lastman posed for a photo tossing his souvenir Angels support T-shirt into the garbage. This brought a HELLS ANGELS WANT LASTMAN TO APOLOGIZE FOR RUDENESS headline in the *National Post*. Lastman claimed he didn't know that members of the Hells Angels made money selling illegal drugs, and said he only shook Biancofiore's hand because he was afraid. "What am I going to do?" he asked. "Not give them my hand? I'd be afraid not to." Toronto police chief Julian Fantino said the handshaking and media kerfuffle was evidence of the Angels' deft skill in public relations. Many others said it made Lastman look like the consummate buffoon.

In Quebec, the "Handshake from Hell" was considered further evidence of anglo stupidity and insensitivity, as well as the deviousness of outlaw bikers. The timing of the handshake couldn't have been much worse, as the story broke just as a series of biker trials was beginning. Pretrial arguments were to be heard in Montreal in the first-degree murder trial of Maurice (Mom) Boucher for ordering the deaths of two prison guards in 1997. Pretrial proceedings were also under way in Montreal for thirteen other Hells Angels and associates, including

Stadnick. They faced charges including first-degree murder, conspiracy to commit murder, and gangsterism relating to the war with the now-defunct Rock Machine, who morphed into membership in the Bandidos, a major international club.

The mother of Daniel Desrochers, the eleven-year-old Montreal boy who was killed by a pipe bomb during the biker war, called Lastman dangerously naive. "I'm very saddened by the mayor of Toronto," Joanne Desrochers said. "It's like burying your head in the sand. This is a dangerous thing—very dangerous."

While the handshake photo was a unique humiliation for Lastman, it hurt Biancofiore even more. After he was publicly outed as a Hells Angel, he lost his licence to sell automobiles. "It certainly didn't work in my favour."

Much of the horrendous press around the Canadian Angels centred on Boucher, president of the Montreal Nomads charter. Boucher had declared his own personal war on the state, without first consulting the rest of the club. He conspired to kill politicians, a broadcaster, a judge and respected crime writer Michel Auger of the *Journal de Montréal*, among others. For Campbell, it was clear that Boucher had forgotten his place in the world. "Biker wars are biker wars. I've been in them. Participated. Never backed down from the violence. But to have delusions of grandeur that you want to take on the government? We're just Hells Angels and a motorcycle club. We're apolitical. Hells Angels have always been that way. Once you get political, you're going to lose. What happened to Michel Auger is horrendous—a horrendous, cowardly thing to do."

Campbell was tasked with pulling together a Sudbury charter for the Angels. The central Ontario city didn't have any existing charters for one-percenter clubs in the early 2000s, but it did have a lively biker history, including a bloody clash in 1992 between the Choice and Johnny Sombrero's Black Diamond Riders, who had faded into the background but refused to become extinct. The BDR had ostensibly been in town for a baseball tournament when the violence erupted. By the time things cooled, eight members of the BDR were in hospital: four with knife wounds, one shot in the eye and the abdomen, and the others beaten with clubs.

There was also a bizarre incident on December 15, 1996, when someone set off an explosion at the Sudbury police station. Police estimated more than a kilogram of powdered explosives, ignited by a fuse, had been used to blast a hole in the wall of the building. The police station kept on functioning, but the bill for repairs to the station and a bank next door ran to $133,000. Exactly a year later, six Choice members and associates from the Hamilton and Sudbury areas were charged with more than three dozen offences related to the bombing. They included Ion (John) Croitoru, president of the Hamilton chapter of the Choice, a massive product of weight training and steroid abuse who wrestled professionally under the names "Johnny K-9" and "Bruiser Bedlam." Croitoru was one of a new breed of club member. He owned a motorcycle, but Campbell never saw him actually riding it.

K-9 was bizarrely competitive for someone who performed in rigged spectacles. One night inside the Sudbury clubhouse, Campbell defeated him in an Indian leg-wrestling contest and K-9 demanded a rematch. Campbell won again. K-9 demanded another rematch. Again K-9 lost. And again. By now it was tedious for everyone but K-9, who was beside himself. There was no clue rattling about inside his big bald head about why he kept losing, since he was considered by many to be the strongest—steroid-powered—man in the Canadian biker scene and Campbell was considerably smaller, steroid-free and on the senior side of fifty.

"How the fuck do you do that, you cocksucker?" K-9 asked.

"He wouldn't leave me alone," Campbell recalls. "That night he was like a dog following me around."

"There's a technique that your little brain can't understand," Campbell said to K-9.

"You've got to show me," K-9 persisted.

Campbell finally did, just to shut K-9 up. "As soon as you hook, you roll," Campbell said. Then they had another rematch and K-9 finally won. "When I showed him, he almost broke my back."

Police didn't think K-9 and his crew had any particular reason for bombing the Sudbury police station, other than a general unhappiness with law enforcement. Also among those charged was 39-year-old Michael Dubé of Sudbury, who was already in jail awaiting trial for conspiracy to bomb a local nightclub. He had also been a suspect in a 1988 murder. Dubé never made it to trial for the Sudbury bombing, hanging himself in his jail cell in September 1998. "He told somebody he couldn't do any more time."

Attempts to blow up the police station aside, Sudbury became known in biker circles as a hospitable charter. Evelyn cooked up big servings of comfort food for any members passing through, and Campbell supplied free female companionship and booze. A lot of people stayed five or six days, just to soak up the hospitality. "It's often said [in biker circles] if you can't get laid in Sudbury, there's something wrong with you."

Not surprisingly, plenty of men wanted to join the charter, but Campbell was generally unimpressed with the quality of candidates and found himself kicking out a string of them. He preferred to be diplomatic, like a kindly corporate downsizer, and say simply, "It's not working out." That was the hint that it was time to make a graceful exit, before Campbell's patience ran out and he made himself clear with a left hook.

He sounded less kindly when a member posted a picture of Toronto police chief Julian Fantino's home on the club's website. The photo was lifted from a January 2001 edition of the free Toronto listings magazine *NOW*, along with the words "Chief Fantino's suburban bunker." Recalls Campbell: "I freaked when I saw that. I said, 'Get that the fuck off our website today.' Everybody thought it was funny, but I didn't. I thought it was too confrontational. Don't be confrontational towards a man with that much power. We're bikers. Don't think you have that much power in this world."

One full-patch member who stayed on was Sylvain (20/20) Vachon, a former minor league hockey enforcer from Sherbrooke, Quebec. Vachon loved the sport so much he once bought his own hockey team. Eventually, he had to leave the game because no one wanted to fight him, fearing any confrontation on the ice would spill over onto the streets and involve the Hells Angels. His nickname "20/20" came from the American newsmagazine, and it was in reference to the massive publicity his hockey sideline brought him, including a mention in *Sports Illustrated*.

Campbell was also impressed with a striker from Copper Cliff, near Sudbury, named Phil Boudreault. Boudreault had been raised without a father and at a young age assumed the role of man of the house for his mother and two little brothers. He could be a good student when he applied himself, and he could also be a major public menace, as he was quick with his fists and his temper. He channelled his aggression into boxing, fighting for Canada in the light welterweight division at the 1996 Olympics before turning pro, billed as "the Sudbury Sensation."

Boudreault had been with the Satan's Choice while he was boxing for Canada, but kept it low-key so that the Olympic association wouldn't get riled up. Senior members such as Campbell, Doug Hoyle and Bernie Guindon struck him as impressive father figures. "They don't make men like they used to," Boudreault says. "I wish everybody was like that."

He didn't medal at the Atlanta Olympics, but he fought well, winning one match and losing another. He sat beside his daughter and former wife in a Mustang convertible in a parade through Sudbury when local Olympians returned home, waving to fans like a conquering hero. An autograph signing at a wine and cheese party followed, and everything was festive until police arrived with an outstanding arrest warrant.

His ex-wife and daughter were understandably upset by the rude end to the festivities, but Boudreault laughed off the homecoming parade debacle with Campbell, whom he started calling Dad. "I've heard about him since I was a young kid," Boudreault says. "Never anything negative. Always positive, as for the one-percent side. He's just a man standing by his beliefs. He doesn't sway side to side. . . . When I look at him, I see myself as time will pass. . . . I always felt that was me, just an older version of me." Boudreault was also impressed by Campbell's punching power, even in his post-fifty years. "He's got a really, really hard shot. He throws it like it's the last punch he'll ever throw."

Something about Campbell's attitude also clicked with Boudreault. "Life's too short to be asking, 'Can I do this? Can I do that?'" Boudreault respected how Campbell didn't act like a victim when things got rocky, for example during extended stays behind bars. "Lorne gets his time and he never cried about it. Never bitched about it. Just did his time."

Once, at a crowded bar, Campbell bumped into someone or someone bumped into Campbell. Whatever the case, Boudreault immediately corked the stranger with a stiff hook. "Phil, you don't have to do that," Campbell said.

"He bumped into you."

Another evening, Boudreault was at a party with his girlfriend at the clubhouse bar. He earnestly approached Campbell.

"If there's somebody that I want to punch out, can I do it?" he asked.

There are definite rules in the outlaw biker world about whom you can and whom you cannot punch out. If a member hits another member, it can result in as little as a hundred-dollar fine. If two members are fighting, rules forbid the use of weapons and "pile-ons," or others joining in, but kicking, punching, gouging and biting are permissible. If a non-member hits a member, then all rules are off and other members are expected to join in. "Then you'll see a group situation. It's not a pretty sight." When Mother McEwan and others boot-fucked Campbell as he fought with Dave Seguin in 1976 at the Montreal Choice clubhouse, it wasn't just nasty: they were in clear violation of one-percenter rules.

As a senior club member, Campbell had a role in regulating violence, which is why Boudreault showed him the respect of asking him before laying a beating on someone.

"Why's that?" Campbell asked.

"Someone's coming on to my old lady."

"Yeah?"

"Yeah. I have told him [to stop] a couple of times."

"Sure, it's okay then," Campbell said, returning to his beer as Boudreault headed back to the bar.

For some reason, Campbell thought Boudreault was complaining about a non-member sitting at the bar by the fridge. There was no rule against punching out an obnoxious non-member.

"Who do you think it is?" a member asked Campbell.

"That guy at the bar."

"No, it's Terry."

Terry was Terry Pink, a full-patch member. Boudreault was then a "prospect," which was the Hells Angels' equivalent of the probationary rank of striker in the Choice. It was strictly against club rules for a prospect to hit a full member, and yet punching out Pink was exactly what Campbell had given Boudreault permission to do. Making it worse, Boudreault's punches would smash into Pink's face with world-class precision. "Phil was just about to fill him in and I got between them. I explained that I thought it was a different guy." Boudreault respectfully assented to Campbell's wishes and stepped away, leaving Pink with no clue how close he'd come to a righteous pounding.

Campbell then tried to tell Pink to knock it off. He hadn't particularly liked Pink before and now he liked him less, patch or not. "He was arrogant, like his shit doesn't stink."

Boudreault accompanied Campbell overseas in May 2002, when the Hells Angels celebrated the tenth anniversary of their North Coast charter in Holland, which they preferred to call Helland. Amsterdam is a preferred point of entry for bikers going to Europe, and members there are comfortable with their role as biker hosts. There were more than 125 Hells Angels charters in Europe, and the Dutch prided themselves on being unsurpassed in hospitality. "You can't pay for anything. I offered to pay and it was an insult." While the Dutch Angels were hospitable to outsiders, members of the Dutch Nomads charters were often brutal to each other. Campbell was in Holland with Ian Watson of Barrie when Watson felt he needed to say something. "He said, 'I can't believe them Holland Nomads. They punch each other all the time.' I said, 'Don't look behind you, it's happening again.' The [Dutch Nomads] president was punching a guy in the head six times or so."

In Amsterdam, Campbell met a biker from California nicknamed "Tiny" who was bigger than Paul (Sasquatch) Porter of Ottawa, and Porter tipped the Toledos at somewhere close to five hundred pounds. "I couldn't believe the size of the motherfucker. He was the biggest Tiny I had ever seen."

The Dutch bikers loved Boudreault's swagger and suggested that

Campbell give him a death head patch on the spot, signifying full membership in the club. Normally, that's something that's done only after a prospect's home charter holds a vote. Campbell was certain they would approve his membership and was swayed by the enthusiasm of the Dutchmen, several of whom were charter presidents. They were already offering Boudreault free drinks in the clubhouse, even though strikers and hangarounds are expected to refrain from imbibing on club property. "They really liked him. They were treating him like he already was a member."

Campbell asked Boudreault to meet him in what they both like to describe as a "seedy Amsterdam motel room." That's when Campbell welcomed him into the club and handed him a death head patch. It was the silk-threaded version that's popular in Europe, rather than the Canadian cloth model. "He was shocked." Both men revelled in the moment. "He reminds me of when I was younger. He don't back down from anybody. People will make money off of him and his reputation without him even knowing." Says Boudreault: "I don't care if everybody [else] doesn't respect me. As long as he respects me, I can go to bed."

It was while travelling overseas that Campbell got a measure of the respect in which Canadian Hells Angel Walter (Nurget) Stadnick is held in the club worldwide. Stadnick wears "Hell" rather than "Hells" on a patch under his ribs, a comment on the hell he went through when he was severely burned after his motorcycle collided with a car driven by a priest. The accident took place when Stadnick was riding to a biker funeral and the priest was driving to the papal visit. Campbell heard about an incident when another biker in Europe had a "Hell" patch too, and Stadnick successfully ordered the biker to immediately remove it so that he alone could wear it. "He flipped out when someone else wore 'Hell' instead of 'Hells.' [It was like] 'If you've been through the hell I've been through.' He was a god wherever he travelled. I maintain that the reason is that he did everything for the Hells Angels."

It was easy to imagine Stadnick as a wartime general. In a sense that was true, and the war was far from over.

———

245

Like many television watchers across the Commonwealth, Campbell and Evelyn perched themselves on the couch in July 2002 to watch a parade for Queen Elizabeth II, celebrating her half-century on the throne. Nothing about that moment was as interesting as watching her gold-gilded carriage roll past a sea of red and blue bunting and Union Jacks, led by a procession of her subjects. Of particular interest that day was Alan (Snob) Fisher, a full-patch Hells Angel from west London. Snob rode at the head of a pack of fifty motorcycles—one for each year Queen Elizabeth II sat on the throne. Absent from any guest list was Johnny Sombrero, the Toronto biker who had written to the Queen some four decades earlier, asking for a charter to rid Canada of outlaw bikers. "Ev and I were at home watching it from the start just to see the Hells Angels lead the parade. It was a proud moment."

The Bloc Québécois was not amused by the invitation to the Angels to participate in the Jubilee's celebration of alternative culture. The separatist political party had unsuccessfully tabled a motion in the House of Commons asking the Queen to rescind Snob's invitation. For his part, Snob told the press he was honoured and surprised by the invitation, although he shunned a suggestion that he wear a golden helmet or any kind of uniform other than his leather Angels jacket. "I will ride with pride," said Snob.

Campbell and Evelyn particularly enjoyed hearing of rocker Ozzy Osbourne's role in keeping Snob in the parade. When he heard of the movement to boot Snob and some other Angels out of the celebrations, Osbourne reportedly threatened to pull out himself. "I thought it was pretty cool for Ozzy Osbourne to do that. It was the right thing to do."

In defence of Snob's invitation, a Palace representative told the press that he was a successful businessman, not a criminal, noting that he ran a Harley-Davidson shop in west London called Snob's Ultimate Customs. The club had been in England almost a decade longer than in Canada, and it had enjoyed a far gentler ride. There were almost twice as many Hells Angels in Canada as in England, with 450 in the former colony and 250 in England. The English bikers were generally much better behaved, with nothing to compare to the carnage of Quebec's biker war, in which some 170 lives were lost.

English Angels like to note that they were originally invited into the country by no less a personage than George Harrison, "the quiet Beatle." Harrison met some Angels while in California in October and November 1968. A month later, Harrison circulated a memo to Apple Music staff, noting that a dozen or so of the California bikers might soon be dropping into their offices at 3 Savile Row. "Hell's Angels will be in London within the next week, on the way to straighten out Czechoslovakia," he wrote on December 4, 1968, an ambitious reference to undoing the Soviet Union's invasion of Czechoslovakia earlier that year. "There will be twelve in number complete with black leather jackets and motor cycles. They will undoubtedly arrive at Apple and I have heard they may try to make full use of Apple's facilities. They may look as though they are going to do you in but are very straight and do good things, so don't fear them or up-tight them. Try to assist them without neglecting your Apple business and without letting them take control of Savile Row."

The Angels did arrive at Savile Row, although there's no record of the outcome of their plans to "straighten out Czechoslovakia" or even take control of Savile Row. They did tighten up the club's brand in the U.K., however. There were a number of bogus Hells Angels in England at the time, wearing knock-off Angels patches as nothing more than a fashion statement. The bona fide Angels scoped out the situation and two British bikers were sent to San Francisco to prospect with a real Angels charter. On July 30, 1969, they were back in England as charters were granted for South London and East London—the first true Hells Angels charters in Europe. Not long after that, the only people wearing Angels patches in London were true Hells Angels.

Canadians seemed to be corrupting influences on the Angels of the Mother Country. In 1985, Quebec Hells Angel Robert (Snake) Tremblay was found hiding out in a flat in Bermondsey, a neighbourhood of London, fleeing murder charges in the slaughter that year which sent five members of the club's Laval charter to the bottom of the St. Lawrence River in weighted-down sleeping bags. At the time of his arrest, British Angels had provided him with a place to stay and a false passport and had plans to smuggle him to France.

In February 1995, Quebec Hells Angels Pierre Rodrigue and David Rouleau were arrested at a London Hilton hotel while planning to smuggle more than five hundred kilograms of cocaine into England in a scheme that involved Angels pulling together their own fleet of trawlers. A search of their hotel suite netted police contact lists for all of the Angels' twelve British charters.

While the level of criminality of the British Angels was nowhere near that of their Canadian counterparts, it was on the rise. This included a propensity for violence. In January 1998, thirty Angels confronted members of the rival Outcasts in south London with baseball bats, knives, metal bars and a hatchet. Two Outcasts lay dead by the end of the evening, after violence that one witness called "ritualistic."

Despite the occasional spasms of violence, the public face of the Hells Angels in England was more quirky than threatening. For many of their early years, the club's spokesperson was Dr. Ian (Maz) Harris, a Ph.D. in sociology from Warwick University. Dr. Maz certainly looked the role of an outlaw biker, with shoulder-length hair, tattoos, a small beard and wraparound sunglasses. His curriculum vitae as a biker was impossible to challenge. Born in 1949 in Bexleyheath, Kent, Dr. Maz dropped out of school at age fifteen. Not long after that, he founded the London biker club the Anarchists, and then gained membership in the Angels.

Dr. Maz was killed on May 31, 2000, when test-driving an extremely high-powered Buell motorcycle, a subsidiary of Harley-Davidson specializing in racing bikes. As there was only seating for three hundred in the picturesque Church of St. Paulinus in Crayford, Kent, his funeral service was piped outside to mourners. It included a playing of the Doors' "Riders of the Storm" and Richard Burton's reading of Dylan Thomas's play *Under Milk Wood*, which includes the lines, "We are not wholly bad or good/Who live our lives under Milk Wood."

CHAPTER 27

Unwanted Attention

I wanted it to be the way I pictured it in my mind. It never is.

LORNE CAMPBELL

Membership in the world's largest outlaw motorcycle club attracts plenty of attention, much of it unwanted. Campbell was on the porch of his home in rural Baysville, near Orillia, about a year after the mass patch-over to the Hells Angels. He was chilling out and cleaning his 30-30 hunting rifle when his phone rang.

"Who are you?" the caller asked.

"I'm Lorne Campbell."

"I've got a deal for you."

"What are you talking about?"

The caller explained that he wanted to get into the illegal drug dealing business. He sounded as if he was in his early twenties and his tone suggested he was plenty eager, if not wise in the ways of the world.

"I don't do things like that," Campbell said.

The caller babbled on a little longer until the conversation became too annoying for Campbell to continue. He still didn't even know who was on the other end of the line. It sounded like an idiot or a set-up, and neither was welcome.

"Where are you?" Campbell asked. "Get over here."

Not long after that, a stranger rolled up to Campbell's home. Campbell levelled his 30-30 at him.

"Get out of the fucking car."

The man got out of his car.

"Who gave you my fucking name? I'll shoot you. I will shoot you."

The stranger yammered something about a woman he knew who had heard that Campbell was in the Hells Angels. Then he said again that he wanted to get into drug dealing, as if he was at a trade show, inquiring about opening a pita or doughnut franchise.

Campbell demanded to know how the man knew where to find him.

"I googled you."

"Googled me?"

"I googled you."

The man bragged that he could find anybody's address on the Internet.

"You're kidding," Campbell said, then kicked him off his property at gunpoint.

As the Angels expanded, Campbell was getting a reputation for shutting down charters. He ousted most of the Simcoe County charter when he got the feeling that members were hiding behind their patches rather than making the club stronger. He didn't like how several Simcoe County members weren't attending club functions and weren't even riding their bikes. A breaking point came when he was at the bar at a Simcoe club function and a member's wife turned with a smile to her husband and said, "Tell them what happened the other day."

The Simcoe County Angel started laughing, telling how he was getting beaten up in a fight. "He had me down, kicking the shit out of me. All I did was show him my patch and he stopped."

Campbell was blown away by how wrong this was. It was pretty much the opposite of the way things should be, and the man and his wife didn't have a clue. They should be ashamed and yet they were proud, in a profoundly stupid way. They somehow thought it was funny, when the joke was on them. How could they expect anyone to respect the club if they hid behind the patch like this? "I was embarrassed. That's what was protecting him—the Hells Angels patch. [He felt that] it's the club that makes the man. It should be the man that makes the patch."

In a sense, Campbell's philosophy is the outlaw biker version of John F. Kennedy's 1961 inaugural address, in which he said: "Ask not what your country can do for you—ask what you can do for your country." Unfortunately, in Campbell's view, the Angels lowered the brand after the mass patch-over of 2000, in the same way that fake Angels patches had flooded England and degraded the brand back in the late 1960s. "They feel: 'Now I've got power and backing, so I can do anything.' But Hells Angels are smarter than that. Most Hells Angels worldwide are comfortable in their own skin."

The man, and presumably also his wife, wasn't smiling when his charter was shut down and he could no longer take refuge behind a Hells Angels patch.

Campbell was in Amsterdam in 2005, preparing to travel on to Barcelona and Benidorm on the Spanish Riviera for a World Run. He was at the Amsterdam airport with a Dutch member named Harry when Harry got a telephone call.

"Fuck, the Amsterdam clubhouse just burned down," Harry said.

Campbell felt his stomach drop. "What! It couldn't have," Campbell replied, thinking, "I was just there last night. It was intact."

Campbell's mind flashed back to how he had been smoking at the clubhouse bar. Could he have accidentally caused the fire with a cigarette ash or butt? "It was all wood."

"I think I just burned it down," Campbell announced.

He didn't consider hiding his suspicion that he was to blame. "It turned out I was wrong. It was a wiring problem. We found out that in a day or two. I've never ever lied to a brother. Never have, never would."

The Benidorm get-together was in an ancient castle, close to cabins owned by Spanish Hells Angels. Each morning, artists would go onto the beach and build elaborate sand castles, often with religious themes. It was in Spain that Campbell met Hells Angels from the San Bernardino—or

"Berdoo"—charter, east of Los Angeles. San Bernardino is home to two American exports that have become fixtures around the globe: the world's first McDonald's restaurant and the Hells Angels' "Mother" or original charter, formed back in 1948. Campbell told a half-dozen Berdoo members a joke that, when he had shared it with Andre Watteel of the Ontario Hells Angels, had almost made Watteel physically sick. It went something like this: "So I'm screwing my buddy up the ass and he's giving my dick a tug. And then he turns around and kisses me on the lips, the faggot."

The Berdoo Angels proved to have stronger stomachs than Watteel. "One of them fell off his stool, he was laughing so hard."

It was on the Spanish Riviera that Campbell learned his cousin Shawn Campbell had recently got his Angels patch back home at the waterfront property known as Hells Half Acre. Campbell couldn't understand why he hadn't been told in advance so that he could attend. Not long afterwards, he knocked on the door of the Spanish motel room where Shawn was staying.

When the door swung open, Campbell punched Shawn quick and hard. "I fucking gave him one right on the side of the head. He fell."

When Shawn got back on his feet, Campbell said, "Congratulations," and the cousins laughed and shook hands as if the non-invitation and the hard left had never happened. "He's a fighter. He's been there before."

Arriving in Spain with Campbell was an Oshawa prospect known as Sims. If Sims looked nervous surrounded by 1,500 Hells Angels from around the globe at the World Run in Spain, it was totally understandable. Sims was black, while the Hells Angels were close to all-white, like many posh golf and country clubs. California Hells Angels had already told Canadians, in effect, "Send him here and we'll kill him."

The Downtown Toronto charter had an Asian member, who worked on their computers and always seemed to be taking courses. There were a few other members at the World Run who looked black but whose clubs maintained they were really Hispanic or some other non-black colouring that was okay with the Angels.

The English were also pushing to get a black man accepted as a full member of the club. "The guys in England must have loved the guy. We loved Simsy. We fought for it. But it's just a passionate subject. It gets Hells Angels yelling at other Hells Angels at important meetings." The old guard, including Barger, simply wouldn't hear of admitting black members, saying the topic was closed and they didn't want to hear it reopened. When they returned to Canada, Sims was told he would have to leave. "Everyone that met him thought the world of him. He's a great guy."

Not too far from the Toronto Angels' downtown clubhouse on Eastern Avenue in Riverdale was a ragtag group of Bandidos, who gathered occasionally in the basement of a Greek restaurant. The Bandidos Motorcycle Club had absorbed the Rock Machine of Quebec into their ranks, also inheriting their drug turf war with the Hells Angels in downtown Montreal. In the Texas Gulf, where they began, the Bandidos were a serious club, and several of their members had high-paying, demanding jobs in the oil industry. Their new counterparts in Toronto, however, were a pale, sad imitation.

The newly formed Toronto Bandidos defiantly called themselves the No Surrender Crew, borrowing the name from a faction of the Irish Republican Army. Their leader was John (Boxer) Muscedere, a small-town factory worker on disability leave who had been an outlaw biker for less than a decade. He inherited the presidency from Wayne (Weiner) Kellestine when Kellestine was briefly sent to prison on an assortment of drug charges. Now, Boxer was scrambling to hold together a club of misfits who could never hope for Angels membership.

It was a struggle for Boxer to get Canadian members of his motorcycle club to actually ride motorcycles. This mystified Campbell. "Motorcycles are the key. The 'MC' stands for something." Campbell was impressed by the loyalty Boxer displayed towards his clubmates, although it was clearly misplaced, especially with Kellestine. There were plenty of stories about Kellestine, few of them flattering. He had been punched out by a lesbian at a sleazy London, Ontario, bar, crashed a gay pride parade with a collection of fellow white supremacists, and threatened to shoot a disc jockey at a party for playing non-white dance music. He was considered too unstable to reason with or threaten. "A guy like him, you have to kill."

The Bandidos were just an obnoxious presence in Riverdale, mouthing off and acting tough with friends of the Angels. They were annoying enough that the downtown Angels called a meeting with the Bandidos to rein them in. It was held in the basement of the Bandidos' usual Greek restaurant, and Campbell and other Angels were decidedly unimpressed. Campbell didn't pack a gun as they just didn't seem worth the effort. "They looked like drug addicts. I thought, 'Why are we having this meeting? They're not bikers.'" The Ontario Hells Angels couldn't help but wonder what would happen if the Americans at the top level of the Bandidos could see them. "I used to tell people they won't last very long because they're drug addicts. I told the guys they'll implode."

The Canadian Bandidos became more than a mild irritant when they cozied up to the Outlaws. The two clubs tried a show of force at the London, Ontario, motorcycle show at the Western Fair, organized by Larry Pooler, vice-president of the Downtown Toronto charter of the Hells Angels. Ian Watson of the Angels was in a booth when the Bandidos showed up and started taking photos.

"Hey, fuckhead. Take a picture of this," Campbell said.

The Bandido smiled.

"Take a picture of me."

The Bandido stopped smiling.

"You're a fucking coward," Campbell continued.

The cops were there now, but Campbell didn't stop trying to goad them into violence.

"Hey, Musclehead. You want a problem with me? I'm the real deal."

The Bandido just seemed to want out of the building now.

"Don't worry about getting thrown in jail," Campbell heckled, "because I'll make sure we get bunked together."

A police officer was genuinely nervous now. "There's families here. There's children here. I'm asking you to stop."

"Okay, but they started it."

There's a motorcycle tradition in Port Dover, a fishing town on the shore of Lake Erie a couple of hours' drive southwest of Toronto. Every Friday the thirteenth, from spring to fall, outlaw bikers—and far more bikers of the non-outlaw persuasion—congregate here in a middle-aged sea of black leather and chrome. The Ontario Bandidos showed up, wearing their Fat Mexican crests and trying to affect swaggers. The very sight of them was too much for a Quebec Hells Angel, who approached them. "The Quebec guy just leaned over and said something. They were gone within minutes."

Hells Angels were the initial suspects when the bodies of Muscedere and seven other Bandido members and supporters were found in April 2006 in vehicles abandoned by a farmer's field, about a ten-minute drive from Kellestine's farm. They had all been shot, and the initial suspicion was that it must be the result of a battle over drug turf. A Hells Angels spokesperson ridiculed the suggestion, implying that the Bandidos had no turf worth taking.

The story eventually emerged that the eight bikers had been murdered by fellow members, including Boxer's supposed friend Kellestine. Despite his low opinion of the Bandidos, Campbell was impressed by accounts of Boxer's final moments, and how he had stuck up for a Jewish prospect, Jamie (Goldberg) Flanz, to Kellestine. Campbell and Evelyn had met Flanz once at a party years before, and considered him a good guy. Boxer's defence of a Jewish brother enraged Nazi-loving Kellestine. Then Boxer had the balls to laugh in Kellestine's face as he looked into a loaded gun, an instant before Kellestine pulled the trigger. Campbell thought back to how, after Jimmy Brockman had shot him outside the Royal Hotel in Whitby, he had suddenly become calm and dared Brockman to pull the trigger again. Perhaps Boxer felt the same way in his final seconds of life. "I have respect for the guy [Boxer Muscedere], just for how he went out."

Campbell found there was something naive, and yet familiar, about how Boxer Muscedere was blinded by talk of brotherhood from the mouths of men like Kellestine, who ultimately betrayed him. "I've been excessive in my loyalty to people. Look at Boxer. I identify with him because of the blind loyalty. So many times I've had that. I don't think that Boxer had that meanness in him that I have. He was a romantic. Wanted it to be the way he had imagined. I wanted it to be the way I pictured it in my mind. It never is."

In 2006, Campbell packed for a trip to Costa Rica with a friend named Howie, who was confined to a wheelchair. It was intended as a pleasure trip. "I planned ten days. I wasn't even gone ten hours."

He could tell there were problems as soon as he got to the customs counter at San José. "She's typing and looking at me. Looks at the screen again. I said to Howie, 'Something's up.' She called a guy over. The guy said, 'Stand here.'"

Campbell and his friend waited for the next ninety minutes, until a non-smiling man approached him. "He said, 'Come with me.' He had ten guys with him. He said, 'You're not welcome in my country,' three times. I didn't ask him why."

The man said Campbell would be flying back to Canada on the same aircraft that had brought him to Costa Rica. Rain was falling as he was marched out to the jet, and Campbell was handed a plain umbrella. "At least I'll get a souvenir," he thought. An official gruffly demanded the return of the umbrella when they reached the aircraft.

"They put me by one of those marshals. He was reading and farting all the way back."

In Toronto, a customs worker asked Campbell, "Where are you coming from?"

"Costa Rica."

"How long were you there?"

"About an hour and a half."

"What?"

"Yeah, I didn't like it there."

"What? Go stand over there."

The next official Campbell spoke with was interested in his luggage. He went inside an office, and when he emerged he said, "You didn't tell me you're a Hells Angel."

"It took me five days to get my luggage back."

———

Campbell had been thinking hard about switching to the Nanaimo, B.C., charter of the Angels. The charter had pre-approved his membership, and Campbell had lined up a job there driving a truck. There was plenty to like about the move, from the charter's beautiful wood-lined bar to Vancouver Island's spectacular natural beauty. On the other hand, it was tough to think of being on the other side of the country from Janice and Kylie and the grandkids.

Campbell sensed something was odd when he rode to B.C. in 2006 for an anniversary party of the Haney charter. Haney is a particularly serious charter, and their secluded clubhouse in the woods is nicknamed the "House of Pain." "When you go there, you go to party." Court records would later reveal that Campbell was subjected to a "mud test," or given rough, hazing-like treatment by charter members. New members in B.C. are often mud-tested, or challenged physically. Sometimes they're beaten. Sometimes those beatings come from members wearing rings.

Court records show that Campbell was physically shunned during his Haney visit. Two members in particular repeatedly walked away from him. Finally, he confronted them individually with words along the lines of, "What's the problem? If there's a problem, get it the fuck on."

The members replied with something like: "We're sick of new guys from Ontario coming out to parties talking like they've been in the club for fifteen years."

"I'm not a new guy," Campbell replied. "I've been around for forty years. If there's a problem, let's get it the fuck on."

Instead, it was smoothed over. Nothing more came of it during that visit, but things weren't resolved between B.C. and Ontario Angels either. As Campbell rode back to Ontario, tensions in the club remained close to the surface, ready to explode.

CHAPTER 28

Ratwell

I liked him. Everybody liked him. He had a great personality. Great sense of humour. We had a lot of laughs together.

LORNE CAMPBELL on a Hells Angels turncoat

Campbell was in the Angels' Keswick clubhouse, an hour's drive north of Toronto, when a visitor he had never met before started talking to him.

"You from Oshawa?"

"Yeah."

"You know Lorne Campbell?"

"Yeah. When was the last time you seen him?"

"I'm with him all the time."

"Oh yeah? I'm Lorne Campbell."

The man held out his arms and said, "Punch me in the face, man."

Campbell declined, although he agreed that the stranger deserved a five-knuckle massaging. That sort of thing was getting more commonplace now. Once, at a party, a woman gestured towards Campbell and argued with Evelyn that he wasn't really Campbell at all. Campbell enjoyed eavesdropping on the debate between his wife and the stranger who talked about Lorne Campbell as if she were an authority on the man.

A Hells Angels patch brought increased attention not just from police but also from hangers-on, some of whom were eager to turn informer for the chance at big dollars from the police. Others who sidled up to the Angels were trying to use the club's tough reputation to seal their own shady business deals, pretending they had a tight connection to bikers that just wasn't there.

A police operation by the provincial Biker Enforcement Unit served as a profound wake-up call for the Angels about the dangers of informers within their ranks. Dubbed Project Shirlea, it ran for three years, culminating in charges laid in April 2003 against members of the Keswick, Toronto Downtown, East Toronto, North Toronto and Simcoe County charters on a variety of charges relating to cocaine, marijuana and prescription drugs flowing from Quebec into Ontario. While Campbell wasn't charged, Shirlea also effectively dismantled the Road Warriors, the eastern Ontario affiliate club that Campbell had run for a short while.

A guard at the Newmarket courthouse escorted Hells Angel Dave (Shakey) Atwell to the basement bullpen to join other prisoners facing Shirlea charges. Atwell was the sergeant-at-arms of the Downtown Toronto Angels, a position intended for tough men. He weighed in the neighbourhood of 285 pounds, which made him look imposing enough for the job of enforcing club rules, but Shakey Dave couldn't stop sniffling or crying like a little boy who had been given a schoolyard wedgie as he told the guard about how his father was a respected businessman. Shakey Dave also boasted, between tears, of playing university football for the Western Mustangs, which would have been news to anyone who was actually familiar with Ontario university football. The guard told him he should dry his eyes before he joined the other prisoners in the bullpen, sounding very much like a concerned teacher comforting a skittish child on his first day of kindergarten.

After Shakey Dave got bail, Campbell was disgusted to see him in the courtroom hallway, joking with police. "I called Atwell over. He was talking to the cops like he was their friend. I asked why he was talking to the cops. He said they took his father's computer and he was trying to get it back."

Campbell was even more disgusted that Shakey Dave tried to defend his behaviour. "That's your fucking lawyer's job. You don't walk over and talk to the cops. They're not your friend."

Despite his tears and comfort with police, there was still something likeable about Shakey Dave, who had previously belonged to the Para-Dice Riders. Shakey Dave was among the PDR members who folded into the Angels in 2000. He was the kind of guy who needed to be liked, and certainly lots of senior Angels seemed to enjoy his quick banter. Donnie Petersen, the well-respected spokesman for the Angels for Central Canada, was the best man at his wedding, while Atwell was master of ceremonies at the wedding of Downtown vice-president Doug Myles.

Shakey Dave did have a willingness to pitch in on club business. He alternately held the posts of the charter's co-treasurer, road captain and sergeant-at-arms. A road captain's responsible for making sure club runs are well attended, while the duties of a sergeant-at-arms are security and discipline. Security tasks were natural for him, since he was a long-time salesperson at a local store that specialized in secret listening and filming devices. His club duties included regularly sweeping the Hells Angels' Eastern Avenue clubhouse for hidden recording devices.

He tried to say that he was called Shakey Dave because he was a tough guy who could shake people down, but no one seemed to buy that. A more likely explanation was the pronounced twitchiness that his fondness for cocaine gave him. Somehow, despite his proportions, he exuded vulnerability. Part of the reason was his tendency to talk like a guest on *Oprah* or *The View*, spouting psychobabble like, "I was having a pity party" and "I was in a bad place personally."

Shakey Dave would say he was in a bad place physically in the fall of 2005, when another Toronto Hells Angel approached him about how someone should go about killing a police agent involved in the Project Shirlea operation. That only made Shakey Dave shakier. He had been working as a police informant since the previous March, feeding bits of information to the cops. None of the bikers had a clue that Shakey Dave had once applied to be a Durham police officer and hadn't made the cut. Anyone who has ever been a prison guard or a cop, or anyone who has ever applied for those jobs, is barred from entry into the Angels or any other outlaw biker club.

Shakey Dave's Project Shirlea drug charges had fizzled when the court found that the wiretap used against him was improper. That should have calmed him down, but instead Dave got even shakier. After the other Angel told him of the murder plan, Shakey Dave became an active police agent, working full-time to put his clubmates in a bad place, namely jail. His information now appeared in police files under the heading "Agent 3859."

Around that time, the Sudbury charter of the Hells Angels was folding, as Campbell was profoundly dissatisfied with the quality of membership candidates. Little did Campbell know that, as he was discussing shifting his membership to the Angels' Downtown Toronto charter, Shakey Dave was wearing a police body-pack recording device to Downtown meetings. He also wore it when he partied and snorted cocaine with the Redline crew, an Angels-affiliated club in London. Shakey Dave would later say that at times he snorted coke in clubhouses to "keep up appearances," since he had a reputation as a frequent cocaine user.

Shakey Dave remained an outgoing, chatterbox type of guy, and on April 5, 2006, he was able to pull Mehrdad (Juicy) Bahman into talking about submachine guns. Bahman belonged to the Richmond Hill Foundation, a Hells Angels junior support club. He boasted to Shakey Dave that his Uzi was beautiful and he would show it to him sometime, then added that he had plenty of security cameras at his home.

On May 31, 2006, Shakey Dave's body pack picked up Toronto Hells Angels discussing the folding of Campbell's Sudbury charter. Members of the Downtown Toronto charter weren't all excited about the prospect of absorbing Sudbury's remaining members.

"I don't think we should take four guys as a package deal," said Scottish-born Toronto member Mark Stables. "I think we should assess each one of these guys by themselves because, ya know, I don't have a problem with Lorne Campbell. I get along great with him. Ian Watson, on the other hand, I'm not impressed with that guy really." (In the end, Toronto accepted just Campbell from the Sudbury charter.)

Member Carl Stoyan told charter president John (Winner) Neal that he'd also welcome Campbell. "Fucking Lorne Campbell is a fuckin' heavyweight. . . . I'm fuckin' happy to have the guy fuckin' here."

Vice-president Doug Myles was captured by Shakey Dave's hidden recording device saying he welcomed Campbell as a solid member, although he was considered no financial wizard. "Lorne is a great guy, just don't do any business with him. He's . . . no good with money, but stand beside ya in a bar and everything and uh he's a great guy."

In mid-April 2006, the Downtown Hells Angels heard a rumour that there was an informant in their midst and that he was a former Para-Dice Rider. A police source also told them they could expect a raid at the Eastern Avenue clubhouse in six weeks. Rumours are part of the fabric of life for an outlaw biker, and this one didn't generate any particular fear at first.

A report filed to the Ontario Provincial Police biker squad on September 27, 2006, read: "Agent 3859 attends a Hells Angels meeting. Larry Pooler tells the Agent about going to the Indian Reservation with Lorne Campbell and getting a whole bunch of cigarettes. He buys them for ten and sells them for fifteen or twenty a carton."

Shakey Dave's hidden bug picked up Donnie Petersen saying he had a certain respect for Bernie Guindon's old rival Johnny Sombrero, who was still alive and kicking on the fringes of the outlaw biker scene. "[Johnny Sombrero's] a strong man. His whole life he's been strong." The charter's vice-president, Larry Pooler, replied that he had heard stories about how Sombrero "checked in," or requested to go into protective custody (PC), while behind bars. Campbell has nothing but scorn for those who check in. "That's about the weakest thing you can do in jail. . . . There are guys who would rather die than go to PC."

The hidden bug picked up Pooler laughing at the thought of Sombrero requesting protective custody and Petersen answering back: "Not Lorne-Campbell-tough, I guess."

On the surface, Shakey Dave didn't seem too worried about the rumour of a rat in their midst. Under the surface, he felt increasingly alone and stressed. The more stressed Shakey Dave felt, the more he snorted cocaine, and the more he snorted cocaine, the more Petersen and John Neal (no relation to Carmen Neal) chided him to clean up his act. Oddly, Shakey Dave was getting the same anti-drug advice from his police handlers.

On September 27, 2006, a police bug picked up a conversation at the Hells Angels' clubhouse where the topic was Paris Christoforou, the sergeant-at-arms for the London, Ontario, charter, and Peter Scarcella, a

Toronto-area mobster. The two men were both in prison for their roles in a case that had mortified the Ontario Hells Angels and the general public and left a mother of three permanently injured.

Back on April 21, 2004, Louise Russo had been standing at the counter of a sandwich shop in Toronto when a van pulled into the parking lot and two men inside opened fire. Christoforou's bullets missed, but a second shooter, mob associate Antonio (Jelly) Borrelli, shattered Russo's spine. Both men were aiming at Sicilian Mafioso Michele Modica, who was trying to evade a gambling debt. Modica escaped without a scratch, while Russo was paralyzed for life.

At the time of the shooting, the Angels were in the midst of a public relations blitz aimed at countering the bad press coming out of the Quebec drug wars. The club had posted a billboard alongside the northbound Don Valley Parkway in Toronto with the words "Still Fighting for Democracy & Freedom." They had also taken out newspaper ads, run toy drives for sick children and made an online push in support of food banks. Immediately after the shooting, the Hells Angels' Central Canadian branch issued a statement saying the club "extends our heartfelt sympathy" to Russo and her family. The statement described the shooting as an "indiscriminate dreadful action," adding that the club was "sickened by the senseless act of violence that has violated Mrs. Russo's life."

Scarcella only became involved in a plot to murder Modica after Russo was shot. Once caught, Borrelli was sentenced to ten years in prison while Scarcella and Christoforou each plea-bargained for nine-year prison terms. Each of these sentences was on top of time served awaiting trial. Their deal also included a $2-million contribution towards Russo's medical care. The botched hit, appalling publicity and prison time didn't help relations between the Angels and Scarcella's mob group.

"It is true Paris did punch out Scarcella," Petersen was recorded as saying. Shakey Dave's wire picked up Angels talking about how Christoforou had been transferred out of Ontario to Donnacona Institution in Quebec because he was considered "incompatible" with an inmate.

For his part, Campbell considered the accidental shooting of Louise Russo to be another sign of declining standards in the outlaw biker world.

In a well-done hit, there are no family or children or bystanders in the line of fire. The shooter has the nerve to walk up close to his target and isn't afraid to look his target in the eyes. Any fool with a gun and a vehicle can do a drive-by. "That's why I hate drive-bys. If you have an enemy, walk up and shoot the enemy in the head. Don't shoot somebody else."

In July 2006, Campbell had plans to go fishing with Evelyn, Shakey Dave and Shakey Dave's wife. They rented a cottage and Campbell brought along some rare Hells Angels movies. Things started badly when Shakey Dave dropped Campbell's big-screen television and VCR while unloading it from their SUV. Evelyn, much less than half his size, carried them inside instead.

When the TV and VCR were hooked up, Campbell pulled out his prized copy of the 1983 movie *Hells Angels Forever*, starring Ralph (Sonny) Barger. Shakey Dave recoiled like a vegan served a heaping platter of steak tartare and abruptly said no, he wasn't interested in watching that.

Rain made the three-day trip seem much longer, and the nearby pickerel and trout remained safe from the bikers. There was some excitement when Atwell's little pug, Brutus, ate Campbell's eyewear as Campbell was stepping out of the shower. No one thought much about Shakey Dave's dog being named after an infamous traitor, but its eating habits were jarring. "I just heard *crunch, crunch, crunch*. His little pug was eating my glasses."

That same summer, Shakey Dave managed to maroon his truck in a ditch by Campbell's home. That didn't come as a shock, since he had somehow steered Campbell's hand-held snow blower into the same spot the previous winter.

"How do you do that?" Campbell asked after the truck became stuck.

"Maybe I'm dumb," Shakey Dave replied.

"Maybe you are," Campbell thought.

William (Mr. Bill) Lavoie hosted many demons in the seething cauldron between his ears. None was worse than the real-life haunting provided by Steven (Hannibal) Gault, a biker he had sponsored into the Satan's Choice. Gault was a career rat who had been informing to police since his high school days, and Mr. Bill was a career outlaw biker with thirty-three years in the Satan's Choice before he joined the Angels in 2000. Mr. Bill didn't catch wind of Gault's true nature until after he had sponsored him into the Choice and suddenly he was faced with a challenge much like putting a pin back into a grenade.

Gault had once belonged to the Travellers, a group of swindlers who targeted seniors living on farms in eastern Ontario with renovation scams. One elderly farmer was bilked for $260,000 for repairs to his property that were never done.

Gault's behaviour only got worse when he joined the Choice. "After he got his full patch, he thought he was king of the world," says Gault's former wife, Linda. Gault was nicknamed "Hannibal" for his taste for blood, which he demonstrated one evening in the eastern Ontario town of Campbellford when he bit off a chunk of a man's ear in a bar fight. "When we would make him steak for supper, his was just with spices, raw, not even on the grill for a little," Linda recalls.

After Gault was allowed into the Angels in the mass patch-over of 2000, there was plenty more partying, cocaine and transgression, including a 2002 conviction for attempting to harass a Durham Region police officer and his family. A year later, Gault had a restraining order filed against him, forbidding him from having contact with Linda's family after she said he threatened to blow up their home with them inside.

After their breakup, Linda began telling others in the biker world about her ex's deepest secret: that he was working undercover for the police. It might have sounded like something the angry ex-lover of a biker would say, but it also happened to be true. In fact, Gault received more than a million dollars for his undercover work with police that helped land twenty-one Ontario Hells Angels and associates behind bars for drug, weapons and criminal organization charges.

One of the few people who listened seriously to Linda's warning was Mr. Bill, but his behaviour was already so bizarre and paranoid that he wasn't taken seriously now that he was right. "Mr. Bill was trying to tell people Gault was a stool pigeon, even though he was the one who got him in."

By September 7, 2006, Mr. Bill had retired from the Angels in good standing. He was sixty now, making him somewhat of a greybeard in biker circles. Mr. Bill was killed that same day while riding his red Harley on County Road 8 near his home just south of Warsaw, near Peterborough. A car was stopped at an intersection, waiting for two trucks to pass through. When the trucks were gone, the car pulled into the intersection and crashed into Mr. Bill, killing him.

The name of the driver who killed Mr. Bill wasn't released to the public, presumably to shield him or her from angry bikers, but charges were laid against the driver for failing to yield. Something about the story didn't sit right with Campbell as he attended Mr. Bill's funeral with more than a hundred other bikers. It wasn't an official Hells Angels funeral, since Mr. Bill had retired from the club, but they all wore club colours and black arm bands with the words "In Memory of Mr. Bill" as they rolled through Peterborough. Roads are filled with inattentive drivers, and it's easy to see how a motorcycle could be hidden from view behind two trucks. Still, the weather had been good on the day of the crash and Mr. Bill was riding on a familiar stretch of road. "Mr. Bill was a good bike rider. He was eccentric, but he was a safe rider."

Shakey Dave's recording device picked up bikers discussing a shooting at the Club Pro strip club in Vaughan on December 2, 2006. Bouncer Frank (Cisco) Lenti, formerly with the Bandidos, Satan's Choice and several other clubs, had opened fire on West Toronto Hells Angels and associates, believing he was the target of a hit. Squeezing off seven shots in six seconds, Lenti killed David (Dred) Buchanan of the Angels and gravely wounded prospect Carlo Verrelli, while sending Angel Dana Carnegie running for his life. Many bikers, including Campbell, liked and respected Lenti even though he wasn't with their club. Shakey Dave's police notes for December 4, 2006, stated: "Petersen says up until this happened he had a good relationship with Frank and that Frank saved his life once."

On January 30, 2007, police were able to record a phone conversation between Campbell and member Robin Moulton. The topic of discussion was the need to toughen up membership requirements. "I agree we could tighten it up," Campbell said. ". . . I agree with tightening it up."

On February 6, 2007, Shakey Dave's bug caught Campbell again. This time the topic was drug dealing. Shakey Dave said he would pay Campbell to set up a meeting with Shaun Robinson, a fellow member, for a cocaine deal. On February 12, 2007, Robinson said he had spoken with Campbell "about grabbing some white," and agreed to sell a "plate" of cocaine to Shakey Dave.

Nothing happened for the next week.

At 10:50 a.m. on February 20, 2007, Shakey Dave made an audio note with a tape recorder: "I received the device and my instructions to talk to Lorne Campbell about a price of cocaine that he received from Shaun Robinson." Shakey Dave noted that he drove to a Tim Hortons dough-nut shop on Weston Road in Toronto, where he met Campbell, who was parked in his Oldsmobile Cutlass.

"I parked and went up to him," Shakey Dave continued in his audio note. "He looked stressed . . . he was speaking very low and he whis-pered the . . . number thirty-four. I didn't hear him, so I stuck my head in the car window. I said, 'Speak up, for fuck's sakes.' . . . He says, 'Thirty-four thousand,' and he put up his index finger, meaning for one. I said, 'Yeah, that's it. That's good.' I said, 'What about you?' and he said, 'Well, what about me?' I said, 'Okay, well, I'll give you a G-note on top of that,' and he said, 'Yes.'"

Shakey Dave then added that he gave Campbell fifty dollars for gas to drive to Kitchener. "I know he's tight for cash. I didn't mind doing this. It's, ah, sort of an investment in credibility."

Shakey Dave's body pack recorded him talking with Campbell:

"Yeah, okay," Shakey Dave said. "All right. Part of the thing was not to get you too involved. . . ."

"Yeah, yeah," Campbell said.

"See, I'm smart and I don't get anyone else involved. . . ." In true Shakey Dave fashion, he praised himself for his discretion and smooth-ness. "Or try to be, anyway, except for the constant lying."

Campbell responded to the joke, saying, "Oh yeah, fuckin' liar."

On February 23, 2007, the deal was over.

"Yeah, we'll do this again next time," Shakey Dave said to Campbell.

"You're the man," Campbell replied.

On February 26, 2007, Shakey Dave called Campbell and got himself invited to see him at his home near Orillia. There, Shakey Dave made what appears to be an effort to pull Campbell into some sort of incriminating statement.

First he handed over a payment for arranging the meeting. "That's the two hundred."

"Oh, okay."

Then he commented on the kilo of cocaine he'd purchased from Robinson. "There was a fish stamped in it. Do you know anything about that? Was that anything to do with you?"

"That sounds pretty fishy to me," Campbell said.

Shakey Dave pressed on: "Buddy, I looked at it. I went, 'Wait a minute.'"

"Yeah," Campbell said.

"Big fish."

"Yeah, I don't know, man. I have no idea. . . ."

The next day, Shakey Dave was crying on Campbell's shoulder, like a nervous schoolboy. Others in the club suspected he was a rat and Shakey Dave let on that his feelings were bruised. They suspected him because he was trying to start up drug deals with Angels who weren't drug dealers. There were also questions about how he somehow managed to buy a new truck and a new Harley, after scrounging for money not long before that.

"What did you do? Win the lottery?" Campbell asked.

Shakey Dave mumbled something about having a job but didn't go into any details, looking even shakier than usual.

Evelyn and Campbell gave Shakey Dave and his bride an abstract glass sculpture in March 2007 for their wedding the previous summer. Shakey Dave and his bride were there for the weekend, and Evelyn had stuffed two chickens so that there would be plenty of seconds and even thirds if their hefty guest brought his appetite.

Shakey Dave and his bride showed them an album of photos of their wedding in the Dominican Republic, and the Campbells presented them with their belated wedding gift. Then, without any warning, Shakey Dave stood up and made up an odd excuse about how something had just come up. "They really liked it [the gift]. Then they took off."

"There was something wrong," Evelyn says.

Finally, Myles confronted Shakey Dave about the rumour that he was a rat. There was no conclusive outcome to the conversation, but discussions about such topics seldom end nicely. Myles clearly offended Shakey Dave. Shakey Dave's debriefing notes record that Campbell offered to listen to him in person, but Shakey Dave was too busy tending bar at the clubhouse to take him up on it. "The Agent tells Campbell he just finished a heart-breaking meeting with Doug Myles. The Agent says that guys are talking behind his back and he's very upset. Campbell tells him to come up and the Agent says he can't because he has to do his bar shift tomorrow but he'll talk to Campbell tomorrow night for sure."

The Angels kept the Downtown Toronto clubhouse open twenty-four hours a day, ready to receive members from out of town whenever they might drop by. This was Shakey Dave's turn to make sure Angels could get in and police and hostile bikers stayed out. When his shift was over, Shakey Dave disappeared forever from the outlaw biker life.

CHAPTER 29

Don Jail Inmate # 0994271886

I told them, "You guys jump me, I'll hunt each one of you down and I will kill you. I am no bluff."

LORNE CAMPBELL

On Tuesday, April 3, 2007, Campbell was cleaning his $40,000 gun collection, which included some rusted-out ones he had inherited from Mr. Bill. "The guns were in terrible shape. He would talk about guns all the time, but they weren't cared for. They were very rusted. I wouldn't fire any one of them. I wouldn't even give them to somebody."

The cleaning done, Campbell forgot to store them safely again, and so when Evelyn tidied up, she put them back in their locked cases. The whole incident didn't seem like a big deal at the time and might easily have been forgotten, if not for what happened hours later.

Campbell couldn't shake the feeling that something was about to happen. A lot of things didn't quite sit right. He had a nagging feeling that his fishing buddy Shakey Dave might have turned rat. There had also been rumours of a pending raid for months. Indeed, an Internet blogger had posted a supposedly confidential judge's order allowing federal authorities to seize the Hells Angels' fortified clubhouse on Eastern Avenue. The court document was posted on at least five Internet sites, including one for true-crime aficionados, where it appeared on March 25, 2007, only eleven days after it was drafted. The blogger who posted it identified himself only as "drmm," "drmmfamm" and "a researcher from Toronto, Canada."

Then there was the strange mud test by Haney, B.C., members, and the cryptic comment that members there were tired of junior Ontario members coming west and acting as if they had been in the club for fifteen years. Why would someone say something like that to Campbell, whose loyalty was unquestioned and who had been on a Harley longer than many of them had been alive?

And what about Shakey Dave's increasingly shaky behaviour? He had refused to hug Evelyn a couple of times over the past few months, saying he had a bad cold. "That's because he had a wire," Evelyn says now.

Just in case there was a raid, Campbell had already moved a lot of his Hells Angels gear, such as sweatshirts and T-shirts and photos and even golf balls, out of the house. That included Angels charter photos from around the world, club guidelines for Canada, membership rules, contact information for bikers in Canada and abroad, incorporation papers, and the 2007 Ontario Hells Angels calendar, with bikers posing like pro wrestlers by their bikes while enraptured strippers looked on in the background. Still inside the house were more mementoes and clothing, as well as his colours, which he still wore whenever he climbed on his Harley.

Campbell dozed off on his couch watching television one night and was awakened at six the next morning by a loud banging sound. "What the fuck's that?" he thought. Next came the tiny sparkles that are released by police percussion bombs. "I looked up and there was little sparkles coming down. I wasn't so stunned that I didn't know what was going to happen."

His senses hadn't yet cleared when a strange man shouted from inside his house, "Lie down on the floor!"

Sparkles still hung in the air and now there were also police in riot gear, with helmets and facial shields. Campbell refused to lie down, but as his hands were pulled behind his back and cuffed, he didn't fight back. It wasn't the best way to start the day, but it wasn't the worst morning of his life either. "I just thought I was not going to be found guilty and I would get bail the next day."

Evelyn was new to this. Fortunately for Campbell, she had stored away his gun collection or that would have led to a new raft of charges for unsafe storage. Evelyn demanded to see a search warrant before police carried out his vest with his club colours on a coat hanger. Evelyn ordered the officers to stop immediately. "They belong to the club," she said, grabbing the vest.

"Yes we can," said the officer, pulling them back. He showed her the search warrant, which allowed them to take anything with "Hells Angels" on it. They carried out club plaques and photos, as well as twenty-three shotguns and rifles and a compound bow. Evelyn's cellphone was ringing non-stop now, with friends and members wondering what was going on. The Downtown Toronto charter of the Hells Angels on Eastern Avenue had also been raided that morning, as had the homes of other members. The raids were the culmination of an eighteen-month operation called Project Develop, which involved some four hundred officers and relied on information from a paid police agent. The only home in his club circle that wasn't raided was that of Shakey Dave Atwell.

As her phone buzzed, Evelyn turned it face down so that police couldn't read the numbers on its call display. It was a shock, but it could have been worse, as Campbell had prepped her on what to do during a police raid. "'Don't get intimidated. You don't have to say anything. You don't have to go off the handle.' I felt for Ev. I had been through stuff like that before. She hadn't."

After that morning's pre-dawn raids, there were 111 charges laid against twenty-eight members and associates. The foundation of the case was the betrayal of Shakey Dave, soon to be referred to in the club as "Ratwell." Some Angels tried to convince themselves that Shakey Dave must be suffering inside, but Campbell didn't buy that for a second. "A lot of guys would say he can't look at himself in the mirror. I don't believe that. The guy loves himself."

Campbell later said the worst was yet to come for Shakey Dave, and it likely wouldn't be in the form of a beating or a bullet from former buddies. Some people in the biker world expect a Hollywood-style happy ending when they go into a witness protection programme. "They think everything's gonna change. They're going to get a place with a white picket fence. But they're the same guy at the end of it all."

On the surface, the charges against Campbell didn't look so bad. He was charged with a drug trafficking conspiracy for agreeing to take a thousand dollars for introducing Shakey Dave to Shaun Robinson for the cocaine deal. He had been captured on video and audio with Shakey Dave, telling him the price for a kilo of cocaine was "thirty-four," or $34,000. That would be hard to beat. There was also a charge of contributing to a criminal organization, something all of the accused faced. The criminal organization charge was one that Campbell felt they all had to fight for the sake of the club. If they were branded a criminal organization, then added time could be tacked on to any future criminal convictions, on the grounds that crimes were committed to benefit a criminal group. Something about the criminal organization tag rattled Campbell on another level as well. Outsiders might consider it strictly semantics, but Campbell felt there was a crucial point at stake. "It's a motorcycle club with criminals in it, not a criminal organization. That's an important distinction." Campbell may have looked stoic as the fight began, but he was concerned his club might be taking a serious hit. "I have the same emotions as everybody else, but I don't show them."

Locked up in Toronto's Don Jail, Campbell was denied bail, which was troubling, but he remained optimistic he could have that overturned. What concerned him more was that Evelyn now had to make a two-hour drive down to see him, and then drive back home alone. "She would never complain to me. Never once."

On one of her first visits at the Don, Evelyn told him of the strange experience of driving through crowded downtown Toronto. "I gave this homeless guy ten dollars so he could take the subway to Pickering," she told Campbell. She noted that the stranger told her a taxi would cost a hundred dollars, which was far too much.

"You idiot. The subway doesn't go to Pickering."

It was an almost predictable thing for Evelyn to have done. She wasn't a city person and was still soft-hearted when it came to all strays, even human ones.

"Don't fucking open your window for anybody," Campbell sputtered.

His lawyer, Andrew Perrin, brought in top-flight criminal lawyer Tony Bryant, and Campbell told him immediately that he wanted to get to trial quickly. Rushing to trial meant they couldn't weigh the Crown's evidence in a pretrial, but it also saved money in legal fees and potential jail time awaiting trial. That idea fizzled, however, as the Crown denied attempts to sever Campbell's case from those of the others or to forgo a preliminary.

Authorities didn't have to explain why Campbell was the lone Hells Angel deposited in the Don Jail. Clearly, they didn't want him with the other Angels as he could be expected to push them to plead not guilty to anything involving conspiracy or contributing to a criminal organization. He also was pushing for everyone to take trial by jury on criminal organization charges, since club members always seemed to lose when they left that determination up to a judge.

The Don Jail was a tough place to be alone, especially for a Hells Angel in his late fifties. Originally opened in 1864, the Don had deservedly garnered generations of bad press. In 1928, a grand jury called it a "disgrace"; in 1931, a mayoral delegation reported, "Many of [the cells] are so narrow a fat horse could not be backed into them"; and in 1935, a grand jury called it "an overcrowded dungeon . . . like the Black Hole of Calcutta."

Globe and Mail writer Kirk Makin once wrote that the people who ran the Don back then weren't trying to make it a nice place:

> *In its heyday, the prevailing ethic at the Don Jail was simple—prison should be a harsh and intimidating experience that no sane person would want to repeat.*
>
> *To that end, the last thing an offender saw as he entered the Don from the outside world was a mawkish stone figure of Father Time carved into the stone above the front door of the jail. Inside, numerous wrought-iron serpents and dragons emerge from the dark, connecting walls to balconies and catwalks.*

Floggings were conducted on the floor of its central rotunda, with inmates watching the gruesome spectacle from the balconies. For a long time, talking was prohibited.

There were thirty-four legal executions in its gallows, and in the early 2000s fifteen skeletons were discovered in an outside exercise yard. There were also some seventy murders, with prisoners getting beatings or worse from other inmates for offences such as looking at someone the wrong way, taking too long in the shower or sitting in someone else's chair.

By the time Campbell arrived at the Don, prisoners were housed in a new wing, built in 1977, but the bad karma wafted over from the old dungeon. Politicians had been promising since 1996 to tear the whole place down, and in 1997—a decade before Campbell walked inside—the U.S. State Department wrote in its annual human rights report: "Conditions were described as so depressing that some inmates purportedly pled guilty in order to be sent to other facilities and thus avoid awaiting trial in the jail."

All municipal and provincial jails lack the rehabilitation programmes and other recreational facilities found in federal penitentiaries, since they're a place for defendants awaiting trial or convicts serving short stays. That meant anyone, from an underworld hit man or a terrorist to a lifelong pervert to a parole violator or drunk driver, could be found within the Don's walls, breathing its stale air.

There seemed no end to the ways that jail was worse than prison. In prisons, inmates can purchase calling cards to phone their loved ones and lawyers at pre-assigned times. In jail, they have to call collect, and the Don had only four phones to use. These were often monopolized by prisoners such as Eric Boateng, one of the Jamaican gang members who call themselves gangstas. Boateng, who was just in his late teens, seemed to be on one phone all day, as if it belonged to him alone.

In prisons, interested inmates apply for cooking jobs and they're fired if there are too many complaints from the customers. "If they don't do a good job, they don't keep it." In jail, food is often served up by inmates who are indifferent at best and hostile at worst. In the Don, Campbell refrained from consuming any coffee or tea, fearing what mystery ingredients might lie in the dark waters of his cup.

In jail, inmates are separated from their loved ones during visiting times by thick Plexiglas. Physical contact is impossible, although women often pull open their blouses and lift their skirts in the wheelchair-accessible area, which has a particularly wide viewing area. "You never get to hold your wife, your kids."

Prisons have weight rooms, tracks and basketball courts, and sometimes also handball, mini-putt and nine-hole golf. Jails have none of these. Motivated prisoners are forced to improvise workout programmes they can follow in their tiny and often crowded cells. Prisons are often cleaner than jails such as the Don, where mice were part of the general population. Campbell found himself developing ear infections and scabs in the corners of his eyes not long after he arrived. Prison inmates can wear regular clothes, while in jail they wore only clown-like orange jumpsuits and blue slippers. In prison, inmates can have radios and televisions, and can work on leather and wood crafts. In jail, they can't even have pens, and must do their writing with a shortened pencil.

Just a few years before Campbell arrived, there was a move to desegregate the Don. Black gangsters had been housed in an area nicknamed "Motown," while repeat offenders who had done federal penitentiary time were kept in the "Pen Range." The problem, authorities concluded, was that this arrangement only made gangsta street gangs such as the Malverns and Crips feel stronger and more special. So, by the time Campbell arrived, the prevailing thinking was that other inmates, including bikers, should be housed in the gangstas' midst, to dilute their power. At fifty-nine, Campbell was almost triple the age of many of them.

The trouble started on his first full day of custody, when he saw a tray of hot cross buns in the meal line on the range. The gangstas who were in charge of handing out food seemed in no hurry to pass him one, so Campbell reached out and grabbed a bun for himself and placed it on his food tray

"Yo yo!" a voice behind him shouted. "Yo! We don't reach for the food here."

Campbell wheeled around and glared in the direction of the voice. "Don't you fucking 'yo' me."

"Where are you going with that?" asked Eric Boateng, who seemed to have a particularly elevated status among the gangstas. Boateng was one of more than a dozen gangstas arrested after the fatal shooting of fourteen-year-old bystander Jane Creba on Yonge Street on Boxing Day 2005.

"I'm going to fucking eat it," Campbell replied.

Within seconds, he was encircled by a half-dozen Jamaican gangstas, all in their late teens or early twenties. It often seems the lower you get in life, the more the little things matter. Now, in the belly of the city's worst jail, gangstas and an aging Hells Angel were ready to go to war over a sweet-tasting pastry.

"I'll take on this whole fucking range. I wasn't born the day I got to the Don. You guys jump me and I'll hunt each one of you down and I will kill you. I am no bluff."

A jail captain pushed in between them and faced the gangstas. He was wearing a white shirt, showing he was higher in rank than the blue-shirted guards. "He's got friends and he ain't no fucking show."

"I don't depend on my friends," Campbell snapped at the captain. "Let's get it fucking on."

The captain made it clear there wouldn't be a brawl on his watch, finally asking, "We don't have a problem here, do we?"

The next day, Campbell was handcuffed to a gangsta in his early twenties as they were transported in a police van to the Finch Avenue courthouse. The gangsta at the end of his wrist seemed polite enough, so Campbell introduced him to his Hells Angels clubmates in the courthouse bullpen. The gangsta, who was facing a murder charge, was the only black prisoner in the jailhouse bullpen and clearly appreciated Campbell's courtesy.

That night, without Campbell knowing, this polite senior gangsta got word to his friends on Campbell's range at the Don Jail that they should back off the old Hells Angel.

The next day, Boateng walked over to Campbell and asked, "Are you being treated okay?"

"What do you fucking care?" Campbell replied.

"You getting everything you should be getting?"

"Yeah, why?"

"I'm just wondering."

There was now a sea change in how Campbell was treated by the jailhouse gangstas. Other inmates routinely had their "jug ups," or night-time snacks of tea and cookies, stolen by them, but Campbell was spared such indignities. Boateng continued to steal desserts and snacks such as peanut butter from other inmates, but he and his crew were now invariably polite with Campbell. It was like being back in training school, when he stood up to the bullies. "They would deliver my desserts. If I didn't get it, I would say, 'Where's my fucking dessert?' They would say, 'Hold on,' and give me two or three."

In the mornings now, Campbell was allowed to use the showers first. Anyone trying to wash before him was told: "Get the fuck out of there. Mr. Campbell's coming." The gangstas took pains to guard the seat where Campbell sat alone and played solitaire. Anyone who approached the chair was sternly told it was off limits: "It's Mr. Campbell's seat." They now also made sure he had access to the phones, pretty much whenever he wanted. "I'd go, 'Who's on the fucking phone after you?' They'd go, 'You are.'"

A few months after Campbell's arrival, Boateng was on the street again. He went back to the Don once to visit an inmate while on bail, even though that was against the rules. After this visit, Boateng was shot dead on a Riverdale residential street by men in a van. Word reached Campbell of his death. Despite the special treatment he'd received from the gangstas, Campbell's first thoughts were about the hot cross bun incident and how Boateng had made the Don an even worse hell for fellow inmates by stealing their food.

"The killers should have stuffed peanut butter in his mouth."

CHAPTER 30

Cards and Letters

It's going to blow up.

Advice to Lorne Campbell from DON JAIL GUARD

Campbell befriended the man in the next cell, an African-American librarian's assistant in his late fifties named Gary Freeman. American authorities wanted Freeman extradited to face charges of shooting and wounding a police officer in Chicago in 1967. After the shooting, Freeman had fled to Canada, where he changed his name to Joseph Parnell, fell in love and raised a loving family that included a professional football player, a teacher and a provincial bureaucrat. He maintained that he fired on the police officer in self-defence during a racially charged time that white Canadians four decades later could never fully understand. Police claimed he was a member of the Black Panthers. In reality, Freeman was never a Panther, but he was impressed by much of what they did for inner-city communities, such as running food kitchens.

Despite their widely different backgrounds, Campbell and Freeman quickly learned to respect each other. Both were big on physical fitness, fashioning dumbbells from wet newspapers and plastic bags. "He did lots of push-ups and sit-ups. He worked out hard every day." They also both refused to handle the marijuana "spliffs" prisoners would pass from cell to cell once the lights went out.

Campbell was impressed by how Freeman kept to himself and didn't get involved with any gangs, including the gangstas, who obviously looked up to him. "You could see he had nothing but respect [from them]. They wouldn't let anybody near this man."

Many bikers had abusive fathers, while gangstas often didn't even know who their fathers were. Perhaps that explained why biker clubs had a rigid paramilitary structure with titles like "sergeant-at-arms" while the gangstas didn't seem to have much structure of any kind. Whatever the case, Campbell was underwhelmed by how the young gangstas ran their groups. They clearly didn't trust each other. They didn't seem to have a real brotherhood. When they had to go somewhere, they wouldn't trust a fellow member to guard their marijuana stash. "They'll pass it to a white guy before one of their friends. They don't trust their friends."

Campbell also wasn't impressed with how some of the guards had sold out to the gangstas. One criminal on the range lectured a guard for being too slow with his pot and tobacco delivery, the way a customer might chastise a pizza delivery man. "You were supposed to be here yesterday," the gangsta snapped, and the guard did no more than mutter apologies.

One gangsta Campbell spoke with was born and raised in Toronto's Jane–Finch high-rise corridor, and knew precious little about the world outside its boundaries. He wouldn't take even a short trip out of his neighbourhood for fear that fellow gangstas would rip off his drug turf. Membership in the Hells Angels had taken Campbell to Paris, Amsterdam and the French and Spanish Rivieras. The Toronto gangsta, by contrast, "was born and raised in Toronto and he had never seen the CN Tower."

Campbell descended into what would likely have been diagnosed as depression had he received counselling. He scratched at his cell walls and plucked out his eyebrows and obsessed about the day he would again be free of the rodent-infested jail. "I've got a family. I'm doing every day, minute by minute." Christmas was particularly bad, even though his stepdaughter, Kylie, gave him a collection of framed family photos.

It wasn't just the prisoners who were wound up tight. At least one white guard slipped threatening notes into black guards' lockers. The black guards were on a work-to-rule campaign, meaning all prisoners were locked down in their cells.

Campbell was okay with some facets of lockdowns, even though they were usually meant as punishment. Three prisoners were cramped into each small cell, with one having to sleep on a mattress on the floor, but at least there was welcome relief from the usual noise. The range meant four televisions blaring four different stations at full volume and fifty prisoners trying to talk over them. "I read a lot and enjoyed the quiet. I really didn't mind being locked down except for the lack of showers. In those years it was the only time there was relative quiet. When the TVs were on, you can't get away from it. I had control of the first TV. I'd put it on mute with the captions, but the other three would still be going. During a lockdown, if you want to talk to somebody, you don't have to yell because the TVs aren't on. That's why God gave us lockdowns."

Campbell had a collection of paperbacks to read during lockdowns, including *Relentless* by Dean Koontz, *Deadlock* and *Blood Game* by Iris Johansen, *True Detectives* by Jonathan Kellerman, *A Perfect Spy* by John Le Carré, and, less predictably, *The Kite Runner* by Khaled Hosseini and *A Mixture of Frailties* by Robertson Davies.

One guard liked to call out to prisoners with comments like, "John Smith, the witness protection people are out there to see you." It infuriated some inmates, but Campbell was amused. Anything that broke the tension wasn't all bad.

Another male guard at the Don started painting his fingernails with ginger-coloured polish. The guard's head was shaved and he had the refrigerator-like physique of a championship wrestler, which he had been as a teenager. As the months passed, the guard shaved all his visible body hair and donned a reddish wig, which called to mind a full-figured Lucille Ball. His facial appearance and body hair might change, but his punching power, grappling skills and position of authority still commanded obedience.

At this point, Campbell was no longer surprised by flamboyantly bisexual or gay guards or inmates, and he respected anyone who was true to him- or herself. That said, the prospect of cavity inspections from someone transitioning from a male to a female body was a first. He joined other prisoners in refusing to submit to the full-body searches from the transitioning guard. "You've got to bend over and strip. Here's your asshole to this guy standing there with makeup and a wig."

The guard's gender transfiguration became an emotional issue for many of the other guards and inmates, but Campbell had too much on his mind to be pulled into the drama. "If you made fun of that, the whole range would be locked up." Better to keep his mouth shut and keep to himself. "It's like living in a box for all of that time. . . . All I did was play solitaire."

Campbell found himself becoming extremely food conscious. He went strictly no-dairy immediately after seeing prisoners handle a jug used for delivering milk. "They've been scratching their balls and their asses all night and they'd run out and take it. They'd never wash them. I was told by one of the staff, 'If you wash them, they just get dirty again.'" For a brief time he went vegan, and then shifted to a high-protein, fish and chicken diet. He also thought often and fondly of Evelyn's cooking, such as mashed potatoes with her special horseradish, sour cream and cheese, and spaghetti sauce with a secret ingredient she jealously guarded.

Sanitation inside the Don was a constant bother, with mice scurrying constantly underfoot. More than once, Evelyn came out of the women's washroom in the visiting area to warn other visitors, "Watch it, there's wildlife in there."

Jail time did entitle Campbell to receive a newsletter called *Brothers Behind Bars*. It went out to full-patch bikers imprisoned in Australia, Canada, England, France, Finland, Germany, Norway and Sweden belonging to fifty-eight clubs, from the Avengers and Bandidos to the Boozefighters, Brother Speed, Hells Angels, Hessians, In Country Vietnam, Outlaws, Pharoahs, Sadistics, Sacramaniacs, Unforgiven, Vietnam Vets, Warlocks and Wino Crew. The newsletter's circulation was just three hundred, and its bold motto was "Free All Brothers Behind Bars." While its readership was exclusively outlaw bikers, much of the content was lifted gratis from mainstream publications. Also included were poems and song lyrics that couldn't make it into any mainstream—or few fringe—publications and which would make a hardened Teamster blush. They included "Perfume on My Colors" by SOS MC DAGO, a song with the chorus: "She woke me with a shotgun, / And she scared me half to death / She says I come home drunk last night / With Pussy on my breath."

He sometimes received the *H.A.M.C. B.H.C. Newsletter*, which stood for "Hells Angels Motorcycle Club Big House Crew." It arrived from the United States, with pictures of American World War II fighter pilots who'd nicknamed themselves "Hells Angels." It also contained articles lifted from the mainstream media, such as a story about the Hamilton arrest of a biker for wearing no pants or underwear; fitness plans of Danny Lawson of Manitoba, a bodybuilder formerly of the Los Bravos MC; articles about police charged with assault and insubordination; and an upbeat piece about Harley-Davidson profits being on the rise.

The newsletter also contained a suitably crude humour section, including jokes like this: "As an airliner is about to crash, a female passenger jumps up frantically and announces, 'If I'm going to die, I want to die feeling like a woman.' She removes all her clothing and asks: 'Is there someone on this plane who is man enough to make me feel like a woman?' A man stands up, removes his shirt and says, 'Here, iron this!'"

On a loftier note, the Big House Crew newsletter included a quotation by deaf-blind American author Helen Keller: "Security is mostly a superstition. It does not exist in nature, nor do the children of men as a whole experience it. Avoiding danger is no safer in the long run than outright exposure. Life is either a daring adventure, or nothing." Requiring less contemplation was a note from a military journal, which advised: "If you see a bomb technician running, try to keep up to him."

Campbell received plenty of personal correspondence too, including a sketch of a warrior-like nude woman sent by Chris (Mad Dog) Pedias of Ajax and a postcard from a biker in the Netherlands, with toned women's butts bursting from orange thongs like ripe cantaloupe. He got cards from countries he had never visited, written by people he had never met, like HAMC Black Forest in Lahr, Germany. Campbell also collected poignant reminders that he wasn't home for big moments, such as photos of his granddaughter Chaedra's first Communion.

He found it hard to reply to all the letters, constantly surrounded by the racket of young convicts nearby. He did write to Evelyn, though, on

June 12, 2007: "Well, I guess we talked enough on the phone for one day. But this card says it all. I Love You, Lorne XOXO Oh! Happy Father's Day." He drew a happy face beside it. Evelyn sent him a Father's Day card from their two dogs.

Campbell had expected quick bail, since his charges weren't that severe, but he didn't get it. It particularly irked him when five suspects from the Driftwood Crips street gang did get bail. Moreover, the province was ordered to pay each of them two thousand dollars towards their legal costs after a judge ruled their constitutional rights had been violated because they had waited too long for bail hearings. They'd been charged with cocaine possession, participation in a criminal organization and weapons trafficking.

A guard Campbell got along with warned him to keep trying. "You should try to transfer out," the guard said. "It's going to blow up."

The smoke was so thick in Campbell's range on July 24, 2007, that he couldn't see two metres in front of his face. A prisoner had deliberately set two mattresses and some bedding on fire. "It was horrible. We couldn't breathe. They took the Russian—we called him Boris—away on a stretcher. We wet our sheets in the sink and put them up to our faces. In no time, they were black. We had to keep switching spots on the sheet."

Staff brought in a half-dozen huge fans to blow the smoke down an elevator shaft as inmates remained locked in their cells with dampened sheets over their faces. It was still dark a couple of hours after the fire began, when Campbell heard a strange *click, click* sound on the floor. A prisoner warned him to put his hands over his ears, but there wasn't time. "It almost blew my ears out. It went off right before I got my hands on my ears." The bombs released little sparkles, like the ones that had filled his home when he was arrested. The prisoner warned Campbell that soon the jail's tactical unit would appear. Sure enough, paramilitary officers in riot gear were on the range quickly, making sure prisoners didn't attempt to bolt or seize control.

Evelyn was just outside at the time, and her blood pressure rose as she saw paramedics wheeling the Russian from the jail on a stretcher. Once she was told it wasn't her husband, she could only wait and worry that he'd be the next to be carted out, wounded, burnt or suffering from smoke inhalation, and lifted into an ambulance. Campbell's diary for the day reads simply: "2 percussion bombs."

Three days after the fire, Campbell handed in his work for his "Gospel Echoes Team Certificate" and received a small diploma with a gold seal and a Bible with a black cover, with "Lorne Edgar and Evelyn Darlyn Campbell" embossed on it in gold. To get it, he had to write a series of tests. Among the questions: "Think of a church you have attended and describe what made you feel welcome or unwelcome with that group." Campbell's answer: "I've attended church in the past and felt that I didn't fit in. It seemed to me the members hung together without helping some new person."

Another question: "In the space below, describe the most forgiving person (friend, father, mother, etc.) that you know other than God." Campbell's answer: "My wife Evelyn is the most forgiving person I know. No matter what the circumstances, she sees the good of the situation."

Question: "Tell about a fear you struggle with and how you are facing it." Campbell's answer: "I have a fear that comes when the lights go out in complete darkness it frightens me a bit because I can't see anything and when I hear a noise it gets worse. Now when that happens I just pray to God and I find that I feel peaceful and fall asleep real easy."

Among the others was a question that elicited a response which was particularly mindful of those less fortunate: "Tell about one area of injustice you would like to see changed." Campbell's answer: "I would like to see the homeless people taken off the streets, fed and clothed. If they have special needs then let all the fat cats in government positions cut their paychecks in half and donate it to the cause."

He gave the Bible to Evelyn for Christmas.

It was all quite touching and inspirational, as far as it went. It would have been far more uplifting if Campbell had actually completed the course himself. In truth, the answers were written for him by his cellmate, a homeless armed robber named Donny, who had *Old School* tattooed on his arm. "I never wrote one word of that," confesses Campbell. He became interested in the course when he saw Donny receive his own personally embossed Bible. "I said, 'Where the fuck did you get that?' You get so fucking bored in there that you want to get stuff that nobody else's got. I got him to do that whole thing. He was happy to do it and he was religious."

Campbell nourished an interest in Native spirituality, studying a publication called *First Nations Scribbles*. It included articles on cultural genocide as well as more feel-good topics like "Chasing away the blues." Included were tips that were impossible for him to follow in the foreseeable future, such as "Increase exposure to natural sunlight" and "Take a winter vacation (somewhere warm!)."

He received a card dated September 7, 2007, with the cute little face of a dog on it. The card was clearly not from Evelyn. It read:

Hi Pal

This dog is wondering why this photo is in this card after being thrown out of the car window coming home from Doug + Lois's. I sent Ian a picture of the horse I used to screw when I rode the Range.

Respect always
Randy Quaid.

Odds were that the card wasn't from the troubled actor, but rather from Campbell's close friend Larry Vallentyne. He was in the habit of sending him rude cards and signing the names of celebrities and notables, including Elvis, the cast of *The Andy Griffith Show* and Luca Brasi, the chilling mob enforcer from *The Godfather*.

Campbell received a more earnest letter dated September 10, from Doug Myles, the Downtown Toronto Hells Angels vice-president. Myles was writing from the Metro West Detention Centre to explain why he was leaving the club: "Bottom line I have 3 kids, my two youngest . . . 10 and . . . 4 are suffering because their Dad is not there. I have to put them first. It tore my heart out to hear them cry, it tore my heart out to retire! . . . the club has been my life for the last 20 years plus, I will miss it big time!"

Campbell thought of Evelyn, and it hurt him to imagine how she must be feeling. He wrote to her in an attempt to cheer her up on September 18:

> *Hey You: I know its upsetting . . . I know it doesn't seem like it but there are better days ahead.*
>
> *The good thing about it all is that we have each other and if nothing else, that matters.*
>
> *You're the best thing that's ever happened to me and it keeps me going . . . I Love you Lorne XOXO*

On Thursday, October 19, it all became too much for Campbell. He was ordered out of his cell for a search, and when he returned, his glasses were gone. "I had put my glasses on a little steel table. Your cell is small. You don't lose your glasses. I looked all around my cell anyway."

The guards told him to look again.

"Listen, my glasses are not here," Campbell protested. "You probably put them in the garbage by mistake."

It wasn't just about the glasses. It also wasn't just about the noise, which never seemed to stop, or that those making the noise were so young and spoke in such a thick island accent that he struggled to make out what they were saying, even if he didn't really want to follow their conversation anyway. It wasn't even that he had no clue when he would finally walk out of this hellhole or hug Evelyn or play with his dogs or sit on his Harley or feel the sun on his face. It was about everything.

"You move me off this range!" Campbell shouted. "Get me downstairs where there's more mature guys!"

The guard balked.

"You motherfucker! I'll stab anybody in the eyeballs!"

Campbell was moved downstairs the next day.

On October 25, Campbell was called on by the jailhouse chaplain, which was always a bad sign. As they walked together to see Campbell's lawyer, the chaplain couldn't stop talking about drug dealers he knew in Oshawa. Campbell couldn't figure out where this was going until they joined the lawyer and together they revealed the chaplain's purpose. Campbell's mother had just died of dementia while sitting in a basement chair at the age of eighty-three. He'd never got the chance to say a proper goodbye. His journal entry for that day reads simply: "Mother died."

His request to attend her funeral was denied.

Campbell received an outpouring of correspondence from bikers around the world, many of whom he had never met. A Hells Angel from Colorado wrote: "I am a member of the Denver Colorado charter and I heard about your mom. I lost my mom about a year ago. It was tough for me. I got thrown in jail on the way home from her service!!! Still in a bunch of shit over it!!!"

Sympathy cards also arrived from Angels and supporters in Illinois, including a "Mean Green" and "Friend Curtis," as well as from Eastside Germany, Sonoma County (California), North Toronto Brothers, Hartford (Connecticut), the Redline support club in Milton (Ontario), Southwest Wales, Alberta Nomad, and a Prospect charter in France that included a Cisco, TiTi, Rocco and Paolo. There were also condolence notes from the Swiss Riviera, Stuttgart, London (England)—signed by Boz, Marcus, Grant Hangaround, Dodgy Dave and Jon—East End Vancouver, Kitchener, Kelowna, Antwerp, Essex (England), Haney (B.C.), Southend Brothers (Denmark) and Aalborg (Denmark)—where three members had the nickname "Beast" and one the moniker "Bastard." The Angels charter in Rome wrote, "A warm embrace!" and signatories included a Graziano, Giuseppe, Ugo, Gabriele, Maurizio and Nico. There was also a note from Millhaven that read, "I can't believe these fucken creeps won't let you go to your moms funeral, maggots, pieces of shit," signed "Shawn C."

"I was surprised only because I never thought people would know about it. I wasn't surprised the Hells Angels sent stuff because that's what Hells Angels do around the world. It was nice."

Perhaps jails have always been a dumping ground for the mentally ill, but things had got far worse since Campbell's earlier jail stays, which had come before a number of long-term care facilities were shut down by the province in the 1990s in a cost-cutting move. Every night, a particular inmate in the Don lay on his stomach and banged his head furiously on the bed until he went to sleep. Another was an accused arsonist and drew brightly coloured pictures with crayons of fires consuming houses and families.

An inmate who was over seventy years old lost control of his bowels in the shower and was beaten mercilessly by third-floor gangstas. It was as if he was being punished just for being old. "There's no morals at all in the county buckets. No morals at all. They're all brought up with no fathers and no morals."

There were also strange omissions of security by inmates, for instance how gangstas were willing to turn the other cheek after an inmate was caught stealing things from their cells.

"Why do you want him on the range?" Campbell asked.

"We know his family."

"He's a box thief. He's going off the range." Campbell turned to a guard and made it clear that the inmate had to go. "This guy don't belong here."

The thief was immediately transferred to another part of the jail.

Campbell read news of the outside biker world in articles delivered by Evelyn in her care packages. He felt a sense of personal loss when he learned that London, England, Hells Angel Gerry (Gentleman Gerry) Tobin had been shot in the back of the head while riding his Harley on the M40 motorway on Sunday, August 12, 2007. The former Calgary resident had been heading home from the four-day Bulldog Bash motorcycle festival with a prospect and a hangaround, one of whom was visiting from Poland and the other a Polish immigrant who had lived in England for six years.

There was also a sense of surprise as Campbell read of Tobin's murder. Campbell had known him since the late 1980s, back when Tobin was still a member of the Grim Reapers. He always considered Tobin a nice, inoffensive man, and his murder seemed so out of place for the English Hells Angels. Campbell thought back to how Queen Elizabeth II had waved at Snob and other bikers during her Golden Jubilee celebrations and wondered how things had gone so wrong.

The attack had been carried out with military precision, as a green Rover 620 pulled up alongside Tobin's Harley and someone leaned out of the window, squeezing two quick shots from a handgun. One of them hit Tobin in the back of the head, just under his helmet, killing him instantly and sending his Harley careening down the crowded motorway. When police looked into the background of 35-year-old Tobin, they found nothing sinister. In Alberta, he had weathered a troubled childhood, and by his early twenties he was leading Bible studies and spoke of becoming a missionary. Tobin moved to England ten years before his death, working as a mechanic at a Harley-Davidson dealership in Mottingham in south London. While he had given up on his dream of becoming a missionary, Tobin had no criminal record in either country.

It was natural to once again curse the Outlaws after hearing news of the shooting, and there was speculation in the press that the hit had been ordered by American "overlords" in the club. The Outlaws had about 200 members in England, compared with 250 Angels. The Outlaws had moved into England only in 2000 and quickly claimed the area around Stratford-upon-Avon in Warwickshire as their turf, even though the Angels were already operating the highly profitable Bulldog Bash there. The location of the bike festival put both clubs in an untenable position. Under the biker ethos, turf is of paramount importance. So are appearances. If the Angels moved the location of their Bulldog Bash, they would lose respect. If the Outlaws looked the other way, they would seem bullied and weak.

In the end, an investigation showed that Tobin had been killed by members of the South Warwickshire chapter of the Outlaws solely for the colours on his back. Tobin's killer had never met him, and that didn't matter; he wore a Hells Angels patch and that was enough. The fact that the killing wasn't personal somehow made it all the more chilling. "I've had enemies. Outlaw enemies. I've had Bandido enemies. I've had Golden Hawk enemies. I've had Loners enemies. I would never wait and shoot someone on a fucking road because the club's an enemy. It's very, very cowardly. And anybody that's done it in any club I've belonged to is a coward. Just don't do it. Be a man about it and if you're going to shoot someone, be close enough to see what you're doing."

CHAPTER 31

East Detention
Centre

We're all Hells Angels. Suck it up. Act solid. Act together. Don't let
anyone see us disorganized. Do not argue in front of people. Do not
talk about Hells Angels.

LORNE CAMPBELL giving a pep talk to co-accused

C ampbell showed up for one bail hearing with no footwear after
a guard took his shoes to X-ray them for security reasons and
was slow bringing them back. The floor was cold and Campbell
was cranky.

"They took my fucking shoes," Campbell grumbled. "It's like fucking
Nazi Germany." His lawyer, Tony Bryant, could only hope against hope
that the Jewish judge a few feet away didn't hear.

"I thought, 'Oh no, this is not a good start,'" recalls Evelyn.

There was no bail that day. The worst part for Campbell was seeing
how hard it was on Evelyn. He hated jail, but at least he was familiar
with the routine. "I'd look at Ev and Ev would be distraught. It hurts."

News came in a March 10, 2008, letter that one of Campbell's co-
accused, a Hells Angel nicknamed "4X4," had denounced the club.
Campbell knew that this sort of thing had the potential to make them

all look bad. The black guards' protests were still continuing on and off on May 1, when Campbell wrote Evelyn:

Hey There:

Pretty hard to get a visit around here. I guess they're still having their problems.
    It's 2:00 pm so I don't think the dentist is in the picture for 2-day. I'll have to wait till after the prelim is over. . . .
    And that's it for now. Here's a smile for you. [happy face]

I Love you
Lorne XOXO

On May 2, Campbell's journal summarized his experience in the Don, which was about to end:

3 to cell—original built for 1
—clothing changes 1 every 3 wks
—yard . . . sometimes not for wks
—lock down due to job acshone by guard—threats on black guard
—lockdown no visits because guards refuse to work because concerns over weapons in jail
—slept on floor beside toilet when 3 to cell
toilets flood whole range, piss, shit everywhere (2 inches, 5X)
constantly sick, dirty have to steal clean and disinfctant to clean cells.

After thirteen months in the Don, Campbell was finally transferred to the Metro East Detention Centre. Lockdowns at the East weren't quite as severe as at the Don. The cells were a little cleaner and less crowded, and the ventilation was better. As best he could, Campbell took up the same routine he had followed in the Don. When he was permitted to leave his cell, he spent much of his time in a special seat, where Campbell and Campbell alone could sit and play solitaire.

The transfer to the East signalled the start of his preliminary hearing, which began May 5. Finally, the legal process was moving ahead. There were daily trips to the Eglinton Avenue courthouse in suburban Scarborough, papers to study and talks with the lawyers.

On the first day of the preliminary, Campbell joined his co-accused in the prisoners' bullpen in the basement of the courthouse. He made it clear what he expected from them. They hadn't been through the court system as he had, and none of them had done serious prison time. "Throughout this, nobody is going to see you arguing," Campbell said. "We're all Hells Angels. Suck it up. Act solid. Act together. Don't let anyone see us disorganized. Do not argue in front of people. Do not talk about Hells Angels."

On their way to court each morning in the back of a transfer vehicle, the Angels picked the locks of their handcuffs and leg restraints with a plastic comb so they could stretch out and ride in more comfort. When they were pulling up to the jail, they'd click them back on again. It felt good to be free, but also to outwit the system, if only for a few minutes. One day, a guard opened the wagon earlier than expected and saw them all relaxing with their wrists free.

"Fuck," was the best Campbell could say.

If the guard had wanted to press the issue, they could all have been charged with attempting to escape, even though the Angels all silently put their manacles back on. "He never said a word."

One day on their ride into court, a young black prisoner rode with them. They didn't talk to him but undid his cuffs as a courtesy. "You guys without a doubt are the coolest motherfuckers I ever met," he said as they continued their conversation, ignoring him.

Campbell was saddened to hear how the grade nine daughter of Adolfo Rengel, a court officer who handled him, had been murdered on New Year's Day 2008. Stefanie Rengel had been lured from her home, stabbed six times and left to die in a snowbank just metres from her home. She was the victim of an obsessively jealous teenaged girl she had never met who was dating her former boyfriend. "He was a good guy. He always would talk to us, driving us back and forth to the preliminary. He'd remember our names and say, 'How are you doing?' Just a nice guy. A lot of these guys are ignorant. He wasn't. I said, 'Sorry to hear what happened.' He said, 'Thank you.'"

The preliminary was a chance to get out of jail for a few hours and see fellow club members, but there was a price. Each day, when they came back from court and put their court clothes away, they had to pull down their underwear and bend over for an up-close inspection. "The women guards are right there. It's extremely, extremely demeaning." It was the same routine when a team of a half-dozen guards made surprise checks on their cells. Prisoners were ordered out, one by one, and told: "Drop your boxers. Now bend over. Pull back your ass cheeks."

"Why do six guys have to look at your asshole?"

Family pictures and letters were eyeballed. All of their things from the canteen, such as gum and potato chips, would be mixed together in a pile, along with their bedding. "You didn't know what sheets are yours. What property is yours. I used to tell those guys, 'In a penitentiary you would not get away with that.' They'd say, 'What do you mean?' I'd say, 'You would fucking be jumped and have the shit kicked out of you. Or you would have a grievance against you. And we are not convicted.' They would never go into your cell in a prison. Guys would freak."

Things were a little better now for Evelyn. When Campbell was at the Don, she would sometimes make the two-hour drive down to Toronto only to hear there was a prisoner lockdown and she couldn't get a visit. Often Evelyn had to make four drives to the Don in one week to yield just two visits. She was waiting tables at a golf club at the time, so it was hard to take when she gave up sleep and made the long trip only to be told she couldn't see her husband. At the East Detention Centre, staff often let her know in advance when visiting privileges were cancelled, to spare her the drive. Other times, they just let her visit anyway.

Campbell wanted to be in shape physically when his trial finally started. He developed a fitness programme at the East, running twice around a tiny yard, which was half the size of a hockey rink, then alternating laps between running and walking. He was only supposed to be outside for twenty minutes a day, so this was as much running as he could get in.

In the winter, he lay on his back alone in the snow in the yard and made snow angels, which brought a laugh from the guards. Perhaps they thought he was making a statement. Campbell swears he was just playing in the snow.

Once a week, he went to Native smudge ceremonies. There was something about the people there that he felt he could trust. "They were really nice people. There were white guys and black guys too. It was nothing in this room went out of this room." While in the Native group, he made a dream catcher for Evelyn, designed to catch evil spirits.

A judge came in once to speak to prisoners and Campbell was curious what she would have to say. A few inmates giggled and heckled and farted loudly to disrupt her, while others asked questions of breathtaking stupidity. "Do you know that the police lie?" one agitated prisoner called out, and then gave a convoluted description of his case that was impossible to follow, except for the fact that he'd thrown illegal drugs away while being chased by police and then been charged anyway. The prisoner seemed to think the judge would be shocked by the injustice of this. "I don't know your case," the judge diplomatically replied.

"She was trying to help," Campbell remembers. He had trouble containing his rage against inmates who ruined the meeting, especially the moron whining about his drug arrest. "I thought, 'You fucker. Fucking bonehead. Is that why you came here?' I had a couple of questions but didn't get to ask them. When we were leaving, I apologized to her. She just smiled back."

On May 24, 2008, Campbell sent Evelyn a plain card:

Hey You:

And this is the card they sent me. It's a good thing that some of us care.
anyway happy anniversary and I so much wish I was out there
with you.
I love you with all my being

Lorne XOXO

On June 2, Campbell wrote his lawyer, Tony Bryant:

We know that the police are trying to put us all in jail. Just because you are not paranoid doesn't mean they're not out to get you. [Happy face]. . . .

We are "tightening up" to protect our way of life. No more— no less.

Then he wrote about transcripts of the secret recordings made by Shakey Dave Atwell, the friend turned police agent. "Him and Rod Barry talking about an eightball. It occurs to me that Attwell [sic] is instigating the so called drug talk in the clubhouse."

On June 4, Campbell again wrote Evelyn. He didn't have much to say, but the letter was a form of contact nonetheless:

Hey:

John and I are sitting here in our cell just thinking that they're pulling the same things on us as they are on them terrorists that are in the papers lately. It seems everywhere we are we're being recorded. Oh well.

There were a couple of paragraphs about a family member who was having troubles, and then he signed off.

A biker friend wrote on June 10 to state: "Remarkable how good and loyal and strong Evelyn has been through this whole ordeal. You have every reason to be proud of her."

The letter writer also noted that the son of a Hells Angel in San Quentin had been killed: "He was shot to death leading a funeral procession for J.R., a brother from Sonoma County that died in prison of cancer." He continued: "These are difficult times and your strength feeds us all. I am proud to be your brother and I know your support will help get through this. One day all of us that are separated by bars and borders will be sitting in a hot tub in a bordello in some place where they can't keep us apart."

———

On Sunday, June 15, Campbell wrote Evelyn:

Hey there:

Well we're just sitting here on Father's Day laughing at our cell mate.
I didn't know till an hour ago that he's in here for robbing a bank.
Listening to him tell the stories is enough to keep us entertained for a while.
Any way here's a Garfield cartoon that I got a kick out of. It's a good
one to hang on the fridge.
So goodnite and I'll see ya tomorrow at court.

I Love You
Lorne XOXO

The inscription on the Garfield card read: "Thinking of you adds a wonderful touch of love to my every day." The drawing showed Garfield the cat preparing to kick Odie the dog and then missing. He walks away in frustration, sneaks up behind the dog again, kicks him hard, and then thinks, "It's tough getting old."

CHAPTER 32

Holding Pattern

the only thing I miss more than you . . . you and me!

card from EVELYN to Lorne Campbell

Evelyn kept sending Campbell reading material, including the June 16, 2008, edition of *Maclean's* magazine, which had the front-page headline BUSTED: THE INSIDE STORY OF THE BERNIER SCANDAL. The headline alluded, not so subtly, to a cavernous cleavage shot on the cover of Julie Couillard, a former squeeze of a senior Quebec Hells Angel, who moved on to date Canadian foreign affairs minister Maxime Bernier. Evelyn also constantly sent cards with stories about their dogs and cars and her jobs, such as waiting tables at a golf course and customer service at Walmart. One card showed kids enjoying a picnic, and it contained the message: "the only thing I miss more than you . . . you and me! I love you." There were only so many ways of saying the same thing, but Evelyn kept on trying. On November 18, she wrote a note that said: "Well, it's pretty lonely without you. Writing cards is not the same eh. But that will change + we can be laying in the bedroom watching T.V. together pretending it's not snowing haha."

She also sent one to their friend and club member Shaun Robinson, who was also in custody awaiting charges from the Project Develop raids. It read: "Welcome to your new home."

Plenty of women Campbell had never met also took the time to write him, after getting his name and address from biker-friendly websites. One woman named Ruth (a.k.a. "hotmom") noted she was forty-two and a single mother:

> *Hi Lorne, how are you keeping? I do hope well! I do hope you don't mind me writing you but I want to send some love and let ya know I'm a supporter. I do think they should free all angels.*
>
> *I'm a platinum blonde, 5-2, 109 pds, have 5 tats . . . 2 angels on each top thigh (on the side) and my lower back has a cross with a design on each side going to my hips. Planning on getting more. . . . Do you have kids? Are you married?*

There was also a troubling letter from a woman he had known back when she was ten years old and he was in his late twenties. Tina Fudge clearly wasn't seeking male companionship of the romantic kind when she wrote from the Vanier Detention Centre in Milton, outside Toronto, where she was awaiting trial on a murder charge: "Fuck I tell ya things sure have changed since prison for woman days—this place is a joke. These girls think being Queer is kissing a girl—well I say Come over to my room I'll show you a few licks, oops I mean tricks ha, ha!"

Campbell remembers visiting her home when she was a little girl. "Her father was always in the pen. She and her sister were expected to have sex with visitors to their home when they were just kids. They didn't have a chance to learn any different."

Campbell's sixtieth birthday fell on Tuesday, September 2, 2008. On that milestone day, Campbell's journal entry shows he celebrated alone by doing 1,081 push-ups. His goal had been 1,000, but he added 81 for good measure because "81" is a nickname for the Hells Angels—H being the eighth letter of the alphabet and A the first.

By December, it was so cold in Campbell's cell that he could see his breath. He complained daily to jail officials about the lack of proper heating and wrote the provincial ombudsman. He received a letter dated

December 16 in which the ombudsman suggested he submit a written request to the jail superintendent.

Campbell's comment in his diary for March 27, 2009, reads: "Talked to the Rabbi and signed a paper to start the Kosher diet."

In his constant quest for better food behind bars, Campbell revived an old trick from prison and looked into changing religions. Now, he decided it was high time to become Jewish. That revelation hit him after he was impressed with the look of the kosher meals of fellow Hells Angel Mark (Bullet) Bodenstein. Any religion that allows for so much tasty fish couldn't be all bad in Campbell's books. Campbell told a jail chaplain that he was seeking to become a Jew, and the matter settled deep into the back of his mind until a guard stopped by his cell one day.

"Campbell, the rabbi is here to see you."

Campbell thought it would take much longer to set up the meeting, and he hadn't put much thought into his Judaism conversion story.

"Your name's Campbell," the rabbi noted. Perhaps he already sensed that Campbell sought kosher fish and chicken, not religious conversation.

"My mother's Jewish."

"Well, what's her last name?"

Campbell was flustered. His mind blanked. No Jewish names came immediately to mind. Somehow, he hadn't expected the question. At least not yet. The best he could manage was to ask the rabbi to speak with Evelyn, who was no more Jewish than Campbell.

The rabbi was no fool. Campbell attempted to rally by saying, "I left home when I was just a little kid," as if that would explain why he couldn't recall his mother's maiden name. He tried to gain a bit of control in the conversation by adding, "I'd really like a Jewish Bible. Could you get me one?" The rabbi's face showed things had just gone from bad to worse in less time than it takes to eat a bagel and lox. "He knows I'm lying. I know he knows I'm lying."

That was the last time Campbell saw the rabbi. The chaplain who arranged the meeting also wasn't impressed. Normally a cheerful woman, now she seemed to scowl at Campbell whenever she wasn't ignoring him altogether. It was a side of her Campbell hadn't seen before, and it was unsettling. "She liked everybody."

———

A March 27 story from the *Toronto Sun* noted that Gerald (Skinny) Ward, head of the Niagara Falls Hells Angels, had been sentenced to nine years in prison for instructing others to commit an offence on behalf of a criminal organization. Ward had already pleaded guilty to trafficking cocaine and possessing the proceeds of crime—$304,000 in cash, found in Ward's home after his arrest in September 2006. Like Campbell, a member of the club had turned against him. In Ward's case, it was Steven (Hannibal) Gault, the former Oshawa Hells Angel who made more than a million dollars working for police as a paid agent between the spring of 2005 and fall of 2006. Campbell had only talked with Gault a couple of times, but he found there was something off-putting about the way he wouldn't nod until Campbell nodded first. "He looked sneaky. He just didn't look right."

Other articles Campbell read behind bars included one published in the *Toronto Star* on March 27 about how Raymond Desfosses, a high-ranking member of Montreal's notorious West End Gang, and Frédéric Faucher, former leader of the Rock Machine, had been arrested along with eight others in Quebec in connection with dozens of murders linked to outlaw biker gangs between 1978 and 2003. Five of the victims were killed by accident. Police said the roundup was partly based on information provided by Gérald Gallant, a contract killer who turned police informant after committing twenty-seven murders himself and attempting another twelve. It was obvious that the more clubs got into drugs, the more blood was spilled and the more informer problems they developed. Old moral lines about police doing deals with the devil were now so blurred as to be non-existent.

Campbell couldn't control the outside world, but he could manage his health up to a point. His April 11, 2009, journal entry noted: "Started DIET Squats (240) No bread, potatoes, desserts, chocolate, sugar and no eating after supper." He could also zone out by losing himself in a game of chess. On June 9, he received a printout of "Rules of Chess" from Tony Biancofiore, the Angel who had been photographed shaking the hand of Toronto mayor Mel Lastman.

Campbell sent a letter to Evelyn on Monday, August 10 about Prison Justice Day, an event organized by his old friend Rick Sauvé. It was an attempt to call attention to violence against inmates and involved a day-long fast. His note to her mentioned how authorities tried to cut a deal with charter president John (Winner) Neal, the former Para-Dice Rider member who was caught up in the same sweep that put Campbell in jail:

Hey!!!

Scare ya? Well here it is "prison justice day" again. No food for the day. Actually I don't mind it. As it is I haven't eaten after supper since last Sunday and I think I've lost weight. And I do my abs everyday too.

The new glasses finally came which is a big relief. Tell me that wasn't like pulling hen's teeth. [happy face]

John just came back from his visit and told me he just found out they finally offered him a deal. Twelve years for conspiracy to commit trafficking, and leave the criminal org. up to the judge. Outrageous but that's just my opinion.

And that's about it for now. If I tell you everything that's going on there wouldn't be anything to put in the next card. [happy face]

I Love You
Lorne XOXO

Evelyn kept writing, sending cards and articles and puzzles and health recipes, with news of their dogs and anything else she thought he might want to hear. His Christmas cards in 2009 included one from his ten-year-old granddaughter, Chaedra: "Grandpa—you mean so much. . . . I love you Grampa. I miss you soooo much and I wish I could see you at Christmas Love Chaedra." Then she drew three hearts and concluded: "oxxxxxoooooxxxxo"

On an earthier note, another card read: "Your Luxembourg Brothers wish Merry Xmas and a fucking new year."

His Christmas reading also included an article sent to him by Evelyn, written by Sandro Contenta for the December 20 *Toronto Star*. In it, an academic likened shepherds at the time of Christ's birth to outlaw bikers in the twenty-first century. The comparison was that both the shepherds and the outlaw bikers had outsider roles, at the low end of the social ladder.

Contenta's article included this:

> *"It's perhaps an exaggeration to say, 'When you hear shepherds, think biker gang,' but they were really on the margins of society," says Rev. Andrea Budgey, the Humphreys Chaplain at Trinity College, who, as it happens, grew up on a Nova Scotia sheep farm.*
>
> *Shepherds were poorly paid, transient and armed to protect their flocks—characteristics that made them widely suspect and feared. . . .*
>
> *We even have documents from the Roman period where a prefect would say, "If you catch shepherds, flog them on the suspicion that they're bandits." You don't necessarily have to have evidence that they are—the very fact that they're shepherds tells you that if they're not criminals they're thinking of being one.*

The year 2010 began with heightened fitness goals. This should be the year Campbell finally went to trial, and he planned to show up in shape when he was judged by a jury of twelve strangers. His journal for January 1 stated: "160 decline pushups-Abs." The next day, it was: "Chin-ups, 6 sets of 5, Squats (240) 300 incline pushups, Abs." He also did incline and decline push-ups using the bars of the cell as leg and arm supports. The man who had been extreme in anger and extreme in drugs was now extreme in his pursuit of health and fitness. The former cocaine enthusiast now perused *Muscle* and *Men's Health* magazines, putting plenty of thought into various recipes for soy milk.

In federal penitentiaries, prisoners had jump ropes, but not in jail. Campbell would pay a couple of chocolate bars for other prisoners to make ropes for him, stripping sheets and braiding. Then Campbell dipped them in water, so they had just the right weight. It was steady work for the rope makers, as they were constantly confiscated. "I had guys that would do that. Just gave them a couple chocolate bars."

By January 16, Campbell was up to 300 push-ups, while his January 30 entry recorded: "Pull-ups 6 sets of 5, Abs 400 incline push-ups." Evelyn helped out, sending him information on the nutritional value of oats and rolled-oat recipes.

His daughter, Janice, wrote on March 10 to say that his granddaughter Chaedra had won a speech competition. London, England, Hells Angels sent him a card marking March 22, 2010, as Angel Day: "Thinking of you on this 22nd day of march 81st day of 2010." Cards of support kept coming in from places he had never visited and bikers he had never met, including charters in Bohemia and Luxembourg and a support charter in Bretagne (the Dreadfuls MC).

There was also news about bikers who had once worn Hells Angels patches and who were now publicly distancing themselves from the club. Terry Pink, the biker Phil Boudreault had almost starched in the Sudbury clubhouse, was among that group. He had been president of the Simcoe County charter, and was pinched through his deals with Steven (Hannibal) Gault.

It disgusted Campbell to learn how Pink had cried in court in February 2009, as he pined to be kept at home with his wife and two young kids. Pink had been convicted of selling 8,340 ecstasy tablets to Gault on four occasions, but vigorously denied committing the crimes. Campbell fumed that his crying threatened to make them all look weak and degrade the Angels brand. "You're a big shot, eh? You're making money. Two-inch chains around your fucking neck. Diamonds and gold and a big fancy bike. See how much you stand up when you get arrested and you're in one of these shitholes. See how much you complain. I didn't complain—only to my wife. I hate a coward. I can't stand a coward. Nothing wrong with fear. You don't have fear you're insane, but there's still no excuse for a coward."

There was also a generational disconnect between Pink and bikers like Campbell. Pink frosted his hair, installed a Louis Vuitton seat on his Harley, and shipped his bike long distances. Harleys in the 2000s were light years more comfortable than the spine-shaking, oil-dripping choppers of the 1960s and 1970s. Bikers like Merv (Indian) Blaker had built their rides up from rejected clunkers into something special. You wouldn't have caught Blaker on a Louis Vuitton seat. And you also would never have caught him shipping his bike for long runs. That was another Pink crime against the natural order of the biker universe, in Campbell's eyes. "Anybody that ships their bike, unless they have to be back real fast, I can't have a conversation with."

Campbell may have used Spray 'N Wash a couple of times a year to keep his Angels colours legible; otherwise, they'd go black from the road mud spraying up on them. But somewhere between the high-fashion seat and frosted hair and bike shipping and crying in public, men like Pink stopped being real bikers. "He's just a poser. The only time you'd see him on his bike is when he's on a run."

Campbell also felt severely let down by what he heard of the emotional courtroom performance of Kenneth (Wags) Wagner, another of Gault's targets. In October 2008, federal prosecutors announced that Wagner was the first Canadian criminal to have been found guilty under the "boss law," which involves directing others to commit crimes for the benefit of a criminal organization. Wagner, a first-time offender and father of two, had been a founder of the Hells Angels' Niagara charter in 2001. He pleaded guilty to trafficking four kilograms of cocaine, selling a gun to another Hells Angel and possessing $150,675 in criminal proceeds. Court heard that confidential police documents were found when police raided the Hells Angels' Niagara clubhouse and the homes of Wagner and Ward.

Campbell couldn't stand the image of club members like Wagner looking weak before the courts. "He's just a piece of shit. He was crying on the stand. It goes back to the saying, 'If you can't do the time, don't do the crime.'" In Campbell's books, Ward was cut from totally different cloth. "He stayed solid. He got an extra nine years after three in the bucket, but he still stayed solid."

Andre Watteel, president of the Angels' Kitchener charter, carried himself like a real biker, in Campbell's eyes. He too had been nailed by an informer in his midst whom he'd once trusted. But Watteel wasn't crying or buckling or squealing as he awaited his sentence for selling cocaine. Watteel wrote Campbell on June 6, 2010, from the Barton Street East jail in Hamilton:

We were immediately told there was a paid police agent + his name. It was not kept a secret. Buddy Frank was a friend of mine for 15 to 20 years. It makes me sick to think that a person I partied + drank with for that many years + trusted would work with the police against me. I guess some people have no trouble selling their friendship, that dollar is their only friend.

At the pretrial, the Crown offered to let Watteel off on fifty-six other charges if he pleaded guilty to criminal organization. "The answer was no," he wrote.

In his letter to Campbell, Watteel sounded hurt as he continued:

I never involved anybody else in anything I did. In the bodypacks I found some things that were said to the agent by myself that proved the rest of my friends were not involved in any way + I read in one of his conversations towards the end of the project to another person that Andre is independent + not working with any of his friends. . . .

Then, like a true friend, he dropped the subject and asked about Campbell's family. "How is your wife doing? She is a nice person. I know how hard it is on her + Winner's wife also."

Former Manitoba Hells Angels president Dale (Deli) Donovan wrote Campbell from Stony Mountain Penitentiary, outside Winnipeg, where he was serving an 8½-year sentence for an assortment of offences, including cocaine and marijuana trafficking. Donovan had sent Campbell pictures and designs to use in his former tattoo business, which was a big deal in the skin-inking world. With him was fellow Angel Jeff Peck, whom Campbell had known from Peck's days back in the Los Bravos. Police had managed to pay a career criminal to infiltrate their charter. If Donovan was flustered, he didn't show it as he wrote: "Me and Jeff are making good use of our free gym memberships here too. . . . I lost my gut and even put on some size."

Behind bars, the lines between paranoia and healthy realism all but evaporated. One day, he heard that a prisoner's wife had been caught trying to smuggle six .38 bullets inside. What the inmate planned to do with a gun was anyone's guess. "I don't know if he was going to smuggle the gun in after, a bit at a time," Campbell jokes. A guard asked Campbell if he had a gun and Campbell laughed at the suggestion.

On August 5, 2010, someone slipped a note under Campbell's cell door that read, "everything that you do in here is being recorded and you're being watched." The note wasn't signed. Meanwhile, gangstas remained protective of Campbell. If they didn't trust an inmate who was about to be transferred into his cell, they would warn the prisoner that they didn't want him there. They didn't have to say it as a threat; it was obvious what the words meant. That summer, the gangstas were leery about an older prisoner also named Campbell, who had only been in the jail a couple of days.

"We seen him talking to people," a gangbanger said. "We think he's a cop here for you."

"They told the guards to get him the fuck off the range," Campbell recalls. "They did so. They're not stupid."

Evelyn kept driving down to Toronto for visits. Things warmed up with the Metro East staff after they noticed her weeding a flower garden outside the jail while waiting to be let inside.

CHAPTER 33

Legal Showdown

He felt like picking on an old guy. I hit him six or seven times.

LORNE CAMPBELL

C ampbell's trial was set to begin on Monday, September 13, 2010, at the Toronto Courthouse on University Avenue, a stately limestone building just down the road from the former mental asylum grounds where the provincial legislature now sits. Shortly before the first day of court, Campbell received a card from Rev. Douglas Tebbutt, a heavy-set, leathered man who had been officiating at biker funerals since the 1960s: "There is a strong team on the internet standing in strength for you." Some of the bikers who had once found freedom and brotherhood on the open roads now sought them online.

Campbell marked the opening day of the trial with an entry in his journal. At the top of each page was a religious inscription. On that day: "For the LORD is good, his mercy is everlasting; and his truth endureth to all generations"—Psalms 100:5. Campbell's handwritten entry for that day dealt with something far less than absolute, godly truth. In pencil, it read: "START OF TRIAL." By that were three stars. It continued: "5.55 breakfast. Chest & back pain!!!"

Campbell had elected trial by jury. Almost three years in jail with no bail, nor even time to attend his mother's funeral, had convinced him that trial by judge alone would be suicide. Campbell's trial was being conducted at the same time as the cases against John (Winner) Neal, the sixty-year-old president of the Downtown Toronto Hells Angels; vice-presidents Larry Pooler, sixty, and Douglas Myles, fifty-four; and member Mehrdad (Mark, Juicy) Bahman, forty-nine. Two currents ran through each of their cases. The first one was relatively commonplace and grubby, and involved the efforts by Shakey Dave Atwell to draw as many of his clubmates as possible into low-level drug and weapons deals. Campbell fell into the net when he agreed to take a thousand dollars for setting Atwell up with Shaun Robinson.

The second current was far more serious. It involved allegations of criminal conspiracy and committing crimes for the benefit of a criminal organization. At its core were Juicy Bahman and his dealings with Vincenzo (Jimmy) Sansalone of the Haney, B.C., charter of the Hells Angels and Omid (Mo) Bayani of the United Nations, a new and particularly violent group of west coast criminals.

The United Nations was a gang that existed to commit crimes, with none of the bikers' allusions to brotherhood. Originally called the Global United Nations Syndicate (GUNS), their name referenced their multi-ethnic nature, as the gang had Indo-Canadian, white, Iranian and Asian members. Much of their money came from flying tons of high-grade British Columbian cannabis by private planes and helicopters into the United States, where they swapped it for cocaine to sell at home. This business meant run-ins with B.C. H3ells Angels as they carved out their market.

Bayani had middling power in his group, which boasted about seventy-five members in the Lower Mainland area of B.C. The commonly accepted story behind Bayani is that when he was just five years old, his father was murdered in Iran and the word "Bahai" was written on his lifeless chest by Iranian fundamentalists bent on stamping out the Baha'i faith. Bayani's family fled to Turkey, and when he was sixteen he arrived in Red Deer, Alberta, with his mother and sisters. He found work at a fast-food restaurant and was still in his teens when he drew a four-year term in a medium-security prison for a crime spree. Wearing a balaclava, he'd robbed workers at five convenience stores for cash and cigarettes at knifepoint.

If Bayani was bad on the streets, he was even worse behind bars. He ran up twenty-one more charges as a prisoner, including one for beating an inmate's face with a club that had the words "goof beater" carved into it. He was bumped up from a medium- to a maximum-security prison, where his behaviour only got worse, as he constantly tried to goad guards into fights.

On July 20, 1997, the federal immigration minister signed a deportation application to send him back to Iran, declaring him "a danger to the public of Canada." His lawyer fought back with an application to stay in Canada on humanitarian and compassionate grounds. As the lawyers wrangled, Bayani floated away on bail and began doing business with fellow Iranian immigrant Juicy Bahman when Bahman was just a Hells Angels prospect.

Bayani had fronted Bahman six hundred litres of the date-rape drug GHB, worth eighty thousand dollars, with an agreement to pay him back with the profits from sales. When police caught wind of the deal, they lifted the drug from the Toronto garage where it had been stored and staged things to look as if there had been a break-in.

What happened next was predictably tense. The United Nations threatened to murder Bahman if he didn't pay back the eighty thousand dollars he owed them. Bahman didn't have the money to do so without sales proceeds from the drugs, which had been taken by the police. The B.C. Hells Angels needed some sort of truce to get the United Nations off their backs, since Bahman's dealing threatened their credibility. Furthermore, there was a principle at stake for the bikers. Hells Angels have a "no rips"—or no drug rip-off—rule, and Bahman's predicament reflected badly on all of them.

Despite the mess, Bahman had gone on to get his full patch, and the club in B.C. and Ontario inherited his troubles. Toronto president John (Winner) Neal felt the need to mediate, even though no one in the Toronto charter had been part of the GHB deal apart from Bahman. "Nobody knew about this but Juicy," Campbell explains. "It was no club conspiracy to deal GHB. They don't even know what it was."

There were times during the preliminary, held by Justice Gail Dobney, when the Angels might have been forgiven if they had reconsidered their effort to save Juicy's skin. "He was farting from the prisoners' box during the preliminary. He thinks it's funny. I said, 'That's the judge that's judging you, you stupid fuck. That's the judge that's judging me too. We're facing years. I'm getting double digits if we're convicted, you stupid fuck.' It was funny when he called her Judge Dodge Omni, but the loud farting had to stop. She seemed to be reading papers, but she had to hear it. I spoke to him. He stopped doing it."

Even with Juicy's new-found efforts to control his flatulence in the prisoners' box, he remained a boor at heart. "You can't imagine the pig that the guy is." He revelled in displaying the tattoo of *JUICY* that ran across his ample belly. "He was fond of showing people that." Juicy didn't say how he got the nickname, and there was a good chance not many people would have wanted to know. Perhaps the worst part of sharing close quarters with Juicy was when he ate, and his big round face moved like oatmeal coming to a boil, with every muscle actively involved in the chewing, smacking, sucking and swallowing of whatever was on his plate. It was even worse than eating with Pigpen back in the old Satan's Choice days. "He [Pigpen] eats normally. He was brought up as a gentleman. It was the acts that he did that got him his name."

During the court case, Campbell finally learned why he had been "mud-tested" in Haney, B.C., at the Angels' clubhouse. It was because Juicy, who was then just a prospect, had used the Angels' name to get into the GHB deal with Bayani and the United Nations, only to screw it up and bring heat back on the club. "That's why I got mud-tested. That's why they said, 'We don't like guys coming out here from Ontario and acting like they've been Hells Angels for fifteen years.' I had no idea until the court case. I just knew I was mud-tested."

During the preliminary hearing, Campbell watched as Bayani sat quietly near Evelyn in the public area of the courtroom. Bayani was free on bail and curious to hear what was being said about him. One day, he heard the police intercept of a conversation in which Bahman ridiculed Bayani's clothing and then threatened to chop him up into little bits.

"I didn't know where to look," Evelyn recalls. "He smiled."

Campbell was also watching Bayani's face, and found himself thinking he would be a good man to stand beside in a war. "I've been involved in a lot of violence. I looked at him and thought, 'So has he.' He didn't let anything bother him. I never met him in the life, but I liked his style."

After three months of pretrial wrangling, Campbell was eager to defend himself. Bryant set the tone for his defence when he opened the actual trial before Justice Maureen Forestell by filing a statement from Campbell that became the trial's first exhibit. It was an acknowledgement that he was a full-patch Hells Angel, and proud of it.

As the trial began, Campbell became concerned that Juicy seemed prepared to cut a deal and plead guilty to conspiracy. To protect the club as a whole, Campbell quickly moved to put the brakes on any individual deal-making. By their very nature, conspiracy charges involve more than one person. "I told him, 'Juicy, don't do that. Don't tell me you can make a deal for conspiracy and not involve anyone else.'"

Juicy agreed and didn't go ahead with any conspiracy deal. He immediately pleaded guilty to nine charges of trafficking drugs and possession of the proceeds of crime. He entered not-guilty pleas to possession of brass knuckles and to trafficking drugs and guns to benefit a criminal organization.

In her opening remarks, Crown attorney Tanit Gilliam said that Atwell's undercover operation was halted after Myles grilled him in February 2007 about his involvement in a number of cocaine and GHB deals gone bad. That was around the time Shakey Dave started acting whiny to Campbell about people saying mean things about him. Gilliam told the court that Neal, Myles and Pooler stepped in to arrange payment of Bahman's drug debt: "This was done in order to protect the reputation and good name of the Hells Angels." Lawyers for Neal, Myles and Pooler countered that the Toronto Hells Angels weren't trying to traffic GHB, just protect Bahman's skin from angry drug dealers from B.C. As the Angels saw things, they were now being punished for peacemaking.

Amidst the intrigue and talk of murder plots, there was time for a food fight. Legal affairs writer Tracey Tyler of the *Toronto Star* reported that Toronto jail residents such as Campbell received only $1.19 worth of food for their lunch, which often was no more than a semi-nutritious cheese sandwich and a glass of water with artificial flavour crystals. That paled compared with the $5.89 spent for jailhouse lunches in

Newfoundland, where prisoners often dined on grilled salmon and grilled chicken pitas, roast beef, mashed potatoes and coleslaw, which they could wash down with skim milk. In the end, the Downtown Toronto Angels were allowed to buy their own lunches from the court cafeteria. While this meant healthier, better-tasting food, it also meant an added expense of thousands of dollars for Evelyn as the trial dragged on. Campbell's diary entry for Tuesday, October 19 read: "5.05 Breakfast. Motion to sit beside my lawyer denied. Won the food fight. We are allowed lunch from caf. We pay. No hot."

When Shakey Dave Atwell took the stand in mid-November, he was dressed in a conservative business suit, shirt and tie, and looked like an undertaker, not a biker. He quickly told the court he expected to spend the rest of his life in hiding.

"I'm a . . . rat," he told Crown attorney Faiyaz Alibhai. "I've got to be hiding for the rest of my life, sir."

As Shakey Dave confided his fears, his former clubmates showed not even a flicker of sentiment towards him. This was according to plan. It was like the shunning by a strict religious order of a wayward former member, whose very existence is not worthy of the slightest acknowledgement. Campbell had reminded the others in the box to keep any reactions in check: "'Do not make any emotion towards anybody. Don't huff. Don't make a face.' It was hard. Even for me. It just looks bad, and it's a kid thing to do." He gave the same caution to Evelyn, who was in a front row of the courtroom daily. Atwell craved attention and Campbell didn't want them to give him any.

Shakey Dave fought to keep his voice even as he noted there was a photo of Steve (Hannibal) Gault on the walls of clubhouses across the province. Written over Gault's photo inside the Toronto clubhouse were the words "Rat" and "LIAR."

Evelyn, meanwhile, studied the eyes of jurors. She felt that one of them had a crush on Tony Bryant, as she seemed to have a bad case of "moon eyes." That was good. However, two of them seemed to have a crush on Atwell. That was very bad.

Atwell continued his testimony, noting that some members of the club once wore patches on their vests that read "Filthy Few." He explained: "Those members of the Hells Angels have killed for the club." That had recently been replaced by a patch called "Front Line" after "Filthy Few" began to attract too much police and media attention, he said. In fact, the Downtown Toronto Hells Angels routinely swept their fortified clubhouse for police listening devices and spoke with hand signals and code words when discussing drug deals. "There was a lot of note writing, and you'd burn the note afterwards. There was a lot of talking in code and signals." Code for a kilogram of cocaine was holding car keys, while touching one's nose meant cocaine. Rubbing a thumb over a cheek meant "Mafia," while tugging on a sleeve was shorthand for buying drugs on the cuff, with payment coming later. He added that he personally had upgraded the infrared security camera system around the clubhouse.

Atwell said that the clubhouse had a sliding steel front door and concrete pillars—disguised as flower planters—to slow down any police battering rams heading their way. Cocaine and marijuana were freely consumed inside the Eastern Avenue clubhouse, Atwell continued, and he personally had been a frequent and enthusiastic user. "You go to a biker party, there are guys smoking pot in one corner and guys doing lines of cocaine in another corner."

Campbell's journal entry for Thursday, December 2 was printed below a particularly apt line of Scripture: "There is no peace, saith my God, to the wicked"—Isaiah 57:21. Campbell's entry that day read: "Got in a fight in medical bull pen & put in the hole. Misconduct."

His heart troubles re-emerged and seeing a doctor while in custody was always a strain. "You can't get upset with the doctor in there. They'd take you and throw you in the hole." One day when court wasn't sitting, Campbell went to the jail's medical centre. When he got up to ask a question, a young convict rushed into his seat.

"I'm sitting here," Campbell said.

"Fuck you," the inmate replied.

"He felt like picking on the old guy. I hit him six or seven times." Before each shot, Campbell called out, "Watch out." The younger prisoner wasn't able to connect with shots of his own. "While they were taking me away, I said, 'Nice try, kid.'"

On Friday, January 14, Andre Watteel of the Kitchener Angels sent Campbell a card from jail in Hamilton. Two days earlier, Watteel had been hit with a 6½-year sentence for trafficking in cocaine and possessing the proceeds of crime. He had earlier pleaded guilty to selling almost a kilogram of high-grade cocaine to police during twenty-eight separate deals.

He was ordered to return the sixty thousand dollars that police provided to an undercover agent to buy the cocaine, as well as forfeit a PT Cruiser he drove during some of the coke deals. As he passed sentence, Ontario Court Justice John Takach noted that Watteel had been a prominent member of the Satan's Choice Motorcycle Club before it "patched over" to the Hells Angels in Sorel, Quebec, in December 2000. The judge also noted that Watteel and his wife organized a Christmas toy drive and performed other charitable good deeds in their community. However, Takach continued, these acts of community service were outweighed by the damage drugs cause society. "Cocaine is an insidious poison that has destroyed innumerable lives," Takach said. "Even before one ounce reaches the street, it is indubitably soaked with the blood of others."

Watteel felt the judge couldn't see past his Hells Angels membership, writing Campbell: "In my sentencing the judge focused more on my membership than the crimes. . . . I don't think anybody gets a fair trial."

Back at Campbell's own trial, there were a few light moments on Friday, February 11 when Downtown vice-president Larry Pooler got to play lawyer and cross-examine Atwell. Jurors and prisoners grinned as Pooler presented himself as a model of civility, looking dapper in a pinstriped charcoal business jacket, with his long grey hair pulled back in a tight ponytail. Pooler had been free on strict bail conditions and was acting as his own lawyer in a nine-dollar sports jacket he had bought at a Salvation Army store.

He asked Atwell to think back to his mother's death in 2002. "Did the club not support you? Rally around you? Attend the funeral? That kind of thing?" Pooler asked.

"Some members attended the funeral," Atwell replied, controlling his emotions.

For much of his two-hour cross-examination, Pooler asked Atwell about club rules against having unpaid bills or cheating people in business transactions.

"Would you not agree . . . that I was a stickler for the rules?" Pooler asked.

"For some rules," countered Atwell.

Pooler asked Atwell what he considered to be Pooler's line of work.

"You had a couple of concerts and bike shows," he replied. "I never attended any of them."

"So I was a self-employed businessman?"

"Yeah, that would be fair."

"Have you known me to be a drug user?" Pooler continued.

"I thought I seen you smoking a joint. I could be wrong. I never knew you to be a drinker either."

Pooler asked Atwell if he could remember serving as a bodyguard for a man named Larry.

"That guy who pulled a gun on you?"

Pooler didn't flinch at the reply, moving on to the next question on several sheets of notes in front of him.

Some jurors smiled as Pooler scrupulously observed courtroom protocol, addressing Atwell as "Mr. Atwell," and at one point saying to Justice Forestell, "May I approach the witness, your Honour?"

"Yes," the judge replied.

Atwell had earlier testified that men joining the Hells Angels are required to fill out a form, giving personal information such as the names and addresses of relatives.

"The form also asked if you might have pets or other issues that require attention?" Pooler asked, referring to a club practice of taking care of each other's pets when members are suddenly pinched by police.

Atwell responded with a shrug.

Pooler asked Atwell about a business dispute over a vehicle sale while Atwell was working as a police agent. "Is it true that you took a baseball bat out of your vehicle and proceeded to smash the lights out of that vehicle?" Pooler asked.

"I think it was a bat that was [already] there and it was another vehicle," Atwell replied, as if the clarification made a significant difference.

Pooler quizzed Atwell on whether he managed to settle all of his debts before he disappeared into witness protection, including one to a man named Lou.

"You owed some money to the underworld?" Pooler asked.

"I didn't," Atwell said.

"But he [Lou] believed you did?"

"He can believe anything he wants."

Atwell sounded a bit testy now as Pooler asked if Atwell knew if Lou was connected to serious players in the underworld.

"I met Peter Scarcella through him," Atwell replied, referring to the former driver of murdered mobster Paul Volpe. Atwell stopped there, not elaborating on any alleged underworld debts.

Campbell and Bryant had thought of lightening things up by playing the jury an audio recording of Atwell singing karaoke at a bar with fellow Hells Angels. Shakey Dave had worn only a sheet as he lay on his back and belted out the Ray Stevens novelty tune "Ahab the Arab." But without video, they decided not to. It might not have made any great legal point, but it would have been fun.

Bryant had wanted to put Campbell on the stand, but Campbell nixed the idea. The only other time he had testified in court was at the trial for the Bill Matiyek shooting, and that couldn't have gone much worse. Besides, lead investigator Al Rennie of the OPP likely knew plenty more about the Hells Angels internationally than he did. If Campbell was asked questions that he couldn't answer, that would only make him look evasive. In the end, none of the Angels took the stand.

One day in the prisoners' box, Campbell felt a great weight crushing his chest. There hadn't been anything particularly exciting or stressful going on when the pains hit. He didn't want to think it might be his heart, but that was the obvious conclusion. Doug Myles pushed him to tell a court officer. Court was halted as an ambulance was called. Paramedics took his vital signs and then rushed him to the hospital. Two East Detention Centre guards stayed with him throughout. "I was shackled and handcuffed to the hospital bed, but that is standard procedure."

The scare happened on one of the few days Evelyn wasn't in court. Tony Bryant called their close friend Elizabeth Sanchez, who broke the news to her. For a frantic few hours, Evelyn tried to figure out where her husband had been taken and how he was doing. They weren't any help at the jail, where a guard said words to the effect of: "All we know is that if he doesn't come back, we put him down as escaped and we go looking for him." Finally, Evelyn got through to his hospital ward, where a nurse said: "Oh, he's fine. He's joking around with all of the nurses."

Campbell received a letter sent April 10, 2011, from Sean (9 Fingers) McLay, writing from Gravenhurst minimum-security prison. McLay was in custody for cocaine trafficking and Evelyn had taken him on as a foster child of sorts. She bought 9 Fingers black jeans and T-shirts from Walmarts and Value Villages and Giant Tigers so that he wouldn't look too raggedy in court. She did the same for other inmates who didn't have anyone to look out for them. She found that inmates were notoriously bad at estimating their sizes, and she often had to make an educated guess. "He always appreciated that," Evelyn said.

From his cell, 9 Fingers wrote to Campbell:

> *I'm here with 'Forehead' and Eddie 'the King of Regent Park', they both say hi!*
>
> *I'm out in 25 days so this will be the last letter from me for awhile as I can't be in contact with anyone while on parole (14 months). I'll just be keeping a low profile and working.*

After all the bullshit is done with we should meet up for a drink of
scotch. See you then.

Respects
Sean 9 fingers

In his closing remarks in May 2011, Bryant acknowledged that the
jurors must be sick of the legal system after nine months of hearing
evidence. He quoted from Shakespeare's *Henry VI, Part 2*, which includes
the line: "The first thing we do is kill all the lawyers." That was always
sure to get at least a smile from tired jurors. Then he drew from Lewis
Carroll's *Alice in Wonderland* and the passage on the trial of the Knave of
Hearts, who was accused of stealing the Queen of Hearts' tarts:

"Consider your verdict," the King said to the jury.
   "Not yet, not yet!" the Rabbit hastily interrupted. "There's a great
deal to come before that!"

Bryant then introduced jurors to writings from the trial in 356 CE of
Numerius, a governor in the Roman Empire. "Oh, illustrious Caesar! If
it is fit to deny, what hereafter will become of the guilty?" the prosecutor
asked, to which Emperor Julian replied, "If it suffices to accuse, what
will become of the innocent?"

Next cited was the fictional lawyer Horace (*Rumpole of the Bailey*)
Rumpole, created by British writer and barrister John Mortimer.
"Fictional character though he may be, he did one thing in every case he
tried. He would always talk of the golden thread that winds its way
through our criminal law: the golden thread of proof beyond a reasonable doubt. Let me repeat that—proof beyond a reasonable doubt.

"That idea that someone can only be convicted on the basis of proof
of the offence beyond a reasonable doubt is a hallmark of the Anglo-
Canadian criminal justice system—a bulwark that separates our system
from those of other societies considerably less free and democratic."
Bryant was serving the jury feel-good stuff about Western civilization
and the basis of British jurisprudence. "Its importance is unchallenged.

This golden thread is very much a part of the fabric of Canadian society and was permanently enshrined in our Charter of Rights and Freedoms though it existed long before it was written back in the early 80s."

Once Bryant finished his remarks, all Campbell could do was return to his cell and wait. "I was relaxed. He [Bryant] made every point. He was shocking and he was brave. He can be arrogant and condescending, but he has a sense of humour and he is loyal and he is extremely smart. A lot of people don't see his sense of humour. They don't see his intelligence and his loyalty to his clients. He was there every day. I would rather have no other lawyer on that case."

When the jury finally returned on May 23, 2011, after four days of deliberations, none of them looked towards the bikers in the prisoners' dock.

"This isn't good," Campbell thought.

CHAPTER 34

Riding Off

It used to be you knew who your enemies were.

LORNE CAMPBELL

Four years, one month and seventeen days after the mass arrests and the shutdown of their former bunker-like clubhouse on Eastern Avenue, there were tears in the eyes of at least one Crown attorney as the five Downtown Toronto Hells Angels were all acquitted on charges of belonging to a criminal organization. Campbell was found guilty of conspiracy to traffic cocaine, while Neal, Myles and Bahman were convicted of charges relating to trafficking GHB; a charge for possession of a restricted firearm stuck against Pooler.

It was as good a result as Campbell could have hoped for, considering the evidence. He knew from the start he didn't have a realistic shot of beating the cocaine charge, since he was caught on tape discussing the price of a kilo of cocaine with Atwell. "He [Bryant] couldn't fight that," Campbell says. "They had it on audio and video. How could he fight the thirty-four? That's the price of the cocaine." The length of his pretrial custody more than covered the amount of time he would have got for his cocaine conspiracy conviction, which meant he was a free man. "They still owe me some time on my next conviction," he says jokingly.

He never did get any of the $1,000 Shakey Dave had promised for setting him up for the coke deal or the $425 for the eyeglasses eaten by Atwell's dog. Of course, Shakey Dave and Brutus were now vanished into a witness protection programme. For Campbell, the big thing was that the criminal organization charges didn't stick. That had mattered most to Campbell right from the beginning, and in the end nobody pleaded down to any conspiracy charge. Members obviously committed crimes, but Campbell felt strongly that the Hells Angels was an organization that included criminals, not a strictly criminal enterprise. For many members of the public that's just wordplay, but for Campbell it's a very personal and important distinction. Not to believe this is an insult to his many friends in clubs over the years, no matter what the police might say. They were friends and brothers first and criminals second, if at all.

In an attention-craving world where there's no greater insult than to ignore the existence of someone, Campbell and Evelyn say they plan to pretend Shakey Dave Atwell was never born. Evelyn Campbell says she considers Shakey Dave utterly insignificant in the big scheme of things: "Dave came into our life and went out of our life. He caused problems and those problems are gone."

"We don't even think of that fuck," Campbell adds.

On the other side of the country, Omid (Mo) Bayani of the United Nations was due in court on September 7, 2011, for sentencing after his drug trafficking conviction related to Campbell's trial. True to form, Bayani drifted away again. He still hadn't reappeared fifteen weeks later and was sentenced, *in absentia*, to seven years in prison, while Haney, B.C., Hells Angel Vincenzo (Jimmy) Sansalone was hit with a six-year sentence for setting up the meeting between Bahman and Bayani that ultimately led to what a judge called the biggest seizure of the date-rape drug in Canadian history.

Campbell's Downtown Toronto clubmate Mark Stables hadn't been picked up in the raids that netted Campbell, but he was in legal troubles as well after security at Vancouver International Airport found Hells Angels paraphernalia in his luggage in November 2006. A background check revealed that Stables hadn't taken out Canadian citizenship since being brought here from Scotland when he was seven years old. Forty-two years after his arrival in Canada, Stables faced deportation to Scotland because he was a high-ranking Hells Angel who had served as treasurer and sergeant-at-arms for his charter. He had no criminal record and was a fitness enthusiast with black belts in karate and jiu-jitsu. He supported himself by running a downtown Toronto gym whose clients included professional mixed martial arts fighters and several Toronto police officers. Stables said he left the Angels in 2009, but the Immigration and Refugee Board ruling disputed this, arguing that his club tattoo showed no "exit date." He was put on a jet back to his birthplace. "This guy I don't think even gets speeding tickets," Campbell says. "He's a good family man. He didn't drink, didn't do drugs. Worked hard all his life. Paid all his taxes. Nothing criminal about that guy. He hated criminal activity."

When Campbell returned home with Evelyn, he felt more than a little stunned, like he was trapped in a twilight zone. "It was unreal. It was like you don't know how to act. I might have looked normal, but I didn't know how to act." So much had changed, including himself. Time behind bars had conditioned him to blank out his peripheral vision and walk with his eyes aimed down and straight ahead. It also made him extremely possessive about his things. "In jail, nobody touches your stuff." Even a little thing like getting up to speed on computers or learning how to use a smart phone was a challenge. "I threw one across a room. I didn't have any patience."

Some things remain constant amidst all of the change. It remains a given that connivers are people to be shunned. Loyalty remains a virtue. A true man plays the cards he's dealt and doesn't whine. The best things in life are measured in quality rather than quantity. It takes more courage to love than to hate. There's power in an honest story, even if it's not always flattering. If you have a few rock-solid people around you, you're a lucky man. Campbell walked out of jail still believing all of these things.

Once at home, it was only natural to take stock of his life and consider how he planned to live out his final years. Campbell belonged to a club that spanned the globe, with members on five continents. At the same time, he missed the scruffy, un-corporate, often ultra-rude days when partying to excess was a priority. The circus had moved on, and he wasn't convinced it was going to a better place. Some members of the Port Hope Eight—Merv (Indian) Blaker, Gary (Nutty) Comeau, Rick Sauvé and Jeff (Boom Boom) McLeod—are blocked from ever joining a one-percenter club because of parole stipulations. Gordon (Dog Map) Van Haarlem had quit the Choice years before and moved west. Armand (In the Trunk) Sanguigni was dead from an overdose of heroin, while Larry (Beaver) Hurren had died in a motorcycle accident.

That meant Campbell was the only one in the Port Hope case to have moved on to the Hells Angels. He still considers the death of Bill Matiyek a sad waste of life, but he also still doesn't regret carrying a gun that night or using it to protect his clubmates. It remains a deep source of pain that he wasn't believed when he stepped up in court and tried to take responsibility for the shooting. There's also a sense of awe at how his old group hung together and refrained from pointing fingers, even when they faced serious prison time for their silence. "In prison nowadays, it's no respect," Campbell says. "Never would eight guys stick together like that today. It would not happen now. Guys were different back then. They were guys that had a lot to lose and still didn't say a thing. They did their fucking time and never said a word, other than that they're innocent. Innocent completely. That went a long ways internationally. They all earned the utmost respect from every one-percenter club in the world. I'm so proud."

Some old biker haunts such as the Genosha, the Queen's and the Atherley Arms went out of business years ago. Others have had dramatic makeovers like the Cadillac, which is now a social services drop-in centre instead of a hard-core, bucket-of-blood watering hole. Phil Boudreault, the biker who likes to see himself as a junior Campbell, was rearrested for a parole violation not long after being interviewed for this book. So much changes; so much stays the same. Campbell loves to hear how Indian Blaker is cruising roadways into the twenty-first century on the same Harley Sportster that he rode back in the 1970s, and Indian bought it second-hand back then. "Guys back then seemed more comfortable in their own skin," Campbell says.

Campbell can't shake the feeling that his old world has been swamped by waves of paid informants, as clubs expand around the globe. "It used to be you knew who your enemies were. I'm sixty-four years old. I don't want to be seventy-four and back behind bars because of an informant like Shakey Dave. This past four years [behind bars] was because of other people's lack of due diligence . . . Sometimes I feel I can write all my friends' names on the back of a fucking postage stamp, and I'm happy with that."

A few of the changes are for the better, such as the fact that most Hells Angels charters no longer allow smoking at meetings. "A lot of guys are older. It bothers people at meetings nowadays." Some other changes are just signs of the times. He sounds like an old cowboy wistfully noting the shrinking frontier when he observes that there's a general reluctance to sleep out under the stars on extended rides. "When they go on runs nowadays, nobody camps. It's all motels. I don't mind putting my coat over myself by my bike. My helmet for a pillow. You don't need anything else but a helmet."

Campbell's hard-core reputation didn't go away when he stopped wearing a club patch. He was reminded of this when a man approached him at a concert and asked, within a few minutes of saying hello, whether Campbell would kill his wife.

"I'll pay you," the man said.

"Get that out of your mind," Campbell replied. "That's the mother of your kids."

Campbell wasn't totally shocked by the approach, recalling how a middle-aged woman he didn't know had once walked up to him to ask if he'd kill her son.

"Why would you think I'd do that?" Campbell asked.

"I know all about you," the mother replied.

"I just laughed at them," Campbell says. "'I know who you are. I know what you do.' I've heard that so many times."

As a survivor of more than four decades of outlaw biker life, Campbell has spoken privately with people who have done violent things that haunt them. "I've counselled people who've gone over the line. Couldn't deal with what they've done. My advice is: learn to live with it or turn yourself in."

Campbell can be brutally blunt, but he refuses to say a bad thing about Elinor, the mother of his daughter Janice. He freely acknowledges that she deserved far better than his treatment of her. After he got out of the Don Jail, it seemed time to appreciate Evelyn, his daughter Janice, his grandkids Jemelie, Joriana and Chaedra, and Evelyn's adult daughter Kylie, who grew to become an excellent equestrienne in her own right. He knows he has missed far too many family events because of club commitments and wants that to change in his remaining years. "Before, there was always something," Campbell says. "Runs, anniversaries, parties. Now there's time."

Contrary to popular myth, a Hells Angel can retire in good standing if he has the respect of his fellow members. That's what Campbell did shortly after his release from the Don Jail. He handed back his vest and jewellery, his track suits, T-shirts and anything else with the trademarked Hells Angels death head on it. Such material never actually belongs to members, but is always just on loan to them; on death or retirement or expulsion, it must be returned to the club. Campbell also had the exit date 09/06/11 tattooed under his Hells Angels tattoo on his upper left arm, along with the word "left." That's a key word for a former Angel, since "out" means kicked out of the club while "left" is the biker equivalent of honourable discharge, bestowing something akin to Hells Angel emeritus status. That done, an unfamiliar sense of calm settled over Campbell. "Since I got out of jail, I can't be bothered getting pissed off," Campbell says. "Wasting energy on little things. Don't sweat the small things. I'm like that now. I've never been scared of death. Everyone dies. I still have bitterness, but I fight it very well."

Despite the ungodly names of his clubs and his scamming of the Bible in jail, Campbell says he still believes in a supreme deity. His God is like an all-loving parent, who doesn't need him to be humble. Some aspects of his God sound a lot like Campbell himself. "I think God forgives. He's got a sense of humour. I don't get down on my knees and ask for forgiveness. I believe that He automatically forgives you. I don't think that you have to automatically go down on your knees." Campbell also has his own strong views on karma. "What goes around comes around. The good that you do or the bad that you do. The major things." He says he's already reaping positive benefits for at least some of his own personal karma. "As harsh as I've been, I've been very good to the people I love and the people around me. That's come back to me.

"People ask, 'Why would you join a [motorcycle] club?' I had no stable family growing up. Lots of cousins and aunts and uncles, but no stable family. That [club] was the first stable family I had. If you don't love that life, I could see why it freaks people out. Would I recommend that someone young join a club today? Only if you could handle the hardships: the heat from the cops. Bernie Guindon had a saying: 'Lose your job, lose your wife, go to jail.' That's the three things you're taking a chance of losing.

"For my grandkids, I don't discourage anybody, but I don't recommend it. I think you have to be a certain brand to last in that kind of life. It fit for me. There were a lot of good times. I love riding my motorcycle, and the camaraderie. That, I never had growing up. I never regretted it, but a lot of people would. The advice I would give to younger kids is more general: Don't be led astray. . . . Listen to your conscience. Be comfortable in your own skin."

Campbell maintains his friendships with former clubmates such as Wayne Willerton, his old mentor Bernie Guindon and Larry Vallentyne. Willerton never left his day job at General Motors in Oshawa and never struck it rich with his sales and franchising schemes. He retired on a pension in 1996 after thirty-six years on the assembly line.

For his part, Guindon growls that he's broke but proud as he enters his eighth decade. "I don't have a pot to piss in or a window to throw it out of." The Frog's missing some teeth, but declines to have dental work done, in case he gets into yet another fight and has them smashed up again. He also says he's not concerned about any civilian passing judgment on his life. "I don't give a shit. I've done my time. I don't have to kiss anybody's ass. I did it and stood up and didn't rat out anybody. What the fuck? I didn't have to bow down to anybody. I did my time." The man who brought the Choice back onto the road left the Hells Angels in the summer of 2005 in good standing. He's not so happy with where clubs are heading. "There are different reasons for being in the club. They think there's dollars to be made. . . . That's the problem today. If it wasn't for the patch, they would have no balls. The only thing they have is their patch."

Campbell and Vallentyne have been close friends since the late 1970s, and Vallentyne was there when Campbell celebrated his sixty-fourth birthday by a lake north of Toronto. When they weren't strumming and singing tunes by Merle Haggard, Waylon Jennings and Hank Williams, they enjoyed classic country from a CD player on his Ultra Classic anniversary edition Harley. This was too much for a younger guest at the party who was just in her early twenties. She repeatedly replaced what she called the "old man music" with her own CD of more youth-friendly tunes, rankling Vallentyne. Says Campbell: "He never said a word. He just took out the CD and went down to the lake with it. He came back without the CD. The next time he's here, we'll go down to the lake and see if we can find the CD. That's typical Larry. He just makes things funny."

Campbell's heart and back aren't what they once were, but he still cruises on his Harley, with classic country blaring on the speakers, and he still gets his hackles up when he sees riders who don't know how to handle their bikes. "I pull up beside them and ask them if they want me to teach them how to ride."

Like many Canadians, Campbell was shocked by public shootings involving gangstas in Toronto in the summer of 2012. One took place in the crowded food court of the Eaton Centre shopping mall, killing two people and injuring six. Another was at a neighbourhood block party on Danzig Avenue in suburban Scarborough, when two innocent people were killed and twenty-three wounded by gunfire. When he heard reports of the shootings, he said he felt grateful that he didn't succeed in his own efforts to traffic machine guns in the 1980s. "It would have been chaos. I've thought about it often. Just not knowing where they were going to go. Back then, I never thought about that. I was just thinking about making money. I regretted later that money came before my morals. I'm just so glad it didn't happen."

He remains fiercely protective of his pack, and that includes his pets. When a visiting biker threw something at his Australian shepherd, Sparrow, Campbell punched the man in the head and threw him off his property. He doesn't throw punches as frequently or as hard as in his youth, but he still uncorked a righteous smack onto that biker, who was at least twenty years his junior. Nothing trumps family loyalty, even where dogs are concerned. "Until the day that I die, I'll live by that code," he says. "When I'm a hundred years old, I'll smack that guy too."

He also still has an idealized view of brotherhood, even though he never had any brothers by blood. "When I die, I want to be surrounded by men. What's a man? Good to his family, good to his friends and loyal. It doesn't mean a tough guy. That'll never leave me. That's one of the extremes I'll keep." He offers almost no apologies for roads he has travelled because of his extreme nature, but there's at least one thing he'd like to take back. "I've justified everything I've done, except burning the family house. I'm lucky with the life I've led. I've got regrets, but everybody's got those."

Campbell sometimes marvels that he's still alive. So many of his old buddies are now dead from bullets or blades or drugs or bike accidents, and yet here he is. Equally amazing is that his daughter turned out so well and loves him so strongly, considering his severe deficiencies as a young father. He loves to boast how Janice somehow put herself through college while raising a family. He gets a little misty when he talks about how his granddaughter Chaedra once couldn't bear to see him go at the end of a visit. "She cried, 'I won't see you for years.' She just loved me to death."

His voice fills with wonder as he talks of how Evelyn wrote and visited him constantly while he was behind bars. She could have just walked away. These women are easily as strong and protective as any man he has met in his decades among tattooed bikers. There's an irony here that doesn't escape him. Somehow, he has ended up with the stable, loving family he so wanted as a child.

Campbell knows that mainstream society looks harshly on how he has spent his life. For him, it somehow seemed normal and even right at the time, even though many of the stories in these pages are bizarre even to himself in the retelling. In the end, it also felt natural to quietly move on from life in an outlaw biker brotherhood so that he could spend more time with his family. It felt natural because his story has always really been about family. "I love the club, but I love my wife more. I love my family more."

ACKNOWLEDGEMENTS

Lorne Campbell thanks: My wife Ev, the love of my life, and all my girls, Janice, Kylie, Jemelie, Joriana and Chaedra, for their unconditional love; Ovidio and Elizabeth Sanchez for lighting the fire under my ass; Tony Biancofiore, the son I never had; Steve Earle, champion of the underdog; Peter Edwards for your confidence in me; Jim and Mary Liscoumb for getting the ball rolling; Satan's Choice Motorcycle Club; Hells Angels Motorcycle Club; Vagabonds Motorcycle Club; Bernie Guindon for life; Joe Ertel for making the hard times easy; Larry McIlroy for his loyalty, especially in the 1970s; Larry and Brenda Vallentyne . . . friendship is priceless; Jimmy Antonopolis for always being there; Ronnie Mallott and Jacquie Ross, my dear friends; Mike and Regina Ribeiro, for your help through the rough times; Wayne Willerton, for your memories from the early years and your friendship; Scotty and Marisa Jongkind for their never-ending support. Doug Hoyle and Ashley Bailey, forever friends.

Peter Edwards thanks: Mary Liscoumb for getting everything going and insightful comments along the way; my agent Daphne Hart of the Helen Heller Agency for cheerfully finding a home for this project; Anne Collins and Craig Pyette of Random House Canada for seeing its value; Ovidio and Elizabeth Sanchez and Evelyn Campbell for making all those Sundays a pleasure and serving me world-class comfort food, including my first taste of tequila *con serpientes*. Thanks always to Barbara, James and Sarah for love and support, and to Steve Earle, Ron Broitman of Warner Chappell Music Inc., Matt Jones, Seth Faber, Ryan Barkan, Justin Shukat of Primary Wave Music and Jesse Bauer of GoldVE for their co-operation and permission to quote Steve Earle song lyrics. And, of course, thanks to Lorne Campbell for remaining true to his word and telling an honest story.

SELECT BIBLIOGRAPHY

BOOKS

Caron, Roger. *Bingo! The Horrifying Eyewitness Account of a Prison Riot.* Toronto: Methuen, 1985.

Lowe, Mick. *Conspiracy of Brothers: A shocking true story of murder, bikers and the law.* Toronto: Seal Books, 1988.

Norris, Don. *Riding With Attitude: A journey through life on a motorcycle.* Toronto: Toronto University Press, 2005.

Sanger, Daniel. *Hell's Witness: The many lives and curious death of Dany Kane.* Toronto: Viking Canada, 2005.

Scott, George D., with Bill Trent. *Inmate: The casebook revelations of a Canadian penitentiary psychiatrist.* Montreal: Optimum Publishing, 1982.

Thompson, Hunter S. *Hell's Angels: The strange and terrible saga of the outlaw motorcycle gangs.* New York: Ballantine, 1966.

ARTICLES

Blanchfield, Mike. "LSD experiments 'good research back then': Prison's former head of psychiatry stands behind testing on inmates." *Ottawa Citizen*, July 10, 1998, A3.

———. "'I was reduced to a lab rat': Ex-inmate Dorothy Proctor says she was used in LSD experiments. Federal documents appear to corroborate her claim." *Ottawa Citizen*, July 21, 1998, A1.

——— and Jim Bronskill. "Prison doctor sheds no tears." *Ottawa Citizen*, September 27, 1998, A1.

Edwards, Peter. "Blogger leaked order to raid Hells Angels." *Toronto Star*, April 7, 2007, A1.

Gamester, George. "Size was no handicap to little guy with grit." *Toronto Star*, April 28, 1988, A2.

Gladstone, Bill. "Old Lake Ontario town sets out an historic welcome mat." *Globe and Mail*, July 10, 1998, Metro 4.

Hagarty, Britt. "No bleeding-heart liberalism, but a tremendous insight into the prison system—and prisoners." *Globe and Mail*, August 21, 1982, E11.

Kenna, Kathleen. "Savage 'jungle justice' dealt out by inmates in our penitentiaries." *Toronto Star*, October 14, 1986, A1.

————. "There's always 'shine' brewing in Millhaven, its inmates say." *Toronto Star*, October 16, 1986, A19.

Lowe, Mick. "MD accuses parole board of treating man unfairly." *Globe and Mail*, April 21, 1987, A16.

Makin, Kirk. "Jail is demolished, Kirk Makin gains extremely rare access to this infamous Canadian landmark and unearths its chilling history." *Globe and Mail*, April 20, 2011, A8.

Nolan, Stephanie. "Love on the rock: Rogues have mythic appeal, but is dating in the 1990s so dire that women are driven from looking in bars to looking behind them?" *Globe and Mail*, June 19, 1999, A8.

Powell, Betsy. "Jail 'like the Black Hole of Calcutta.'" *Toronto Star*, January 6, 2010, GT3.

Tyler, Tracey. "Jail system creates criminals, lifer says killers' convention would have offered chance to assess rehabilitation." *Toronto Star*, May 27, 1991, A10.

————. "Food fight over chow in prison: The Rock serves salmon while Toronto inmates scrape by on lettuce." *Toronto Star*, October 18, 2010, A1.

OFFICIAL DOCUMENTS

World War II records of Lorne Campbell Sr.

Bath Institution records of Lorne Campbell Jr. (Millhaven and Collins Bay records not available)

MUSIC LYRICS

"The Other Kind" and "Justice in Ontario" from *The Hard Way*, MCA Records, by Steve Earle and the Dukes, 1990.

INDEX